£ 6.95

D1330580

200 24843

Towards a Story of the Earth
ESSAYS IN THE THEOLOGY OF CREATION

Library of
Woodbrooke College
Selly Oak
Birmingham

ESSAYS IN THE THEOLOGY OF CREATION

Towards a Story
of the Earth

Denis Carroll

DOMINICAN PUBLICATIONS

First published (1987) by
Dominican Publications
St Saviour's
Dublin 1

ISBN 0-907271-76-6

© (1987) Denis Carroll

Cover design by David Cooke

Printed by
The Leinster Leader Ltd
Naas
Co. Kildare

231.765

Contents

To my dear father
to whom I owe so much.
And to my beloved mother
who was called to everlasting blessedness
while this book was being prepared for press.

Introduction

Introduction

The threat to people and to nature from nuclear escalation, from denial of human rights, from widespread social injustice, has motivated many people to seek a wider view of nature, of personhood, of social responsibility. The ideal of a just and sustainable society has gripped Christians and others who do not subscribe to the Christian story. Many people feel impelled to contest our present ambient and to work toward a better order wherein the brotherhood/sisterhood of all people would be a reality and not a quaint, even Quixotic, dream. The Greenham women, the men and women of Greenpeace, the Green Alliance, those who struggle for justice at home and abroad, those who have suffered in defence of human rights under totalitarian regimes of the First, Second and Third Worlds, all lay a challenge to articulate 'a new story of the earth'. They protest at the way things are and offer a glimpse of how things might be.

This study offers nine essays set against the backdrop of the Judaeo-Christian theology of creation. The essays are written in the conviction that the tradition carries many elements valuable in fashioning 'a new story of the earth'. The elements developed here are by no means the only ones which could be taken up. An underlying assumption of these pages is that it makes sense to speak of God as existing and of God as creator. The assumption will be contested by many people who, not without reason, contest either the meaningfulness or the worthwhileness of the affirmation of God and of God's creative stance towards the universe. In standing by the assumption one does not underestimate the questions and the refusals from atheists or, indeed, from 'troubled theists'. In a sense, every Christian is a 'troubled theist' insofar as he/she adverts to the pain of the world and to 'the tears of things'. However, one cannot address every question and, I believe, the nine essays in this book contain their own meaning even as they rest on the assumptions above detailed.

Here, then, one starts from within the Judaeo-Christian tradition on creation. Thus, the method is of faith seeking understanding and relevance to the issues of the day. In the first chapter, one examines the several perspectives from which people have considered fundamental issues of truth and value, of origins and destiny. The aim of the chapter is to show that the contributions of the scientific, philosophical, theological and mythopoetic perspectives can be held together without confusion but with much advantage. In the second chapter the biblical and patristic traditions are sketched in broad strokes. In chapter three St Thomas Aquinas and Pierre Teilhard de Chardin are selected as representing the perceptions of creation as *relation* to God the creator and as a *process* of development in freedom towards God, Father, Son and Holy Spirit. In both perceptions the beneficient presence of God is the key assumption. Chapter four outlines some aspects of a creation spirituality which underlies everything else. One can only agree with Edward Schillebeeckx when he argues that an awareness of the created relationship to God is 'the root and breeding place of all religious awareness'.[1] Thereafter, in chapters five to nine, one moves out to consider how the Judaeo-Christian tradition both enriches and is enriched by questions of justice (chapter nine), of care for the earth (chapter eight), of human rights (chapter seven). In chapter five the topic of original sin is reconsidered in the light of contemporary insights and objections. In chapter six one asks if, and how far, the hypothesis of evolution coheres with the attestation that God in creating gave man/woman a privileged nature, function and destiny.

This relatively brief study is presented to whomever wishes to explore the tradition on creation in a fairly systematic way. Teachers, preachers, theology study groups are those who come to mind. The order of the classical text book has not been allowed to dictate what is taken up and what omitted. In almost every chapter one attempts to correlate some new questions with older perceptions. It will quickly become clear that this is not a comprehensive text book in the older format. It will have served its purpose if it helps the reader to see that the religious apperception of our createdness leads both to joyfulness in the gift and to seriousness in implementing the responsibilites entailed by that same gift.

One could not write an essay in the theology of creation without being aware of the gift bestowed by the creative God of life and love. I wish simply to return thanks for the gifts of love and beauty which have come into my own life. To my parents I return heartfelt thanks for their gift of life and for their continuing goodness. I thank others very close to me for their gracious presence. They all have made me aware of the deep meaning to that lovely text on which rests all creation theology, found at Exodus 3:14: 'I will be with you ... as who I am I will be with you'.

Part One

ONE

Creation and Origins: Diverse Perspectives

Beginnings or origins have exercised a fascination both constant and universal. A simple expression of this fascination is the desire of people to trace 'roots', to reconstruct the history of district, parish or region. Again, there is the assiduity of the eighteenth and nineteenth centuries to research not simply the origin of species, of humankind, of the universe, but also of society, religion and language. Witness, too, the thrust in psychoanalysis to recover the original time before the trauma of weaning and the vicissitudes of growth. Sigmund Freud developed the twin ideas of 'blissful origin' of the human being and the return thereto through memory or recall. This applies primarily to the individual's history – Freud made great play of the 'primordial and paradisal' time of childhood.

Long before Freud, however, the return to the origin was esteemed as therapy. In India, traditional medicine attempted to heal the aged and the dying by burying them – momentarily – in a womb-shaped grave. For Taoism, sickness and senility can be relieved by a return to the origin of things. Thus, the Taoist technique of embryonic breathing attempts to replicate the circulation of blood and breath between mother and unborn child. In both cultures, the Indian and the Chinese, the *regressus ad uterum* serves as a model for physiological and psychological techniques, the aims of which are regeneration, longevity, healing and final liberation.

There is a mythopoesis of origins. There are the cosmogonies and the myths, the stories of origins. These arise from a variegated stem but they have in common a quest for wholeness and healing. They carry the intuition that primordial knowledge confers a mastery over being. Hence the perennial value people seem to attach to knowledge of origins. The most primitive way of purveying such knowledge is cosmogony, the theory or story of how the world came to be. We shall look more closely at the dynamic of myth of which ancient cosmogonies are perhaps the most important type for our purposes. For those for whom myth has not entirely shattered, the very enactment of an account of origins regenerates both the present time and the participant in the re-enactment. One regains, as it were, the original time, the *illlud tempus*, the time of sacrality and power. Thus, the participant in mythic re-enactment is endowed with a recharge of vital forces. For this very reason, the narration of a cosmogony and the recounting of world origins frequently accompanied healing, harvesting, setting out to sea, the installation of a ruler, even the search for poetic inspiration. The reiteration of beginnings seems somehow to transform the present. It endows the present with an aboriginal force and purity.

In theology of the Christian tradition, the stress upon origins is balanced by emphasis upon end or goal. As we shall see, the Judaeo-Christian understanding has broken with the sacred circularity of mythic time. On the whole, the Bible has moved out of the shadow of the eternal return. Time elapses. History does not repeat. Notwithstanding the book of Ecclesiastes, the Jewish-Christian concept of time leans towards the linear rather than the circular image. Hence creation theology in attempting to mine the riches of the Christian tradition on origins does so in full awareness of the need both to respect myth and yet to move well beyond it. Creation and fall, creation and covenant, creation and re-creation are dominant themes in the Old Testament. In the New Testament the dominant themes are conversion, discipleship, redemption, salvation and divinisation. These themes always stand under the tension of their insertion into history. It has to be stressed, therefore, that the interest of theology in origins is neither antiquarian nor academic. Creation theology is done with a view to reading better the signs of the present and the prospects for the future.

THE NATURAL SCIENCES AND ORIGINS

Since the seventeenth century, scientists have had apparently good warrant for ignoring the question of origins in any absolute sense. The principle of inertia postulated an innate capacity of bodies to persist unless disturbed by another force. Physical reality could be examined without appeal to absolute origins or metaphysical dependence. However, with the emergence of relativity theory and quantum physics the range of questions pertaining to origins and duration expanded once again. The discovery by Edwin Hubble, in 1929, of a galactic red-shift led to the hypothesis of a general recession of galaxies from a single point of origin. Thus emerged the hypothesis of an expanding – and perhaps infinitely expansive – universe. When in 1965 3^0 K radiation was noticed and identified, the 'big bang' hypothesis of cosmic origins received a strong confirmation. This postulates that from ten to twenty billion years ago a singularity – a primal explosion of a single point of infinite density – originated the expanding universe we inhabit. A moment or point there was when all the material which was to constitute every star or galaxy could have been held in the palm of an infinitely small hand. The movement or expansion thus commenced still goes on – and can continue for billions of years. More imaginatively, some would envisage the coming to be of the cosmos as preceded by a time-reversed world in which the past and the future were interchanged. Just as from the initial 'big bang' has proceeded an immense expansion so, too, in a previous order a contraction had set in train a return to the infinitesimally small point of origin. From a 'big crunch' emerged a 'big bang'! It has been suggested that an endlessly repeatable cycle of universes can thus be generated and regenerated. The cosmos we inhabit is simply one of which there were many and of which many there will be. Thus, in a sense, the past is future and the future past.

The several reactions to the 'big bang' hypothesis are reminders of the long-standing tension of religion and science. Sir Edmund Whittaker, a member of the Pontifical Academy of Sciences, suggested that the model without impropriety could be called 'the creation'. On the other hand, the Soviet scientist V. I. Sviderski referred to the model as 'an unscientific popish conclusion'. With a vehemence that smacked of ideological reaction, Fred Hoyle espoused and propagated the Biondi-Gold model of a steady state universe. In this viewpoint there would be a continual appearance of new hydrogen atoms throughout space to 'balance' the run down caused by the outward expansion of the universe. In Hoyle's opinion, it is a better hypothesis since the 'creation' of these atoms could be explained in intra-cosmic terms. One cannot avoid the impression that Hoyle's strong opposition is influenced by a negative view of Christianity which he believes to have an investment in the truth value of the 'big bang' model. At the other extreme, there is the over-eager reach by some theological apologists for a scientific model of origins which seems to affirm absolute beginnings, the irreversibility of material processes and a broadly determined run down of the universe. This, however, is a temptation to be avoided. For apart from the historic tensions and the dangers of concordism, there is the other danger of distorting what the sciences themselves say. As to absolute beginnings being categorically asserted by the 'big bang' theory, this is quite simply not the case. Much depends on the base of the time scale used to measure the 'age' of the universe. On one base the 'age' of the universe will be finite – from ten to twenty billion years. On another, however, the answer will indicate an infinity of time. Ernan McMullin's reminder is apt: 'What one could readily say ... is that if the universe began in time through the act of a Creator, from our vantage point it would look something like the Big Bang that cosmologists are now talking about. What one cannot say is, first, that the Christian doctrine of creation "supports" the Big Bang model or, second, that the Big Bang model "supports" the Christian doctrine of creation'.[1] The relation between the scientific and theological perspectives on origins is more complicated than may be suggested by 'support', 'accord' or, even, 'contradiction'.

The scientific viewpoint moves from origins in the sense just described to the emergence and development of life. From this standpoint evolution is proposed as an hypothesis. At first blush it seems inimical to the older perspectives on origins offered by the religious tradition. A particularly sharp tension has arisen in the past between people holding the evolutionary hypothesis and others adhering to the biblical doctrine of creation. Evolution supposes that 'all life is shot through with a vital principle which enables it to grow not only in individuals but also in species, so that the individual and also the species adapt themselves to the demands of the environment thus bringing about new forms of life which may be specifically different from the old'.[2] It would further propose that all living organisms derive from one or a small number of original forms, which themselves are presumed to have arisen from inanimate matter. It should be noted that this is an hypothesis and not a law. Yet, accounting as it does for data of several disciplines – biology, zoology, embryology and palaeontology – it must be regarded as an impressive hypothesis. It works well. Hence, according to the logic of science, it must be allowed to stand until it is either falsified or superseded by a more economic or more fruitful hypothesis.

Upon the hypothesis of an expanding universe and of an evolving thrust to higher forms of life, there supervenes a third supposition widely made in scientific circles: the bipolarity of all physical interaction. For long, physicists have spoken of entropy or the run-down of energy: 'the quantified thermodynamic measure of the running down of the energy system' (Monod). There is a progressive dissipation of order which, were it the only factor, would lead to the run-down of the universe. That this does not happen is due to another factor, termed by E. Schrödinger negative entropy and by M. Costa de Beauregard negentropy. There is an equilibrium whereby the run-down through entropy is matched by the ascending force of negentropy. To date, the question of the origin of negentropy is answered by extra-scientific imagery employed even by the physicists themselves. Costa de Beauregard speaks of 'a vast implosion of finality': but neither he, nor physics, nor theology, can demonstrate the cause of such implosion.[3] One might note, therefore, that the scientific perspective tends, at a certain point, to view the cosmos genetically even though the 'genesis' is not amenable to strict scientific analysis. The 'big bang' is, after all, no more than a metaphor. Similarly, with the 'upward thrust of life'. Likewise, 'a vast implosion of finality'. The French cosmologist Jean Ladriere remarks that scientific theory speaks of an origin of the universe that is determinate, undifferentiated and precontaining already the stages of the world's development.[4] The exactitude of scientific language breaks down here and the scientist, reflecting upon 'absolute origins', is pushed back upon descriptive terms from another dimension of human experience.

At the limits of scientific exactitude recourse is necessarily made to the image and the symbol. It is important that science recognize this limitation, for otherwise it will permit itself the luxury of exorbitance, of going outside its proper sphere. Albert Einstein spoke of 'that humble attitude of mind towards the grandeur of reason incarnate in existence, and which, in its profoundest depths is inaccessible to man'.[5] Our measurements define our universe – but they define that universe narrowly and incompletely. At its best science has revealed a complex of interlocking systems which, although interdependent, remain open both as systems and as a system of systems. Here is more than a clever paradox. It is an invitation to do what T. F. Torrance has called 'onto-relational' thinking – itself a move away from the compartmental, atomistic and objectivist approach which has hithertofore dominated scientific method.[6] This kind of thinking has many advantages. It respects more adequately the staggering diversity of the universe as we have come to know it. Again, it forces us to advert to the interrelation of all there is. Our universe is composed of a complex of connections: to realise this is, perhaps, better to respect the interdependence requisite for survival. The interrelatedness of the universe runs deeper than we have realised. As human beings, endowed with rationality and imagination, we are called upon to look again at the question of ends and goals in our science and technology. Here the words of Werner Heisenberg are apposite: 'the decision on aims cannot be made from inside science and technology – unless we are to go completely astray, it must be made where there is a view of the whole man and his whole reality, not just a small part'.[7] The colloquia of scientists, sociologists, philosophers and theologians evidence a heightened awareness of the interrelation of realms of meaning in the human spirit. Perhaps we are learning to differentiate levels of meaning just as we discover that our universe is best conceived of as 'a multi-leveled universe that requires on our part the development of conceptions and structures of thought that are both more open and more deeply and naturally grounded in the astonishing intelligibility of the universe'.[8] These levels of meaning are of commonsense, of theory, of creative imagination, of value and choice. A totalitarian pretension on the part of any one level issues in deep trouble. The warrant of history is clear: brusque commonsense, aseptic theory, blind commitment, all have shown their fatal shortcomings. Nevertheless, the balance of commonsense, science, humane values, creative imagination and action, is irreplaceable for the survival of people, society, even to the earth itself.

PHILOSOPHY AND ORIGINS

Philosophical work on origins has tended to remain within the shadow of theology. The most extended philosophical consideration of origins from Middle Platonism to Spinoza (seventeenth century), has been in the Jewish, Arabic and Judaeo-Christian traditions. This leaves us with the pre-Socratics, Socrates himself, Plato and Aristotle, at the one end, and moderns such as Wolff, Leibnitz and Kant, on the other. With the Greeks one discovers a bridge between mythic and critical thought. Clearly the Socratic approach was already compounded of a demythologizing tendency. Yet with Socrates and Plato the myth is still operative, even if already deprived of its participative dimension. Although Aristotle had worked out a subtle philosophy of nature and, to a degree, had achieved a precision of scientific method, he nevertheless does not get beyond an architectonic view of origins whereby the 'creator' constituted the world and thereafter left it to its own devices.

In modern philosophy there is a gradual extrusion of the question of God from the ambit of relevant philosophical issues. Following Kant – even in disagreement with him - many philosophers seem to find it more engaging to investigate the presuppositions at work in the several branches of knowledge. Kant's assiduity in explicating the preconditions of knowledge is well documented. His method of intentional analysis finds an echo in one of the most influential philosophical movements to spring from the modern Catholic tradition *viz.* the transcendental school, headed by Joseph Marechal and developed by Lotz, Siewerth and others. Again, Kant's search for the preconditions of knowing seems to be re-stated in the phenomenology of Husserl and, even, in certain facets of Existentialism. This turn to the thinking subject has considerable merits. Yet its drawback is that it drives a wedge into human experience thus separating knowledge of phenomena from an unknowable essence of things in themselves. This is an artificial division which has not only earned the criticism of traditional scholasticism but is increasingly seen as inadequate to meet the questions raised by cosmology in the wake of relativity theory and quantum physics.

Modern cosmology has been described as 'a science of the principles of the possibility of the objects of physics'.[9] In a novel way philosophical reflection can come to consider problems of cosmic origins, of indeterminacy in nature, and of the irreversibility or otherwise of natural processes. For example, one asks if the indeterminism revealed by quantum physics is subjective or objective. Is such indeterminism simply due to our ignorance of the factors determining apparently chance phenomena or is it, perhaps, due to an intrinsic property of physical reality. If one entertains the latter possibility then one has also to envisage that there may be in nature something uncaused. How is this to be accounted for? Ladriere correctly points out the insufficiency of any appeal to 'an initial chance distribution which has evolved in a determined manner through time, for there are continually new chance distributions'.[10] The same author suggests that there is a spontaneity in nature which is beyond the purview of physics as such.

It has been remarked that if the universe had expanded at a rate minutely different to that of its expansion after the postulated 'big bang' then human existence could never have eventuated. B. J. Carr and M. J. Rees have argued that even a small variation in electromagnetic and gravitational constants would have precluded life as we know it.[11] The cosmic production of helium would have been either too great or too small, galaxies and stars would not have been able to form, carbon would not have formed in the quantities needed for carbon-based life, the lifetime of planetary systems would not have been sufficiently long for complex organisms to develop. There is, in other words, an isotropy or correspondence between the universe as we find it and the conditions for the human life which declares what isotropic conditions are. Ernan McMullin points out that the isotropy 'is produced only by an extremely small fraction of all the permitted ways in which a universe obeying the equations of general relativity might develop'.[12] An interesting philosophical question is thereby raised: is the universe thus constituted in order that life might be? This is the question of the 'entropic principle' – a question which can be answered in different ways depending on one's perspective. It is raised here not to give an answer but to suggest that philosophy should not be constricted to language analysis, dissection of patterns of thinking or even epistemological theory. Contemporary science therefore raises questions for philosophic reflection, questions which perhaps cannot be answered from within science itself. These questions alert the open and enquiring mind to 'signs of lacunae in the fabric of manifestation, and of the presence in manifestation of a reasonableness that cannot be eliminated'.[13]

MYTHOLOGICAL PERSPECTIVE

There are many descriptions of myth. Several of these bear pejorative connotations. Myth is described as a fanciful tale without foundations. Its pretensions are to be exposed. It is a brake upon progress, a snare for the gullible, an affront to truth. Myth and progress stand to each other in inverse proportion. The development of one spells the demise of the other. A more positive description of myth presents it as 'an untutored effort of the desire to know, to grasp, to formulate the nature of things'.[14] Myth, thus understood, can expand comprehension rather than contract it. Where formal structures of explanation are lacking, where the situation transcends a uni-dimensional explanation, myth can serve a valuable, if not indispensable, function. It has been remarked that structures or scientific explanation emerge from pre-scientific discourse. Pioneers have had to cast around for suitable expression of their results and projections. Very often their explanations were in metaphorical-descriptive rather than formal-mathematical terms. Hence there is a goodly tincture of myth to the expressions of the early mathematicians, astronomers and natural philosophers. In their contexts, myth was a crutch to structured thought and an aid to scientific expression. Again, it is not always helpful to call a spade a spade. There are situations unamenable to purely scientific explanation: contexts where the purely formal explanation of science misses the point, or is shallow, incomplete and insensitive. Contexts of this kind are most effectively met through other modes of thought. Among these modes are the mythopoetic and the mythological.

In his book, *The Historian and the Believer,* Van A. Harvey argues of myth that 'it does not mean a false story but a highly selective story that is used to structure and convey the basic self-understanding of a person and a community'.[15] Hence, the myth is rarely about trivia. It focuses on the deep things of personal and communal living. Always it is a search for understanding. It centres upon and tries to comprehend birth and growth, maturation and senescence, death and destiny. Myth addresses societal institutions – kingship, leadership, trust and fealty. There are nature myths which reveal sacrality through unveiling the hidden works of the gods. Finally, the mundane concerns of work and play, of cooking, eating and drinking, come within the scope of myth-making. Clearly, myth can deal with important elements of human living whether these be individual or social. Of particular interest to myth-making are the crucial times and events in every human life. Therefore it is not surprising that myth operates by the deployment of symbols which root deep in the human psyche. A symbol is always more than a sign. It evokes emotional and psychic response. It can call forth the total engagement of the personality. Likewise with the symbols central to myth. They are multivalent. They link simultaneously to several referents. At all points they engage the emotions and the sensitivities. In addition, they link finite, everyday realities to the transcendent and supratemporal. Through their skilful use the search for individual and communitarian integration is promoted. Every participant in myth seeks to comprehend what links him or her to ancestors, dependents, environment and even the ground of being.

An attribute of myth, shared with saga, legend and fairytale, is the narrative form. Myth is formalised parable where the elements of the parable stand for realities much wider than themselves. As already noted, the symbols of myth are multivalent. They enable a multi-tiered presentation of elusive yet tangible realities. This is done through the telling of story. A sacred history is recounted. A primordial event is narrated. It is more than aetiology: there is dynamic action with an inner life, mobility and versatility. A common starting point to the narrative is 'at that time'. This *illud tempus* is a sacred time, a time of foundations. But it is never simply an *illud tempus,* for in the very narration it becomes a *hoc tempus.* The past becomes present and the present past. The decisions, prescriptions and relations of that time legitimate and interpret the decisions, prescriptions and relations of the present. Events, acts and institutions of the present are rendered meaningful. Significant relations are set up in and through the mythic narration. Clearly, the story narrated is not just a rehearsal of the *saeculum aureum* or golden age. It is a sacred history in the sense of foundations which undergird important concerns of the present. There is no parallel here to 'academic' history. For myth invites participation. A response is called forth in mime, in ritual, in dance. The participants are brought beyond the here and now into the timeless, originative 'then'. The constituting power is not simply invoked. It is *evoked* in order to bestow meaning and order as well as to avert dissolution and disorder. At least in this sense, Cassirer is surely right when he suggests that 'the whole of mythical thought may be interpreted as a constant and obstinate negation of the phenomenon of death'.[16]

In general, then, it can be said that myth is action as well as representation or image. E. Voegelin rightly emphasises that myth has a life and virtue of its own. One is called upon to enter the dynamic of the mythic action rather than to frame the question: is it true? or, even, what does it mean? For, to the mythic consciousness, meaning is disclosed in the action itself. It is not that truth is discounted. Mircea Eliade stresses that societies which cherish myth do in fact distinguish between true and false tales. Myth is among the former – it connotes 'a true story ... a story that is a most precious possession because it is sacred, exemplary, significant'.[17] However, it goes below, or deeper than, the practical or the theoretic dimensions. It is sympathetic to nature and the cosmos, not dominative of them. This leads Cassirer to write: 'the real substratum of myth is not a substratum of thought but of feeling. Myth and primitive religion are by no means entirely incoherent, they are not bereft of sense or reason. But their coherence depends much more upon unity of feeling than upon logical rules'. Or again: 'the consanguinity of all forms of life seems to be a general presupposition of mythical thought'.[18]

In offering a vivid interpretation of the puzzles of life, in grounding the most basic of our activities in a root of meaning, the myth offers stability, rootedness, the sublimation of conflicts, the reinforcement of personal and social identity. It would seem a constant of the human psyche to search for meaning. There is a perennial need to experience the central areas of one's life as significant, as lifted above sheer transience. Myth has met that need to a remarkable degree. By its skilful use of symbol it spoke not only to the intellectual dimension but also to the non-rational, supra-logical elements of human living. It provided a base for permanence in transition, for constancy within change, for solidity in social and ontic flux. In missing this point Rudolf Bultmann's programme of demythologisation entered a blind alley. For Bultmann, myth seems ever a primitive, literalist, univocal language, the references of which are pseudo facts. However, this is a grievous understatement of myth. For myth expresses a preliminary grasp of sacral forces. Similarly, it channels human emotion in the face of the unknown/known: joy, gratitude, celebration and hope, anxiety, guilt and remorse. It presents a dimension of ultimacy, of sacredness, of transcendence, all within the known world of elements and relationships.

In view of the astounding diversity of myth it is surely risky to generalise. On the other hand, for purposes of this study Gilkey's claim may be accepted: 'myth portrays the horizon or the ground of the life-world of man by telling the story of the origins of that world ... it points to powers and events that brought [nature and society] into being'.[19] The cosmological myth is an account of cosmosgenesis – it tells how the world was made, how it developed from the formless, the non-world. Even amongst the cosmogonic myths there is an enormous diversity. Myriad are the accounts of origins and the dramatic narrations of a primal time. Yet, as Andrew Greeley neatly points out: 'whether one sees creation emerging from an egg, or developing from particles that a diver has rescued from the depths, or as parts of the body of a slain monster, or as the result of intercourse between deities, or from a simple divine *fiat,* the creation myths are all attempts to explain the human condition, both in its factuality and its strange blend of good and evil'.[20] For Paul Ricoeur the question of good and evil preoccupies mythopoetic activity. Ricoeur discerns four answers to the question, and classifies the myths as they incorporate one or other of these answers. First, the myths of nature religions locate good and evil in creation itself. Creation is shot through with a dual principle in which good and evil engage in recurrent combat. The Eneuma Elish and the Gilgamesh Epic are good examples of this. Second, there are the tragic myths depicting an irrational universe dominated by the arbitrariness of the gods. Man is burdened with a tragic load from which he tries fruitlessly to escape. To this class pertain the Dionysian and Appolonian myths. Third, there are the Orphic mysteries of ancient Greece, cognate to the cabalistic mystery religions which were to pose a serious threat in the early years of Christianity. Fourth, there are the Adamic creation myths where creation is good, evil introduced by human malfeasance and the beneficent power of God ultimately triumphant.[21]

Our approach to myth, therefore, requires a certain differentiation. We lose a great deal if we fail to advert to the pedagogy inset to mythic discourse. This discourse has aided people to think on issues beyond the purely empirical. To consider ultimate issues, wholeness and totality, requires sensitivity to a dimension which can only be touched by the suppleness of symbol and expressed in a correspondingly flexible medium. The myth has enabled people to transcend their context thus to consider a unifying explanation to the cosmos. Myth, then, is a type of pedagogy. Even more, it provides a model, an imaginative framework within which thought about origins can be pressed to more subtle conclusions. Myth, writes Ladriere, 'begins and makes possible the characteristic operations of thought'.[22] In other words, when sympathetically judged, myth can be acquitted of incompatibility with truth. It is a point of departure for successive refinements in the grasp of reality. Symbolically it tells, in a particular way and from a particular standpoint, what our universe looks like and where we belong in it. Against this backdrop, people can advance to a more critical image of self and of cosmos. Meanwhile, the scholars discuss the roots of mythopoesis. The explanations seem to divide evenly between a psychological and a social root to mythmaking. Is myth the outgrowth of the collective unconscious? Or is it the effect of social and geographical circumstances, as the school of E. Durkheim would seem to suggest? Perhaps the full truth lies with neither alternative. Perhaps the apparently trite depiction of myth as a preconscious and conscious response to overarching reality, fusing imagery, allegory, poetry, humour and pathos, escapes the dilemma.

For the individual, then, myth can be a support in crises of meaning and identity. A truly operative myth can be appealed to at all the truly significant points of life history: childhood, adolescence, adulthood and old age. This may appear a large claim. Yet, it is not necessarily an exaggeration. We stand in need of some comprehensive scheme by which to understand the demands of reality and through which to summon the courage to meet these demands. For a full life, it is suggested, people must have an opportunity to participate in a dimension which runs deeper than the purely empirical. Such needs have been skilfully catered for, at least in part, by mythic discourse. That this is no longer the case is due to several factors. One is the rigidly empirical bent of science and the quasi-scientific assumptions of our age. There is a prevalent restriction of the truly significant to what can be quantified. The really meaningful is then taken to be only what can be observed, measured and planned. Thus arises an implicit disqualification of any transcendent interpretation as naive if not altogether foolish. Another factor, not far removed from the first, is that the environment itself has been 'reduced' by technology and urbanisation. Thirdly, our consciousness of the practical, the *faciendum,* what remains to be done, engenders the feeling that all concerns with origins trammel freedom and creativity. Myth of any kind is then seen as a heavily conservative force, a bar to progress. It is regarded as part of the infancy of humankind, to be outgrown in a scientific and autonomous age.

Thus the myths have broken. Ours is the age of the shattered myth. Cosmogonic myths no longer perform the function they once discharged. The mythic accounts are no longer potent. Critical reason has eroded their content so that they no longer point to ultimacy or mediate sacrality. The tales of the gods and godesses and heroes have become 'lovely, lively but profane'. Any attempt to resacralise them leads only to disastrous results. It produces a pathos-laden *ersatz* religion or the even more dangerous caricature of religion in the coven and the cabal. Hence, the process of demythologisation cannot be reversed. It represents a maturation, an advance in critical awareness. Indeed, in this process of maturation, biblical faith has played a major part. Ricoeur's subtle counterpoint of demythologisation and demythicisation provides a valuable clarification. To demythologise is a real progression. 'Criticism', writes Ricoeur, 'cannot help being a demythologisation; that is an irreversible gain of truthfulness, of intellectual honesty, and, therefore, of objectivity'.[23] In fact, this process rejuvenates the mythic symbol through sympathetic understanding. On the other hand, crudely to demythicise is both damaging and dangerous. Damaging: for violence is done to the symbolic thrust in human nature. Dangerous: for the void is often filled by sinister and demonic replacements. It has been forcefully stated that in our secular age the proliferation of spurious myths goes on unabated. Andrew Greeley draws graphic attention to this in his work *The Persistence of Religion*. Langdon Gilkey perceptively underscores the terrifying myth of the omnipotence of science, of the man in the white coat. In science-dominated culture, for the first time in human history, the essential structures of life remain unthematised.[24] The conclusion drawn by Greeley and Gilkey is that we still need to attend to mythopoesis and to the dimension opened up by myth. With Ricoeur, we might call not for the abolition but for the critical re-interpretation of myth. This is no easy task. For myth cannot be created or prefabricated to order. Neither can we dodge the exigencies of critical awareness. Nothing is more dangerous than spurious mythology. Not only does it transmit a pervasive falsehood – it also legitimises the injustice and oppression of the society which spawns it. Elizabeth Schüssler-Fiorenza accurately claims: 'the absolute precondition of new liberating Christian myths and images is not only the change of individual consciousness but that of societal, ecclesial and theological structures as well'.[25] It remains true that if the values of truth and significance are to be attained we shall have to seek comprehensive interpretations of existence. Today, as before, we need a meaning system which will mediate the transcendent as well as present a coherent view of humankind, nature, destiny, obligation and inalienable right.

THEOLOGICAL PERSPECTIVE

Theology is of its nature eclectic. In relation to origins theology will reach for the fruits of other valid approaches: the mythopoetic, the scientific and philosophical. Theology can only do this if it respects the validity of these other perspectives and does not indulge in dogmatic imperialism, on the one hand, or the dereliction of its proper viewpoint and method, on the other. Of necessity theology will carry mythic discourse. How can the divine 'intervention' in covenant, exodus, restoration and reconciliation, be brought to expression other than in the terms of sacred story? And if Christian faith understands the divine transcendence as immanent to the historical existence of people, sacraments and institutions, it must begin to express the consciousness of that presence through the concepts of mediation, sacrality and symbol. Again, philosophical notions are used in the tradition to explicate the concept of God as transcendent yet immanent to creation, as universal yet personal. Finally, since theology has come to regard its pronouncements as contingent and revisible rather than immutable and untouched by empirical circumstances, it must pay attention to the emergent data of the empirical sciences. Since theology will concede with alacrity that science deals with what theology calls creation, it cannot ignore the development of these sciences.

In regard to the biblical account of origins, it is difficult to say when mythopoesis crosses over into theology. For example, while the Genesis narratives are compounded of mythological elements, they are by no means dominated by these. It has been argued that Old Testament Jewry was interested in salvation history to the point where an independent regard to creation became subdued: creation became merely the explanatory backdrop to Israel's history. On the other hand, one should not overlook the cosmic experience from which all accounts of origins spring and which underlies the early chapters of Genesis. For Christian theology, the expression of the 'cosmic experience' has its own validity precisely as religious – even when found in the Bible. With all the more reason, then, we should be reluctant to subsume the early Genesis narratives within the hegemony of a theology of covenant and redemption. It would be a mistake to suppress the biblical awareness of creation in its own right. Such an independent awareness is clearly documented and should be accorded its proper significance. Edward Schillebeeckx points out that 'it is hardly responsible criticism now to argue that "creation" occupies only a marginal position in the Old Testament'.[26] What applies here applies through theology as a whole. Creation should be seen as a foundation to every other Christian doctrine; 'in its changing historical forms, the experience of creation is the foundation which supports everything. It might be called a fundamental experience of grace ... it is an experience of givenness which is also at the root of all religion'.[27] This 'experience of givenness', implicit in ancient understandings of origins and in medieval theology, merits careful attention. The result will be profitable not only for a fuller understanding of creation but even for our prayer, spirituality and practice.

Creation, then, is at the base of the Christian view of covenant, incarnation, grace and eschatology. Nor can it be divorced from those divine interventions in history which are central to Hebrew religious consciousness. The eternal return and the circularity of time are foreign to the dominant Jewish world view. The Judaeo-Christian tradition cherishes the importance of the 'here and now'. Some exegetes appeal to the absence of speculative thought amongst a nomadic, pastoral people as an explanation for the Jewish awareness of Yahweh's near presence. Whichever explanation one favours, it is beyond dispute that the Old Testament links God closely with the unfolding history of the people. From Exodus to Exile, from Return to inter-testamentary times, there is a vivid awareness of the saving, 'concrete' presence of Yahweh. Israel's history is seen as the implementation of the covenant made with Abraham and renewed thereafter up to Mosaic times. Even here, creation is a stage, an essential presupposition to the Covenant. In the observation of the Covenant and in its definitive fulfilment, creation remains a dominant backdrop. Creation and salvation are ordered to each other. Neither should be suppressed. Neither should be left out of account. Where this mutual inclusion is discounted, salvation becomes a merely formal concept with little relation to human experience. Likewise, the idea of creation is deprived of that reinforcement which the historical bent of the Judaeo-Christian tradition brings to bear on life and death and human destiny.

It is the merit of Karl Barth to have brought a new urgency to the task of relating creation to covenant and salvation. Jürgen Moltmann, too, devotes considerable effort to aligning protology and eschatology, the first and the last things. By so doing, the latter refused to divorce creation and redemption. This refusal has also become much clearer in Catholic theology: '[the] distinction between creation and salvation – often thought to be the ground of the so-called natural and supernatural orders – is not tenable in the full light of God's revelation in Christ. Creation must be seen as a first but essential step in the unfolding of the history of salvation'.[28]

Within the Catholic and Protestant traditions a renewed effort has been made to bring Christology to the centre of theological work. Barth's 'christological concentration' has been frequently noted. With Karl Rahner, Aloys Grillmeier, Edward Schillebeeckx and others, Christ's place in world history and the relation of world history to salvation have been taken up again. It is indeed a *reprise*: both the New Testament and the Church Fathers return time and again to these concerns. St Paul develops the idea of *pleroma* or fullness – the filling and fulfilling of all things through incorporation into Jesus Christ. Here is a concept of immense power which the Church Fathers were quick to expand. Again, in Colossians Paul underlines that Jesus Christ is 'the image of the eternal God, the first born of all creation'. From this emerges the patristic delineation of Christ as ruler of all (*Pantocrator*) and ruler of the universe (*Cosmocrator*). Robert Butterworth rightly points out that 'it is idle to disregard or to neglect the scriptural evidence for the link between Christ and God's creation. To locate creation as a divine activity which is Christoform is a demand both of sound scriptural scholarship and sane Christian theology'.[20] Thus, from the renewal of Christology comes a valuable insight into creation as an enduring reality intimately connected to faith in Christ, the saviour and Lord of all.

Without pretense to imperialism such a theological perspective on creation endeavours to relate the views on origins and goals offered by science, philosophy and myth to its own insights into cosmic history. The work of Teilhard de Chardin is a major attempt at such a correlation. His hyperphysics range from palaeontology to theology in a carefully gradated unity. He skilfully uses the language of poetry and mysticism to present a vision of creation on the move towards fulfilment in Jesus Christ who is at once the Alpha and the Omega. Another progression in the theological perspective on creation has been a new approach to ecology and anthropology. There is a clear message from theology that we must treat nature not as an object to be exploited but as an interlocutor to be accepted in partnership. This is not sentimentalism. It is not a personalising of nature. Rather is it the acceptance of nature as an open system endowed with an intrinsic value which we despoil at our own peril and to our own detriment. Humankind is part of nature, and while human destiny transcends nature it is also solidary with it. On the other hand, creation theology will attempt to develop a theological anthropology based upon the biblical doctrine of *imago Dei*. Thus, on the one hand, a rounded creation theology will be open to ecological concerns, while, on the other hand, it will consider the question of human rights and the struggle for social justice. In this openness and quest the theology of creation may participate in the attempt to fashion a renewed 'story of the earth' so necessary to motivate respect for its inhabitants and care for its future.

TWO

The Early Story: Creation in Bible and Church Fathers

In 597 B.C. King Nabuchednezzar captured Jerusalem and sent the flower of its population into captivity in Babylonia. A decade later a second, more extensive, deportation took place. Amongst the deportees of this time were a prophet, Ezekiel, and another whose name is unknown – but whose very beautiful work, the Book of Consolation of Israel, was incorporated to the book of Isaiah. Found at chapters 40-55 of Isaiah, it has earned for its author the intitulation Deutero-Isaiah, the second Isaiah. It is from the pens of Deutero-Isaiah, Ezekiel and certain others – perhaps another – that the chief sources of the biblical doctrine of creation/origins have come. We know very little about the conditions the Hebrews underwent in the Babylonian captivity. Some did well, many fared badly. Perhaps the opening lines of Psalm 137 express it most poignantly:

> By the waters of Babylon there we sat down and wept
> when we remembered Zion.
> On the willows there, we hung our lyres.
> For there our captors required of us songs and our tormentors mirth,
> saying, 'Sing us one of the songs of Zion.'
> How shall we sing the Lord's song in a foreign land?

The psalm recreates the sad longing, the bitter nostalgia, for their homeland from which the Hebrews had been forcefully torn. There is a poignancy, too, in the supposition advanced by the biblicists that a group around Ezekiel the prophet and the unknown but highly literate Deutero-Isaiah set to rallying their people through the exhortatory literature exemplified by the Consolation of Israel and the book of Genesis. Deutero-Isaiah is precisely that: an attempt to strengthen people whose faith was under considerable strain. Theirs was a simple faith, uncluttered and non-philosophical, expressed in the verses of Deuteronomy 26:5 ff: 'A wandering Aramean was my father; and he went down into Egypt and sojourned there, few in number; and there he became a nation, great, mighty, and populous. And the Egyptians treated us harshly, and afflicted us and laid upon us hard bondage. Then we cried to the Lord God of our fathers, and the Lord heard our voice, and saw our affliction, our toil and oppression; and the Lord brought us out of Egypt with a mighty hand and an outstretched arm, with great terror, with signs and wonders; and he brought us into this place and gave us this land, a land flowing with milk and honey'.

Exposed to the arrogant values of their captors and solicited by the lurid pantheon of Babylon, the Hebrews' faith seemed threatened and perhaps about to falter. Was Yahweh really all-powerful? Was Yahweh indeed all-good? These are questions which acquired a particular force due to the Hebrews' experience of suffering and disorientation. The consolatory answer of Deutero-Isaiah is subtle as well as elegant. His strategy is to bring his addressees through the history of God's dealings with them thus to support the hope he proclaims for the future. What better than a rehearsal of God's past faithfulness, goodness and power, to found the hope that in the near future God would reverse bad fortune and raise up new prospects. From a loyal remembrance and serene hope would come, in the writer's view, a sure vindication.

One underestimates the beauty of the text by limiting its approach to mere strategy.[1] Deutero-Isaiah arises from a personal struggle in faith. It represents the writer's own struggle as well as the agony of his people. The affirmation of God's goodness and faithfulness had to be fought for and renewed in a heart-rending situation where, nonetheless, glimmers of light were beginning to show. Whatever its private circumstances, the text of Deutero-Isaiah holds out a promise. It promises the return to Jerusalem of the captive people, a return which took place from 537 under Cyrus. It looks to a new Exodus, a new covenant, a new creation. In Deutero-Isaiah's logic the foundation of these hopes is nothing other than previous experience of Yahweh's effective faithfulness. However, Deutero-Isaiah argues not simply from the covenant fidelity of God in the past but even from the universal power of God's action in the time of absolute origins, the time of creation. Nothing less than this is required by the nature of the problem. The writer's task was to announce God's saving intentions: as Yahweh had once made possible an Exodus from Egypt, Yahweh would again effect an Exodus from Babylon. In presenting this message, Deutero-Isaiah emphasises not only God's willingness but also God's ability to do what God has promised. Aided perhaps by the breakdown of the securities of home, land and temple, the author fuses creation and covenant in a supremely skilful way. Drawing upon an existing although possibly latent creation faith, Deutero-Isaiah shows that God's salvific power embraces not only this small Jewish people but the whole world. The God of the Mosaic covenant is the God who created – and who therefore has power over – the universe. Over Babylon and its gods. Over Cyrus the liberal king. Over diviners, soothsayers and wise men. Over natural, human and praeternatural forces. Unsought contact with gods rival to Yahweh brought Jewish reflection to recover the universal application of the words: 'I am the Lord ... you shall have no other gods but me ... ' (Ex 20:2-3).

Within this framework texts like Isaiah 48:12 show at once a universality and a particularity:

> Hearken to me, O Jacob, and Israel whom I called.
> I am He, I am the first and I am the last.
> My hand laid the foundation of the earth
> and my right hand has spread out the heavens ...
> Assemble ... and hear.
> Who among them has declared these things?
> The Lord loves him.
> He shall perform his purpose on Babylon
> and his arm shall be against the Chaldeans.

And again:

> Thus says the Lord your Redeemer, who formed you from the womb.
> I am the Lord, who made all things, who stretched out the heavens alone,
> who spread out the earth – who was with me? –
> who frustrates the omens of liars, and makes fools of diviners.
> Isaiah 44:24.

The message, then, is that Israel should have confidence. For the promise is from God who stretched out the heavens and laid the earth's foundations. In turn, this newly strengthened trust that God will save even in deepest adversity enables Israel to see more deeply into the meaning of creation itself.

Of the forty seven times the word *bara* is used in the Old Testament, twenty instances are in Deutero-Isaiah. *Bara* is a technical word from the theological language of the priests. Used almost exclusively of divine actions, it connotes the independence and transcendence of God's creative work, incomparable to anything in human ken. It is not that Deutero-Isaiah initiates a faith in God the creator. Rather, his significance is to have aided the theological progression whereby creation and salvation are fused into one theme in an explicit way. One might say that here the triple base upon which Christian theology rests is first laid: creation, covenant, new exodus or salvation. Deutero-Isaiah represents a progression in Israel's thought wherein the work of God is seen to be effective not just in creation, not just in the narrower concerns of the Hebrews, but in both together – in creation and covenant. The very breadth of Deutero-Isaiah's purview – while it has ever Israel in mind – leads to that more comprehensive view where, in Christ, the new creation and the new covenant spell salvation for people of all times and all places.

CREATION / ORIGINS IN GENESIS

The book of origins – of becoming, of coming into being – sets out a narrative 'genealogy' from the beginning of the world down to the twelve sons of Jacob. It aims to show how the family of Jacob came to be the progenitors of the race singled out by God for special favour. Thus, it proceeds by elimination from Adam, the father of all, through a selected person in each generation, to highlight one man, Jacob, and his family. It is generally agreed that the book is composed of protohistory and prehistory as well as of an extended narrative dealing with the patriarchs or fathers of Israel who lived in 'historical' times. Our interest lies in that part of Genesis which deals with origins of an absolute kind. Yet these early chapters have to be read in the context of the book as a whole. In presenting the accounts of origins and God's dealing with Israel, the 'author' had in mind, just as clearly as had Deutero-Isaiah, to strengthen and encourage a people who had suffered grievously and, perhaps, were still demoralised and distressed as a result of captivity. An unknown 'editor' of the same school as Deutero-Isaiah and Ezekiel would appear to have fused several strands of tradition dealing with Israel's history and protohistory into the patchwork known as the book of Genesis. The strands which immediately concern us are the Priestly and Yahwist texts. The latter had reached definitive form by the time of Solomon (ninth - eighth century B.C.) while the Priestly text did not do so until the end of the fifth century B.C.

Virtually all readers will accept that the Genesis narratives are not literal rapportage. The reply by the Biblical Commission to Cardinal Suhard in 1948 may sound condescending yet its reminder is valuable in regard to these early chapters: 'they relate in simple and figurative language, adapted to the understanding of mankind at a lower stage of development, the fundamental truths underlying the divine scheme of salvation, as well as a popular description of the origins of the human race, and of the chosen people'.[2] The creation narratives of Genesis bear the main positive features of myth. Insofar as the creation accounts detailed in Genesis 1 and 2 are a pictorial, dramatic, even symbolic treatment of something at the very heart of reality, they are myths. And so many writers describe them. Others prefer to say that the minds behind Genesis adapt mythical elements preexisting in their surrounds in order to express a truth which transcends myth. Hence, Erich Voegelin remarks that we have here a blend of history and myth which can be termed world history or existential history. These accounts are not 'pure' myths. There is more to their structure and intent. Creation is linked to history in a way consonant with the historical bent of Jewish national-religious consciousness. There is, in other words, an intellectual advance whereby creation is linked to history. Although not set within time, these origins-narratives remove creation far from ideas of a cyclical return or of an eternal present.[3]

Some scholars describe the Genesis creation narratives as aetiology. This is where an author indicates an earlier event – of which he may have no direct experience or evidence – as the explanation of a present situation. It is the present which is to be understood and interpreted in so far as possible, rather than any claim made for the literal sense of the explanatory causes offered. Thus, in the creation accounts, evil, pain, defeat, sin and even death are rendered intelligible by positing a causal antecedent. There is no claim to know the precise contours of the past happening. The author seems to say: thus and so is the present, so and thus must things have been if there is any intelligibility in the present. The editor of the Genesis accounts presents the original creation and the events which followed from it as the point of departure for a reflective understanding of God's continued dealing with Israel. This means that although the accounts in the early chapters of Genesis are not to be read literally or taken as history in the strict sense, they are nevertheless to be situated within a deeply historical faith. Here is a major difference from the ahistoric cosmogonies of other peoples.

In passing, it is well to note certain other differences. The very context of the Genesis accounts of origins is unambiguously monotheistic. God is transcendent, pre-existent. God's creative work needs no prior matter as substrate. God's very *fiat* is creative: God said ... and it was so. Bodies which in other accounts of origins are divinised, here are treated as creatures of Yahweh. The much feared Leviathan is a relatively tame being in the Old Testament when compared with his role in extra-biblical material. The discriminating choice and careful expurgation of Babylonian imagery is a testimony to the specific quality of Israel's faith in God, the Creator and Lord of all.

Genesis is set to meet a precise purpose. It is a reaffirmation, through recall of past happenings, of the saving presence of God. It is an exhortation to people not to give up heart, not to yield to disillusion, not to cease to hope. The priestly strand seems to address the question: is Yahweh really the mighty God we have worshipped. And, if so, what does God ask of us now. Somewhat similarly, the Yahwist text examines the origin of the evil we experience: does it come from a principle independent of God? Could it come from God? The combined texts answer clearly by presenting the benign sovereignty of God and a subtle account of the origin of suffering, wickedness and death. God is really God. God does care for people. God is all-powerful, God made all things good. Evil and suffering are not to be blamed on God. In a sense, therefore, Genesis is a kind of apologetics – it works towards strengthening an already developed faith in the presence of God who had in the past shown favour. The creation accounts stand against the backdrop of faith in the God of the Covenant who had intervened in Israel's history time and again, who was still with the people – in spite, perhaps, of appearances to the contrary. We should not forget, then, that the account of origins which opens the Old Testament is already linked to the Jewish faith in God. Indeed, the primary concern of the account is not origins but the covenant of old time, and God's fidelity to it. There is more than a hint that in the mind of the compilers of the accounts of origins, creation subserves the choice of Israel and its destiny. With some reserve one can re-echo G. Von Rad's claim: 'presumptuous as it may seem, creation is part of the aetiology of Israel'.[4]

One can summate the thrust of Genesis on origins as follows:

1. It inculcates that the whole world, at once threatening and great, owes its being to the free, sovereign action of God. God creates by God's word. The visible world is not part of God. It is not an emanation in the pantheist sense. Rather, it exists in beholdance to God who in addressing it calls it forth from nothingness. Such a doctrine was of more than a little comfort to the Israelites sorely pressed by powerful neighbours and in forced contact with the gods of Babylon.

2. Whether one views its genre as world history or as aetiology it remains that Genesis bears the epic characteristics of myth as detailed earlier in this study. Amos Wilder writes: 'In biblical narration no significant dimensions are scanted. The private and the public are interrelated, the psychological and the social, the

empirical and the metaphysical. And there is a robust reality sense, a power in being, and it relates to the fact that man in Scripture, precisely in his total perspectives, is still linked with the archaic hidden roots and fibres of his pre-historical and biological inheritance.[5]

3. Creation is basically good. The Old Testament view of creation has a tranquillity and a warmth not found in comparable literature. There is a dark and often lurid quality in creation accounts like the epic of Gilgamesh and the Eneuma Elish. These have a markedly dualistic character: a good principle of order and of light stands against an independent principle of evil and disorder. By contrast, the biblical narrative of origins hymns the goodness of creation: 'and God saw that it was good ... very good'. The sea monsters which abound in most origins narratives are but sparingly referred to in the whole of the Old Testament. When mention is made of these it is very clear that they are subordinate to the God of Israel (cf. Ps. 104).

4. The dark side of life and nature, the cruel edge of things, is not due to God's positive will. God made all things good. The harmony to which we aspire and which we experience mainly as a grievous absence, was part of God's creative gift. Harmony between man and woman. Harmony between humankind and nature. Harmony in nature itself. Genesis appears to share the perennial aspiration for the recovery of harmony. Much later, this theme will underlie Paul of Tarsus's writings: 'the whole of creation groans and travails in pain ... seeking the adoption of the sons of God ...' (Romans 8:22-23). Genesis clearly atttributes evil, suffering and death to a delict, an abuse of human freedom. It was in the abuse of God's creation, rather than in the creation itself, that the fall consisted, that disappointment and failure, suffering and sin, emerged. 'The distortion we experience is not a necessity but a perversion'.[6] The origins accounts identify disobedience to God's plan as the root of all our troubles. It hints at the premature grasp at 'the knowledge of good and evil' and the arrogation of what belongs only to God. The Genesis account strikingly presents the flawed human response to the temptation: 'you will be as God', *eritis sicuti Deus*.

However, questions still remain. Is evil then primarily moral evil? The sheer result of aberrant human decisions? Surely there are other considerations? There is the fractiousness of nature which can issue in ruined lives. There is the heart-breaking kind of tragedy – surely an evil – when the children and the innocent suffer horribly. Perhaps the serpent figure of Genesis reminds us that evil is not fully reducible to wrong choices made by human beings. We are perhaps still challenged to deepen our idea of evil beyond the idea of a single moral fault, a delict at the dawn of the race.

5. The world exists for man and woman but in a qualified sense. These opening chapters of Genesis are human-centred to a degree. For example, the Priestly account reaches a climax in the creation of man and woman. There is an unforgettable beauty to the special blessing pronounced over them and the hymn of joy which proclaims their nobility (Gen 1:26-29). Man and woman are the image of God, they are to increase and multiply and care for the earth. Humankind is suffused of the breath of God, is uniquely living spirit with an especial mission of merciful and faithful stewardship. Rather than a plaything of the forces of nature, man/woman are God's vice-gerent in creation. They have a responsibility for nature and its well-being. Here is the ground for the claim made by many theologians that the first theology of secularity is in the book of Genesis. Nature is not divine. It is not the repository of the sacred in any magical sense. Rather, it is to be respected as the theatre of God's purposes – a theatre of reality where man and woman have leading roles. And so, if Genesis has a human centred bias it is not in any exploitative sense. It inculcates the responsibility of stewardship: 'The earth has been entrusted to man, but it remains God's property. Man has been given no licence to despoil the earth. Man's special status is a call to responsibility towards the natural world. Human dominion ... is meant to be a wise and benevolent rule so that it may be, in its measure, the sign of God's lordship over his creation. Everything in God's created order has its allotted place. Every creature by performing its assigned function, serves and glorifies its creator.[7]

6. The technical doctrine of creation *ex nihilo* is not explicitly contained in these chapters of Genesis. The text clearly emphasises that everything is dependent upon God's creative presence. Yet the first explicit reference to 'creation out of nothing' does not occur until the Second Book of Maccabees.

PSALMS AND WISDOM LITERATURE

It would be excessive to claim that creation in the Old Testament is swallowed up by Israel's longing for salvation – as if there were no real grasp of creation in pre-testamental and Old Testament times. Such a claim would sweep the broad base from under Jewish faith in God's saving acts. It would leave this faith without relation to experience of God in nature and, indeed, in human consciousness. Creation as an article of faith emerged with the spirituality of the synagogue. It is, therefore, relatively late as an explicit teaching. Nevertheless, the Hebrews had long possessed oral traditions witnessing to a belief that we are God's creatures and living in God's world. In so far as these traditions can be reconstrucuted, e.g. from certain psalms, they articulate an experience of 'givenness'. This consciousness of nature and of life as gift is 'at the root of all religion as a relationship with what believers call the creator God'.[8] Even when re-fashioned in the light of later 'salvation' experiences, the creation traditions retain their relatively independent character. Israel experiences the creative power and presence of Yahweh 'in darkness and light, rain and snow, in camel and hippopotamus, moon and stars, in the beauty of flowers, plants and animals, in the birth of a child'.[9] Consciousness of God's creative gift becomes an invitation to thankfulness, trust and obedience in the Psalms and Wisdom Literature. One finds this independent theme, for example, in Psalm 8:

> When I see the heavens, the work of your hands,
> the moon and the stars which you arranged ...
> How great is your name, O Lord our God, through all the
> earth.

It is said that Psalm 19 is part of an ancient hymn from Canaan and is an adaptation to Israel's monotheism. It carries a deep beauty and evinces an impressive creation spirituality:

> The heavens proclaim the glory of God
> and the firmament shows forth the work of his hands.
> Day unto day takes up the story
> and night unto night makes known the message

There is, therefore a distinct consciousness of creation spirituality and theology in the corpus of Psalms. Apart from Psalms 9 and 19, there are Psalms 33, 65, 92, 95, 96, 139 and 149. Taken together they provide a goodly repository for spirituality and Christian reflection. Edward Schillebeeckx's point is appropriate: the Israelite 'integrated a general belief in creation into the monotheistic Yahwism of Israel and above all into its conception of God's history with His people Israel'.[10] This achievement should not be minimised in its witness to the remarkable newness of Israel's faith.

With the Wisdom literature one encounters yet another perspective on creation thought. These books – Job, Wisdom, Ben Sirach, Daniel – are the product of the Jewish disaspora or dispersal through the Greek speaking and Egyptian worlds. They show a marked difference from the rest of the Old Testament.

The influence of Greek and Egyptian 'wisdom' is clear. Whereas the Old Testament is generally spare on abstract concepts, Wisdom literature has a technical vocabulary for such ideas as cosmos and universe. Repeatedly one is struck by its subtlety of thought. The mystery of creation is considered for its own sake. The perfections of the world are extolled. Wisdom literature leads us to God by contemplation of nature as a witness to the divine. Thus runs Wisdom 13:5 ' ... by the greatness and beauty of the creature may be known the creator of them'. The book of Job lists the wonders of creation to justify the transcendence of God to our faltering questions:

> ... where shall wisdom be found ...
> man does not know the way to it ...
> God understands the way to it ...
> When he gave the wind its weight
> and meted out the waters by measure,
> when he made a decree for the rain
> and a way for the lightning and thunder
> then he saw [Wisdom] and declared it.
> He established it and set it forth.
> (Job 28:12)

It would be a mistake if the beauty and religious significance of this literature were devalued. Apart from the role the Wisdom tradition plays in the Christology of the New Testament, the tradition also affects St Paul's view of the 'natural' knowledge of God. His reference to the knowledge of God available from the divine works is continuous with Wisdom 13. Only an extreme dualism of Old and New Testament, of nature and grace, of religion and faith, would deny the value of the Wisdom approach for an understanding of our relation to our world and to God, its sustainer and creator.

CREATION IN THE NEW TESTAMENT

There is little direct reference to creation/origins in the four Gospels. Given their purpose this is not surprising. They set out to present the tradition about Jesus not to develop a theological system. Yet, one can find there a rich source of reflection on creation. The evangelists presuppose the Old Testament doctrine of origins. The genealogy in Luke's Gospel points up the universal significance of Jesus by tracing the unity of the race to the original creation of Adam. Further, the Gospels present God as Father who is present to every particle of the world God has called forth. God has concern for all. For the just and the unjust. For the lilies of the field. The birds of the air are not beyond God's concern. Nor are we. The hairs of our heads are numbered with loving care. Our need of food and clothing is remembered by God. Jesus presupposes the order of creation when he protests: 'in the beginning it was not so' (Matt 19:8). His parables and similes are redolent of God's creative presence, of God's support of, and concern for, the least of things. Jesus would appear to have remained closely in touch with the things of nature and to have had an appreciative knowledge of the processes of nature.

In the epistles and in Acts one uncovers an understanding of creation which became explicit in missionary situations. For example, both Acts 14 and Acts 17 presuppose the Hellenist-Jewish model of instruction for Gentiles wishing to become Jews. In inter-testamentary Judaism there was a tripartite creed adapted for new converts. It expressed belief in God the creator, belief in judgment on those who do not repent, and hope in the proferred salvation. At Acts 14:15 and Acts 17:22-31 Paul uses a Christian version of the same scheme. At Acts 17 he proclaims: (1) 'a God who has created the world and everything that is in it, who is Lord of heaven and earth'; (2) 'who has appointed a day on which he will judge the world according to righteousness'; (3) 'through a man whom he has appointed for that purpose'. At Acts 14, there is a similar approach: 'we bring you good news, that you should turn from these vain things to a living God who made heaven and earth and the sea and all that is within them'. For the Jews of the inter-testamentary period, the first things (protology) are closely linked to the last things (eschatology). The link was conversion in the present. This pattern of creation, conversion, and consummation, was taken up and adapted in the missionary preaching of Paul at Lystra and Athens. The pattern is protology (creation), eschatology (the last things), Christology. It is interesting that creation occupies so large a part of this scheme.[11]

For New Testament Christology, Jesus is the link between protology and eschatology, creation and salvation: 'the bond between creation and salvation is tied by means of the concept of eschatological judgment in Christ'.[12] It is this awareness of Jesus' significance for the whole world that gives impetus to the New Testament belief in Jesus' mediation of creation. Paul speaks of 'one Lord Jesus Christ through whom are all things and through whom we exist'. Thus, one of the first formulations of the faith witnesses firmly to the central role of Christ for the universe: 'for although there may be many so-called gods in heaven or on earth yet for us there is one God, the Father, from whom are all things, and for whom we exist and one Lord Jesus Christ through whom are all things, and through whom we exist' (1 Cor 8:6). From this flows Paul's optimism about the goodness of all creation: 'for the earth is the Lord's, and everything in it' (1 Cor 10:25-26).

Several models are used in the New Testament to proclaim Christ's person and work. Some of these explicitly appeal to the role of Christ in creation. Thereby they witness to the mutual interaction of Christology and creation theology. A clear example is the ascription to Christ of the function of *Logos*. This Word-Christology expresses the universal mediation in Christ in God's plan. In the prologue of John's Gospel there is a studied parallel between the creation account and the new creation in the word made flesh. As one follows the careful artistry of John, one can only admire his skilful adaptation of the Jewish tradition on the creative word of God. It is the Word made flesh in Jesus who created in the beginning. In this allusion is contained the originality of the New Testament as it directly relates what happened in Jesus to the work of God who called forth the world and everything in it. There is an equally striking use of the Word concept in the Epistle to the Hebrews. God spoke in many ways through the prophets, but in the last days through a Son, the heir of all things, through whom this world was created. Word (*logos*), image (*eikon*), and stamp (*charakter*) coalesce here: Jesus is the image (*eikon*) of the eternal God, reflects God's glory as in an image, bears the stamp of God's nature, upholds the world by divine power. 'He is the one through whom God created the universe ... He reflects the brightness of God's glory and is the exact likeness of God's own being, sustaining the universe with his powerful word' (Heb 1:1-3). The author of Hebrews transfers the splendid words of Psalm 102 to Jesus Christ: 'Thou, Lord, didst found the earth in the beginning and the heavens are the work of thy hands they will perish but thou remainest' (Heb 1:10-11; Psalm 102). Christ's part in creation finds its definitive expression here. In him, for the Christian view, the orders of creation and redemption come together in unity.

CHRIST THE RECONCILER OF CREATION

The unity of creation and redemption is clear in Ephesians and Colossians. These letters present the work of Christ as the reconciliation of a multiple disorder: 'He is our peace who made us both [Jew and Gentile] one ... and reconciled us both [Jew and Gentile] in one body through the Cross'. (Eph 2:16). 'Through him are reconciled all things, whether on earth or in heaven, making peace by the blood of his Cross' (Col 1:20). The limitation in Ephesians to Jewish/Gentile relations is superseded in the universal range of Colossians – 'all things, whether on earth or in heaven'. Together these epistles review the effect of Christ's ministry on the cosmic, ecclesiological and ethical dimensions of life. In Colossians the adversary, unnamed but real, is Jewish Pythagoreanism. This was a 'philosophy' or way of life, an amalgam of religion and Hermetic wisdom, which tried to overcome the *polemos* or cosmic disharmony through washings, baths and dietary abstinence. The epistle recognises that there is cosmic disharmony. It endorses the Greek perception that war, hostility and disorder are prevalent. Yet, it contests all spurious reconciliations by presentng the cross of Christ as the reconciliatory event *par excellence*. Jesus Christ has a cosmic significance. Because of this, his death and resurrection can effect a universal reconciliation: 'it has long been an apostolic conviction that Christ is the Lord, *Kyrios,* of the Church, but now Colossians wants to give Jesus a place in the whole of the macrocosm'.[13] Because he is the firstborn of all creation, in whom all things were created, Jesus can reconcile all through his death and resurrection. Much later the liturgy was to acclaim:

> O faithful Cross, you stand unmoved, while ages run their course,
> Foundation of the universe, creation's binding force.[14]

Primarily, the reconciliation is of sinners with God. People once again have accęss to God's favour. This reconciliatory lordship of Christ is exercised through the Church, his body. The reconciliation is cosmic – extending to thrones, dominions, principalities, powers and authorities. The harmony grievously disrupted by the age-old curse of sin has been restored in Jesus Christ. The Christian no longer has cause for cosmic anxieties, no longer need attend to tabus or horoscopes, no longer should fear the forces of destiny.[15] It is worth lingering a moment on the cosmic role ascribed here to Christ. One can say that Colossians accords Jesus a definite causal power in several ways. Everything is for him – Christ is the very goal and meaning of the universe. Everything is in him – Christ is Lord over all earthly powers. Everything is through him – for through him God created all, including the powers, lords, rulers, and authorities which as cosmic forces so intimidated people of the ancient world.

CHRIST THE HEAD [RECAPITULATOR] OF CREATION

'For he has made known to us the mystery of his will, to reestablish all things in Christ, things in heaven and things on earth'. (Eph 1:9-10). The Letter to the Ephesians insists that creation is planned with Christ in mind. Jesus is the presupposition and exemplar of that splendid work. Creation moves to a *resumé* or recapitulation in Christ. God's plan is to bring everything to unity and peace in him. Ephesians speaks of *anakephalaiosis*. It means not so much headship as primacy or principality, with the added connotation of recapitulation or bringing together in one point. Christ is the summit of creation upon whom converge all else. In him the deepest reality of things is restored – their being for God. Creation is, as it were, Christoform. Edward Schillebeeckss's fine treatment of recapitulation shows that the fundamental insight of Ephesians is that Christ is the founder of universal peace. The same author emphasises that the chief lesson of the text is not 'a kind of cosmic omnipresence'. It is rather that through the death and resurrection of Christ, forgiveness and new access to God is gained for all without exception. In Christ a broken world has been made whole.[16]

An allied notion, embedded in both Colossians and Ephesians, is that of *pleroma* or fulness. This is the fulness to which creation is called but has yet to attain. Creation is predestined to a godly existence derived, not from itself, but from Christ who draws all others to share in the fulness with which he is already filled: 'in him the fulness of deity dwells bodily, and you have come to the fulness of life in him' (Col 2:9). Thus Christ becomes the *pleroma,* the fulness of things. He becomes the principle of totality not only for people but for the world as a whole. One can speak of redeemed people and, even, of a redeemed world. Just as the whole of creation shares the aspiration of humankind for the fulness of adoption in the fatherhood of God, the same creation already shares in the redemption attained in the cross of Christ. If one follows Congar's interesting suggestion, one might use the image of concentric circles to express both the *anakephalaiosis* and the *pleroma.* At the outer circle, Jesus is the head who resumes, and fills up, all creation – even those cosmic powers such as 'principalities, thrones and dominations' (Col 2:16; Eph 1:2-7). At the inner circle, he is head and fulness of those who have accepted his lordship through the Gospels. In other words, Christ is head of the Church, the community of people who by faith and baptism have entered into the closest relationship to him. This Church is filled with the power of Christ. Hence it has a responsibility for the world, for creation – in particular to labour so that the peace of Christ is given form in its own life and work. Thus one sees more clearly that neither Colossians nor Ephesians proclaims an individualistic or private salvation.

NEW CREATION (*KAINE KTISIS*), NEW PERSON (*KAINOS ANTHROPOS*)

For all its positive estimation of a continuing creation, the New Testament affirms the need for renewal through recreation or new creation: 'neither circumcision counts for anything, nor uncircumcision, but a new creation' (Col 6:15). Paul is clear that this new creation is more than a metaphor. It is neither a legal fiction nor an 'as if'. It reaches into and transforms our life. In Christ we become - and are - new creatures. The same God who, in creation, said 'Let light shine out of darkness' has given us, in re-creation, 'the light of the knowledge of the glory of God in the face of Christ'. Paul's emphasis on the first and second Adams is the clearest example of this. In Adam, God's good creation has been spoiled; in Christ, it has been restored superabundantly: 'where sin abounded, grace did more abound'. Christ the mediator of creation and re-creation, has given us a new nature, established by him and exemplified in him: 'if anyone is in Christ, he is a new creation' (2 Cor 15:17).

Since action follows being, the ethical dimension of new creation is equally important. Perhaps this dimension merits the greater stress. It is only as we live 'in righteousness and truth' that the new creation is fashioned in us – 'for we are his workmanship, created in Jesus Christ for good works which God prepared beforehand that we should walk in them' (Eph 2:10; cf. Rom 2:12, Gal 5:6, 2 Cor 3:18). In effect, the New Testament has a range on creation that moves from the first things (protology) to the last things (eschatology). It holds these two ends together and accentuates their unity. God's dealing with the world is essentially simple. From creation to re-creation to final fulfilment, God's action bears upon salvation in Christ. The nodal point is the Easter event with its effects in history, in the cosmos and in people's lives. At Easter, a cosmic principle of renewal and restoration has been inserted even though its consummation has yet to come. Whereas the original creation was an effortless evocation (God said, 'Let there be ... ' and it was so) the new creation comes through the weariness and labour of the Cross. It has been ushered in through pain and suffering. It is established gradually. Its power is the resurrection of Jesus and its first fruits communicated through the Holy Spirit not only at Baptism but also throughout our lives. The struggle for a new creation redounds upon nature as well as on humankind. This cosmic dimension of struggle, with its hint of a glorious outcome is brought out by Paul: 'For we know that up to the present time all of creation groans with pain ... but it is not just creation alone which groans; we who have the Spirit as the first of God's gifts also groan within ourselves, as we wait for God to make us his sons and set our whole being free' (Rom 8:22-23).

For New Testament thought, then, creation is much broader than origins. Creation transcends even that religiously valuable sense of the presence of God which the Old Testament hymns. Creation in the New Testament is closely related to the project of reconciliation of man/woman with man/woman, of man/woman with nature, and of all with God. The project laid in creation reached its high point in the ministry and work of Jesus Christ. As our experience tells us, there remains much yet to do. There is a remainder yet to be filled up in the suffering of Christ through the work of discipleship. In the work of discipleship the new creation is being built and the 'new man' fashioned. Hence the New Testament forces our ideas on creation to embrace a cosmic Christology (L. Boff), an eschatology, as well as a new and more exciting perspective on discipleship. It points up the identity of the regenerative, re-creative Holy Spirit with the spirit which hovered over the aboriginal chaos. One can but re-echo the sentiment of Jürgen Moltmann in regard to the interconnection of creation in the New Testament with all the dimensions of the Christian faith: 'Anyone who looks for statements about creation in the New Testament often finds the results disappointing. Apart from the beautiful 'lilies of the field', creation does not seem to be a new theme. But we only get this impression if we are looking for statements about creation at the beginning. The New Testament testimony to creation is embedded in the *kerygma* about the resurrection, and in pneumatology. In these God's creative activity is understood eschatologically as *kalein* (to call to life), *egeirein* (to raise),and *zoopoioun* (to make alive), for they are related to the creation of the end-time or 'the new creation'.[17]

THE EARLY FATHERS OF THE CHURCH

With the monumenta of the Apostolic Fathers – the epistles of Clement, the epistle of Barnabas, the Didache, the Shepherd of Hermas – we meet important works of catechetical and practical theology. These adhere firmly to apostolic preaching. They do not move outside the ambit of the Scriptures and later Judaism. They show an awareness, however, that the *caesura* between the Church and paganisn was belief in the oneness of God. It is true that 'the first article concerning the creation was not proclaimed from the rooftops until the gnostics appeared with their attempt to cut the created world loose from God, and attribute to the demiurge power over bodily and external existence'.[18] Yet the doctrine of creation appears even in these earliest post-apostolic

works. The Shepherd of Hermas insists that the first command-
ment is to believe that 'God is one, who created and established
all things, bringing them into existence out of non-existence'. This
is the first allusion in Christian literature to *creatio ex nihilo*.[19] In
the same vein both the Didache and the epistle of Barnabas teach
that God is the Lord almighty who governs the whole universe.
The first epistle of Clement carries several anthems of praise to
the Creator: 'the Father and creator of the entire cosmos', 'creat-
or and Father of ages', 'creator and guardian of every spirit'.[20]
Although one can take the impression that the Christian dimension of creation is relatively undeveloped, nevertheless it is not
absent: 'He [Christ] called us when we were not, and willed us to
come into existence out of nothingness'.[21] However, the relation
between creation and 'saving history' is not brought out with
sharp definition. An emphasis on the life of the Church communities and a preoccupation with individual morality seem to have
inhibited any systematic address to that question. As a result it
was not until a later time that an engagement took place with the
Hellenic environment into which Christianity had moved.

THE APOLOGISTS

The early second century saw the emergence of apologists for the
new faith. People such as Aristides, Justin Martyr, Tatian and
Theophilus of Antioch addressed the Greek intellectual world.
They tried to show that Christianity was superior to the religious
perceptions of paganism. This task was rendered difficult not by
any inherent deficiency in the Christian teaching but rather by the
many adaptations required to present the Jewish-Greek concepts
of the New Testament in the diverse milieux of the early years of
Christianity. The apologists had a dual concern. They wished to
defend the Christian view of God and creation. On the other
hand, they attacked the prevalent ideas of the relation between
the divine and the worldly. They insist that God is one, not many.
The Greek pantheon is ruthlessly emptied. It is replaced by the
strict monotheism of Israel. As a corollary of this, the Apologists
lay heavy stress upon the *creatio ex nihilo*. Thus the foundation is
laid for Christianity's long-standing opposition to every form of
metaphysical dualism. These Apologists oppose any suggestion
of the eternity of matter or of a principle independent of God. In
this way they contest Greek natural theology and the ancient
cosmogonies. Nevertheless, the very fact of entering even a dialogue of conflict leads the Apologists towards the Hellenic idea of
transcendence so that the *Logos* or Word is occasionally predicat-

ed as intermediate between God and creation. With Arius this was to wreak havoc in the Church of the early fourth century.

The first major theological works on creation were in response to Gnosticism. For this reason alone it will be worthwhile briefly to consider a current of thought with which Christianity had to engage in controversy of the fiercest kind. The lure of Gnosis seems to have fascinated Christians right into the late middle ages. Gnosticism was pre-Christian, yet its most fruitful soil was at Rome and other centres of early Christianity. It was an amalgam of Jewish, Christian, Greek and Oriental wisdom. It developed initiation ceremonies and other ritual practices. It was never a Church. Rather the Gnosis was purveyed by local groupings around individual teachers. Some masters of Gnosis regarded themselves as Christians and practised as such. One finds a peculiar dialectic of attraction and repulsion in regard to Gnosticism in sections of patristic literature. Perhaps the sharpest threat of Gnosticism was that 'behind all the ... sects there lay the common stock of ideas which could fasten upon, adapt themselves to, and eventually transform any religious environment concerned to find an answer to the problem of existence, evil and salvation'.[22]

Gnosticism was marked by an extremely pessimistic view of creation. In large part it was a recoil from suffering, evil and meaninglessness in nature and history. It traced the origin of the material world to a fall or disaster. Creaturehood was equiparated with sinfulness or deformation. Salvation was placed in a long lost paradise or in a new age yet to arise from the ruins of our present evil day. Strands within the Gnosis opposed the creator God of the Old Testament to the saviour God of the New. Since the criterion of goodness was distance from matter, the body was regarded as evil. Redemption was attained through avoidance of the world: 'man's salvation ... consists in raising himself above his human condition and creaturely status'.[23] Leo Scheffczyk asserts that Gnostic redemption is anti-cosmic. Hence it places an unbridgable gap between creation and redemption. Neither the body nor anything material can be redeemed. How, then, can redemption be achieved? It is attained by esoteric knowledge communicated to the 'spirituals': 'the spiritual man is redeemed by knowledge'. Knowledge is not merely virtue. It is very salvation itself. The power of Gnosticism over many of the best minds forced Christianity to clarify its own view on the main points in contention. One of these was the relation of creation and redemption.

Irenaeus of Lyons is the best known and most consistent opponent of the Gnosis. *Adversus Haereses* is his principal theological work. Here he attacks the dualism of the Gnostics, by proclaiming the unity of the Old and the New Testaments. Likewise, he stresses the unity of creation and redemption. Irenaeus establishes that God the Creator and God the Redeemer are one and the same. God's plan for the world is of a piece. It was redemption in Christ which God had in mind at creation. Irenaeus outstrips even St Paul in showing that Christianity grows out of the Old Testament. Whereas Paul brings out the contrast between Adam and Christ, Irenaeus underlines their connection. In Adam we were created in a childlike state of innocence. We were destined gradually to develop towards our full stature. With the advent of sin our progression was grievously hindered. It was the second Adam, Jesus Christ, who restored abundantly what had been destroyed. Irenaeus' presentation of salvation history speaks of the recapitulation of all things in Christ. He re-echoes Paul's notion of summation of the whole cosmos in one person. According to J. N. D. Kelly, Irenaeus allows his thought to pan across history from protology to eschatology: 'Christ recapitulated in himself all the dispersed people dating back to Adam, all tongues and the whole race of mankind, along with Adam himself'.[24] As Adam originated a humanity plunged into disobedience and death, Christ inaugurated a new humanity unto everlasting life.

Since it is the same God who creates and redeems, there is nothing outside the scope of God's creative and redeeming activity. Irenaeus highlights the absurdity of supposing that there is any being over whom God's power does not obtain. If there is any such being, it must be a second divinity. There is no independent vis-à-vis to God in creation. On this key idea rests Irenaeus' deep conviction of 'creation out of nothing'. Matter is not eternal. God needs no pre-existing material upon which to work. God did everything not from need but from the motive of beneficent love. Thus Irenaeus offers a solution to the problem of why God created: 'It was not that God needed humankind, but rather that there might be those on whom to confer God's benefits' (*non quasi indigens Deus hominibus, sed ut habeat in quem collocaret sua beneficia*).[25]

We frequently overlook that there were thriving centres of Christian life and major theological reflection even before the prominence of Rome and Constantinople. At Alexandria there was a vigorous school of catechetics. There, through the work of people such as Clement, Origen and Athanasius, a lively theological tradition was sustained. Another 'school' was at Antioch in

Turkey. Nor should we overlook the contributions made by Tertullian and Augustine in North Africa. It is salutary to recall a vitality now quenched but which influenced the broader stream even in regard to creation theology. Both Clement and Origen had to take account of the challenge of Gnosticism. It is an evidence of their confidence that they attempted to express some of the concepts of Gnosticism in a way consonant with Christian orthodoxy. They sought 'not so much to contradict error as to establish points of agreement and to interpret the other doctrine so far as possible in a Christian sense'.[26] The history of christology at Alexandria evidences both the strength and weakness of their endeavour. It is a tribute to the unwavering Christian sense of these people that they managed to use tenets of Platonism, Stoicism and neo-Pythagoreanism as a sub-structure on which to build an orthodox theology. Clement moves away from a literal interpretation of Genesis. He believes that creation is a timeless act in which all things were brought to be. Creation is a continuing reality, a *creatio continua*.[27] Just as God is committed to the world in its creation, God remains with it in its preservation. Origen too attempted to bring coherence to Christian thought on creation. His approach, while far less scriptural than Irenaeus', was to influence the thought of many generations after him. Above all others, he tried to establish an alignment between Greek philosophy and Christian theology. Here his success was limited. Yet his innovative genius has perdured throughout the centuries. In his *De Principiis* he speaks of providence as most detailed and all pervasive (*minutissima et subtilissima*). Origen thinks in terms of a divine pedagogy guiding things back to an original unity. This is his scheme of *exitus-reditus*: the creation goes out from God – not in an emanationist sense – only to find an original unity in God. It is for this idea of a divine economy or pedagogy in creation that we are most indebted to the Eastern Fathers. Not without its difficulties, the insight has great significance for an apperception of God's closeness to creation.

WESTERN PATRISTIC THOUGHT

In the West there was a less mystical, more strictly rational, view of creation. The neo-Platonic speculations on the pre-existence of souls, on a multiplicity of worlds, on a hierarchy of beings, were considerably restricted. Lactantius, Tertullian and, later, Hilary of Poitiers forsook the Platonic bent of the East, although they continued to use neo-Platonism as a crutch to reflection. In Jerome there is an emerging preoccupation to relate creation theology to a theology of the Trinity. Yet it was Augustine who gave western thought on creation its fullest shape. Augustine combined a leaning to scriptural exegesis with an outstanding ability to make use of diverse philosophic aids. He wrote three commentaries on the book of Genesis: *De Genesi ad litteram, De Genesi ad litteram imperfectus liber, De Genesi contra Manichos*. Augustine's creation theology is mirrored in these works. He is very clear about a 'creation out of nothing'. Even matter, that invisible and unknown territory (*terra invisibilis et incomposita*), is a creature. Creation is neither a semi-divine emanation nor independent of the Saviour God (as in Gnosticism). Rather, everything has come from God, being called forth by God out of its own nothingness. While the *City of God* hints at a developmental theology of creation, Augustine achieves a philosophical depth at considerable expense to the scriptural insight that creation is part of the history of salvation.

Augustine's philosophical genius enabled him to contribute the original insight of the concreation of time and cosmos. The world is created with time rather than in it. Time is neither a space nor a receptacle. It is rather a function of change, a measurement of duration. Rejecting Aristotle and Plato, Augustine offers an analysis which is both metaphysical and psychological. From the metaphysical aspect, he draws a firm distinction between temporal and eternal existence. The creature is inescapably temporal, contingent in being, and subject to change. Only God has being in an eternal Now. From the psychological aspect, Augustine achieves a major advance by linking time and consciousness. Time, he tells us, is the measure of change. Its roots lie in both the external and internal dimensions of reality, the objective and the subjective. This dual analysis of time is crucially important in the consideration of the finitude of all creatures and in contesting an endless succession of worlds, a concept dear to neo-Platonic speculation.

Another achievement of Augustine was to relate creation to Trinity. Creation is a trinitarian act. It is from the Father through the Word. Its eventual perfection is guaranteed by the Holy Spirit. All things bear the mark of the Trinity. The term *vestigium Trinitatis* comes from Augustine and is applied in Christian theology to the whole creation. On the other hand, one should not ignore Augustine's repeated emphasis that with regard to creation 'the Father, the Son, and the Holy Spirit form a single principle, just as they form a single creator and a single Lord'.[28] It is partly because of this link to Trinitarian theology that one finds a basic optimism in Augustine's thought on creation. Unfortunately, such optimism does not mitigate the severity of his judgement on the body and on marriage. His increasing pessimism on these will be referred to later on this study. It is of interest to note, however, that one of the first magisterial pronouncements on creation (Council of Toledo, 447 A.D.) included an affirmation of the goodness of marriage.[29]

Augustine used his own experience of two streams of thought *viz.* neo-Platonism and Manichaeism, not only to combat these but to achieve a middle way between their extremes. He seized upon the neo-Platonic hierarchy of being and used it to rebut the emanationism of the neo-Platonists and the dualism of the Manichees. God is God. The creature is creature. The world was created good. Sin introduced the age-old fissure thus originating evil and decay. Evil, Augustine tells us, is an island of nothingness in a world created good. However, it remains an irony that while his tireless reflection forces Augustine to affirm the goodness of creation yet his personal characteristics and his experience forced him to ever more pessimistic views on the actual state of humanity.

THREE

An Emergent Tradition on Creation

CREATION AS RELATION: ST THOMAS AQUINAS (1225-1274)

It has been argued by Professor Alan Watts that 'the idea of God as maker of the world, and thus of the world itself as an artefact ... with a purpose and explanation ... is the clearest example ... of the architectonic and artificial style of Christianity'. The late Bishop John Robinson in *Honest to God* subjects the traditional view of creation to a similar criticism. Both writers see creation as a static conception which does justice neither to our relationship to the ground of our being nor to the dynamism of nature itself. Clearly, these are objections which must be met. Since St Thomas Aquinas is a major representative of the tradition under criticism, it will be helpful to consider his presentation at some length. One would urge a sympathetic understanding of the purpose and method of Aquinas, as of the medievals generally. Attention to the context in which they worked can show that the medieval theology of creation is a good deal more impressive than is commonly allowed.[1]

Aquinas wrote in the high middle ages. The fifth crusade had petered out just before he was born. It was a time of disorder, famine and disease, which were grimly accepted as part of the natural order. On the other hand, a coherent view of an intellectual, spiritual and political order was being sought. Aquinas represents the culmination of an endeavour to present a worldview. He succeeded in the attempt to a degree hitherto unrivalled for self-consistency and comprehensiveness. And so the paradox stands that, in spite of much misery and underdevelopment, medieval civilisation was one of the most vital in history. In Scholasticism a new level of reflection was attained. The major achievement of the Schools was a systematic, critical presentation of the insights of Scripture and the living tradition, through the prism of theoretic reflection.

Although St Thomas used concepts from the natural philosophy of his time, it would be a caricature of his theology to see it as an exercise in derived philosophy . He drew liberally on an Aristotelianism newly available – the 'new learning' mediated by the Arabian philosophers and scientists. Again, it is true that St Thomas' type of reflection lacks the directness of the Scriptures and the simplicity of the earlier Fathers of the Church. Aquinas proceeds with the objectivity of the scientist rather than with the imaginative fire of the prophet or the pastor. He treats each topic by setting out the countervailing objections before offering his own analysis in a fashion both restrained and austere. Yet his starting point is always the experience of the living God mediated in the tradition of the Church. Aquinas' creation theology is best understood when related to the *idée maîtresse* of his writing on God: the 'I am Who I am' or the 'I will be with you' of Exodus 3:14. Aquinas' thinking on creation springs from a theology of the God of Abraham, Isaac and Jacob, the Father of our Lord Jesus Christ. St Thomas came to believe that creation can be rationally demonstrated. However, it is doubtful that he would attempt a proof of creation apart from religious experience or the tradition in which such experience is mediated.

With St Thomas there is a restrained interest in the question of origins. His fundamental concern is the perduring relation between the Creator and the creature. To this question Aquinas brought a novel approach. It was an approach which extended the existing literature and exemplified his genius for judicious selection from diverse material. For St Thomas, creation is the reception of being from the giver of all existence. Creation is nothing other than a relation to the Creator as the fount of our being. God *is* being. God is the fullness and perfection of existence. All created beings *have* being. They have being as a participation in what God is fully and perfectly. This participation defines creaturehood.

Aquinas came to speak frequently of 'being by essence' and 'being by participation'.[2] This couplet is used recurrently in St Thomas' later writings to express the relation of the creature to the Creator. The notion of participation has a Platonic root. It means to have a part: *est autem participare quasi partem habere.* (*In lib. Boethii De Trinitate,* I, 2). It connotes likeness, similarity, imitation, sharing in nature or perfection. However, on its own it does not make it sufficiently clear that the creature is infinitely distant from the Creator. To remedy this, Aquinas used another philsophical tradition – the newly available and apparently radical doctrine of Aristotle on causality, potency and act. Aquinas can argue that every cause communicates something of itself to its effect but always in proportion to the limitation of that effect. Thus, when St Thomas speaks of creation as participation in being, he envisages a sharing in the being of God in a manner proper to our created nature. In other words, creation is not an act at the beginning of time. It communicates a real but limited sharing in being. The one who *is* being is God. Everything which exists *has* being in utter debt to God's creative gift and in the measure of that gift.

What does Aquinas intend by 'being'? It is the supreme act by which every existent is not simply this or that but *is*. Being is not a predicate. It is not a quality like height, colour, weight. Rather it is act and perfection. Its sheer actuality is brought out by the participial form, 'being'. It perdures from moment to moment, ever to be renewed. Being is the perfection by which I simply am and continue to be. It is intimate to me in a way I cannot measure.[3] Just as personal love cannot be measured but is savoured as God's good gift, so too with being. Its gift is 'that unique and incomparable point of reality where God meets the creature and the creature reaches to God'.[4] In the perspective of Aquinas, only God is his being. Therefore, God is infinite, surpassing, real being. As participants of being, we receive it ever anew. We do not possess it of ourselves. For living, moving and having being we depend upon the One who is being *per essentiam*.

One discovers in St Thomas a two-tiered conception of being. At the predicamental level, the level of the structure of things, there is a real relation of essence and existence, of nature and being. Each individual relates to and is perfected by its own act of being. This act or perfection – esse – confers the ultimate uniqueness of each existent, the otherness which is the basis for all union in independence. There is, however, a second level to the structure of things. Here the relation of creature to Creator is primary. The focus of reflection is again *esse,* the act of being, not precisely as a perfection of the creature, but as a constantly renewed gift of the Creator. In this frame of reference, one looks at things not merely in their 'horizontal' dimension but even more in their coming forth from God and in their continuing relation to God. Aquinas speaks of the 'transcendental perfections' such as being, truth, justice, love and wisdom. These are the simple perfections containing in their definition no admixture of imperfection (*perfectiones simpliciter simplices*). In the creature they witness vitally to God, even if at an infinite remove. Realised in God in sheer identity with all that God is, in us they are radically beholden to God for their being and their perdurance. Thus, our very act of being, and all the transcendental perfections in which we share, are sustained by God. They take on full significance when regarded as giving witness to the Creator

What, then, does Aquinas mean by creation? Creation may be viewed in two aspects: active creation (*creatio activa*) and passive creation (*creatio passiva*). Active creation refers to the creative act of God. Passive creation focuses on the effect in the creature. In the first (active) sense, creation is defined by St Thomas as the production of something from its own nothingness.[5] This highlights the radical nature of creation. It precludes any prior reality from which the new being is educed. An example may be of use here. We rightly speak of the scupltor's work as creative and original. He or she has created a new, sometimes intelligible and possibly beautiful form from what was once shapeless matter. Nevertheless, a more accurate description would be 'evocation' or 'eduction' rather than creation. For, as distinct from creation strictly understood, the sculptor needs something upon which to work. In creation, however, something is called forth, is constituted, where previously there was a void. In the words of the Psalm: 'He spoke and they were made; commanded and they were created'. The credal statement of the French episcopate, *Je Crois en Toi*, puts it well: ' ... God does not make something by creating, rather he exists contagiously, he communicates of himself as do all good educators'.[6] Creation is not an artefact. It is a gift, not of improved or altered being, but of being pure and simple. At this point we are drawn from the mythological view of origins which normally presupposes some form of dispositive material, a world stuff from which the universe was fashioned. Indeed, we are drawn away from origins as such, to the properly metaphysical level of radical dependence upon God at all points of individual and universal existence.

There remains, however, the second aspect – *creatio passiva*. This, so to speak, looks at creation from the aspect of the creature. Creation, in this sense, is not a first 'kick-off'. It is not as if God were a clockmaker who, having set up the works and wound the springs, left the clock to itself until some repairs were needed. Creation, in this second sense, is the answer to the question of the ground of being. It is a relation which arises from the continual gift of and reception of existence at the deepest level. St Thomas writes: 'creation is none other than the relation of the creature to the Creator as to the princple of its very being'.[7] Such a relation subsists throughout the whole of reality without any prejudice to the autonomy of nature and the cosmos. In the Thomist perception, creation is a unilateral relation of dependence: the creature depends upon the Creator, but not the Creator upon the creature. Eric Mascall has pointed out: 'the really basic fact about a creature is that God does not leave it to itself and, therefore, as the object of the creative act, it is the very thing it is'.[8] Creation is not something between us and God interposed either 'out there now' or 'back there then'. It is pure relation arising from the reception of being here and now. This is surely the meaning of Aquinas' remark, 'it is not non-being that receives the divine action, but the thing which has been created'.[9] There is no intermediary between creature and Creator. We relate to God directly as the giver and sustainer of our being. Did that relation cease, we should cease not simply to act but even to exist at all.

This, then, is the background to St Thomas' systematic definition of creation as 'the emanation of all being from a universal cause'. [10] 'Emanation' reminds us of the priority of God: from God all things come. They are beholden to God for their being and in no fashion rival God's transcendence. Aquinas can speak of emanation without danger of pantheism since his concept of participation combines both likeness and distance, co-naturality and disparity. 'All being' implies that every scrap of reality is indebted to the Creator for its being and continuance. There is nothing which does not exist through God. Another facet of this truth is the anti-Gnostic affirmation that there is no principle of being co-equal to God. Aquinas would be the last man to practise *odium theologicum*. Yet he remains a stern opponent of Gnosticism, Manichaeism and Catharism. There is a fundamental optimism to his analysis which derives from his essentially positive creation theology.

'From a universal cause' reminds us of the level at which creation should be situated. There are many agents of change in human affairs and in the course of nature. Some are for development. Others bring decline. Our interaction is for good and ill. We confer and receive increments of perfection in our daily activity. Natural causes sometimes work to build up, sometimes to destroy. All the while there is influence, or better, causation. Creation with a small 'c' and creators with a small 'c'! Yet the truly creative act belongs to God alone and it reaches right through to the core of being. It confers existence as such. Only God can act thus. Other agents cause alteration, can generate and cause to decline. Only God can evoke being where previously there was nothing. Things change. Alteration is brought about by many agents. Its definition is 'mutation from one state to another' (*mutatio ab uno statu in alium*). Things are generated. The definition of generation is 'production of a thing from a pre-existent subject' (*productio rei ex nihilo sui sed subiecti*). Generation always presupposes a predisposing situation. It comes from pre-existent matter. Creation, however, presupposes no prior state of affairs. In speaking of creation, therefore, we should remember that temporal categories are misleading – as if one could say: 'before being there was nothing'. Creation is not about before and after. It is rather about an order of being – of reception from a total source. Hence the further classical definition of creation as 'production of something from nothingness' (*productio rei ex nihilo sui nec subiecti*).

St Thomas deals with the allied notion of conservation.[11] There are at least two senses to the word. The first is close to what we mean when we speak of ecological conservation. Conservation is then the removal or prevention of corruptive agents. One conserves by supportive, sheltering, protective action. There is a second kind of conservational action to which St Thomas refers. This is the imparting and renewal of existence. It is the prerogative of God alone. We stand at every moment in a relation of receptivity to God at this most profound level. This is a relation of dependence such that, were it to cease, we would simply relapse out of being. Every creature depends on God both in its becoming and its perduring. Everything is indebted to God not only for being but for continued being. It will be seen that the distinction between creation and conservation is a distinction of reason rather than of fact. In each case we are speaking of relation of gift and continued reception.

God's activity underlies, without interfering in, our powers and activities. This is not the place to enter the once vexed question of reconciling God's influence and human freedom. God keeps us in being and enables our action – even our free action. It is useful to keep in mind the distinction between primary or transcendent causality, and secondary or predicamental causality. Secondary causality runs the gamut of activity from the gentleness of love to the indomitable forces of nature. Yet, underlying all, enabling all, is the primary causality which is God's alone. In this careful sense one can attribute causality totally to God and totally to creatures. We can say of a good action, a beautiful gesture, that it is from God as well as from the doer. Indeed, in strict theology we can say of an evil action that it is permitted by God since the divine conservation is not subtracted from the evildoer.

Does critical reflection on our sources, both philosophical and theological, allow us to affirm that God's creative and conservational activity impinges on our consciousness? Any kind of 'illuminism', any claim to 'see' God or directly to experience God, should be avoided. Such a claim is unwarranted in the mainstream of Christianity and would encounter serious philosophical objection as well. Nor is it proposed here to treat of mysticism whether natural or supernatural. Yet there is an important article of St Thomas on the presence of God to creation. In the eighth question of the first part of the *Summa,* Aquinas urges: 'God is in all things and is present to them intimately'.[12] God is present in grace, in faith, in hope and in love. Theology emphasises that sanctifying grace is the availability of the Father, Son and Holy Spirit. In this question of the *Summa,* however, St Thomas is asking about a 'natural' presence to all creatures in a way suitable to their level of being. God the Creator is present to his creation *'per presentiam, per potentiam, et per essentiam'.*[13] God is present *'per presentiam'* in that 'all things are naked and open to God's eyes'. God is present *'per potentiam'* in that all things are subject to God's beneficent power. God is present *'per essentiam'* in that God is with all beings as the constant giver of existence. This last mode of presence is the closest – for Aquinas, 'being' is what is most intimate and most profound in all reality.[14] This presence is not available to direct conceptual recall. What arises out of such creative presence to us as rational creatures is not a particular content of consciousness but rather our whole conscious existence. God's presence is then an implicit, unthematised ground of all our knowing and willing.[15]

It is fairly clear that the question of creation arises in a very particular perspective. With St Thomas it arises from the tradition of faith itself. His analysis, for all its metaphysical bent, cites the major scriptural texts known to present day creation theology – Ex 3:14; Eph 1:4; Heb 1:3; Rom 11:36; Jn 17:3; Col 1:16; Gal 4:4 etc. Yet Aquinas' concern also arises from a genuinely philosophic question. One can appropriately speak of his 'apprehension of contingency'. Running through Aquinas' writing is the constant reminder that we neither own nor control our being. It is gift, constantly renewed. Aquinas would understand the modern questions: Why is there being rather than nothing? What is the ground of being? To raise these questions one must have faced up to the fragility of being. As one attends to the writings of the Schools – at Chartres, at Paris, at Cologne, writings which find their maturest synthesis in Aquinas – one cannot miss their two dominant tones. One is the ancient faith that God, the Father of Jesus Christ, is the author of all being. The other is a feel for life, personality and nature, a positive assessment of being, crafted with sensitivity to the intimate nexus between God and the world.

Even today, Aquinas' perception enables a confidence in personal being which is under attack from meaninglessness and *ennui.* He invites us to accept ourselves – our selves – as God's good gift. Self-acceptance is of the greatest importance for the way we accept God and others into our life. It is not that for grace to strike home there must be perfect emotional and psychological balance. Nevertheless, a positive self-love is of immense benefit both in nature and grace. We quest for a fulfillment which lies ever ahead of us until the perfection of the beatific vision. Yet the basic gift is given to us in our very being. Our task is to receive this gift in joy and, to the limit of our powers, to construct something worthwhile for time and eternity. Louis Dupre's remark is apposite: 'to exist is to participate in an act of divine communication. This unique mixture of loneliness and presence is what believers attempt to express in the notion of a free creation'.[16]

To realise that existence is an irrevocable gift comes from an awareness that creation is gratuitous communication. God creates out of love. The motive of creation is a selfless love. And the most natural thrust in all creation is to return thanks for that creative, pre-existent love. God does not repent of God's gifts. It is a constant tenet of creation theology that, while our universe is shot through with growth and decline, God never annihilates being, once given. In theology as well as in Christian philsophy it is stressed that personal being does not end in death. No eventuality which affects our being is outside the concern of the Creator. At the level of personal being, no joy, no misfortune, is beyond the scope of God's healing presence. We may enjoy the gift of 'living, moving and having being' (Acts 17:28). We may return accepting thanks for these gifts and use them now and for the future. J.H. Newman's thought, if not his language, is consonant with Aquinas' conception of God's dealings with people: 'God beholds thee individually whoever thou art. He calls thee by name. He sees thee and understands thee, as he made thee ... He views thee in thy day of rejoicing, and day of sorrow ... He interests Himself in all thy anxieties and remembrances; all the rising and falling of thy spirit ... Thou dost not love thyself better than He loves thee ... thou art not only His creature, thou art man redeemed and sanctified, His adopted son ... '[17]

CREATION AS PROCESS: PIERRE TEILHARD DE CHARDIN (1881-1955)

It is said of Teilhard de Chardin that his life-long search was for synthesis: of reason and authority, of matter and spirit, of science and faith. This shows itself in his exigence of continuity: between matter and spirit, between past, present and future, between body and soul. His range of vision is all-comprehensive and has a tincture of mythopoesis. Teilhard spoke of his system as 'hyperphysics' – the perception of the structure of reality in its main lines, as they stand out from comparing the results of the experimental sciences with the thrust of the Judaeo-Christian tradition. There are those who complain that Teilhard crosses the bounds of science, philosophy and theology into the less defined fields of poetry and mysticism. Certainly the breadth of his intellectual concern, the symbolism of much of his language, and the fervour of his aspirations liken his views to aspects of mythmaking. Teilhard the scientist becomes Teilhard the apologist, even Teilhard the mythmaker. His perspectives merge: religious, philosophical and scientific concerns come together in his work. Note for example a passage like the following: 'Alone, unconditionally alone, in the world today, Christianity shows itself able to reconcile in a single, living act, the All and the person. Alone, it can bend our hearts not only to that tremendous movement of the world which bears us along, but even beyond it to embrace that movement in love'.[18]

While Teilhard is an enthusiastic visionary he is also a humble one. He wishes to offer a strong but personal view. Intellectual coercion is foreign to his nature: 'I am not pushing a thesis of any kind; rather what I offer is my own personal witness. I am offering the invitation of a traveller who, having left the beaten track, has quite by chance stumbled upon a point of view from which everything suddenly becomes strikingly luminous and who calls out to his companions, "Come and see" '.[19]

Teilhard views the cosmos as a process which mirrors the inner life of God. Despite all its pain, failure and even apparent absurdities, creation is destined to share the life of the Trinity. One is reminded of St Paul's idea of creation groaning for the redemption of the children of God. Teilhard believes that the explanation of things is found not in their origins but in their total history just as the greatness of a river is only discerned at its mouth, not at its source. The goal of the universe discloses its meaning. The question remains of how this goal, and hence, this meaning can be discerned. Teilhard believes that an anticipatory understanding can be achieved through attention to the overall pattern emergent on 'an immense time graph'. The experience of a palaeontologist of front rank dominates Teilhard's speculative imagination here. Dealing with the relics of millions of years, he can more easily attempt to draw the co-ordinates of such a time-graph.

Side by side with this attention to *process* Teilhard holds the traditional doctrine of creation and conservation. God creates *ex nihilo* and is supportively present to the development of the universe. To the concept of a world in development Teilhard brings a refreshingly new approach. The confluence of his several interests – in particular, his theology, his philosophy and his

science – leads him to speak of 'evolutive creation' (*creation
evolutive*). Creation is co-extensive with the duration of the
world. It has never ceased. It unfolds as a continuous activity
spaced over the totality of time. It still goes on: 'the world is
constantly, even if imperceptibly, emerging a little further above
nothingness'.[20] All life, then, is developmental, in Teilhard's
vision. It is process. Its direction is centripetal. It tends towards a
creative centre and moves by convergence upon that centre.
There is an interesting passage where Teilhard subordinates evolution to creation – an order which exemplifies the strong theological element in all his writings. Teilhard argues: 'evolution is not
really creative as science at one time thought; rather, it is the
expression, in terms of our own experience, of creation as it
unfolds in space and time'.[21] If one accepts this idea of creation as
development, under God, of the evolutionary process, one is
speaking of a *creatio continua* much as did the early Fathers of the
Church and the medieval schoolmen.

Teilhard urgently desires to show that God is really committed
to the destiny of the universe. He desired also to show that
Christianity is a life-affirming faith. And so he emphasises that
the world really matters to God. The very least Christians can do
is positively to accept God's creation, to love it and develop it to
the best of their powers. Chardin's religious perception is at
farthest remove from deism or any conception where God, having
made the world, leaves it to its own devices. *Le Milieu Divin*, an
essay like 'The Heart of the Matter' or any of his writings on the
Sacred Heart, exemplify the vitality of Teilhard's idea of God's
creative presence. Strangely, he is not happy with the traditional
stress upon love as the motive of creation. Its imprecision seems
to dissatisfy his exigence for rationality. It is not that Teilhard
identifies love with irrationality. Rather he is reacting to all
suggestions of arbitrary creation. He wishes to bring out clearly
that creation is a patterned process. Take a passage like the
following: 'classical philosophy (or theology) has invariably tended to represent creation ... as an almost arbitrary gesture ...
creation is understood on the analogy of efficient causality and
appears to be a totally arbitrary act ... an "act of God" in the
pejorative sense'.[22] Teilhard wants to exclude any hint of whim
and, instead, urges the purposiveness of creation. Thereafter, he
has no difficulty in showing creation as the working of God's
loving plan to bring all things to fullness in Christ as a showing
forth of the inner life of God.

It has to be said that Teilhard's definition of creation is somewhat tortuous. Creation means that a '*possibly* existing pure

multiplicity' is brought to be an '*actually* existing pure multiplic-ity.' This is the question of origins put in novel form. The basic categories are no longer being and non-being but unity and mul-tiplicity. God is the primal unity. Undeveloped creation is the multiplicity. There is a potentially existing multiplicity – the re-duction of which from potency to act is the first creation. Only then can development towards unity commence. Such a way of expression leads Teilhard into difficulties he would well avoid. For instance, no theologian will be happy with a passage like the following: 'In the beginning ... there were two poles of being, God and multiplicity. To create is, according to all appearances, to condense, to concentrate, to organize, to unify'.[23]

There is an unintended ambiguity here. To speak of two poles of being is to hearken back to the old ghosts of Gnosticism with its semi-divine principles of good and evil, Certianly, Teilhard does not intend this. Yet his imagery does not serve him well. Claude Tresmontant writes: 'the idea of a struggle between the One and the Many is reminiscent of those Babylonian cosmogonies in which we find the demiurge joining battle with chaos. We find then in Teilhard what amounts to a metaphysical mythology'.[24] It should be said, however, that Teilhard is well aware of the ambig-uity and tries to minimise it. Thus he equates possible multiplicity with non-being in order to hold on to the doctrine of *creatio ex nihilo*. Pure multiplicity, then, is a logical postulation rather than a real entity. It is a limit concept, the polar opposite of the perfect unity of the Trinity. Notice too Teilhard's own admission of the constriction of language to express the mystery of creation: 'I have no illusions about the fact that such a conception of a sort of positive non-being, which is the subject of creation, raises some serious problems ... However, is there really any way to avoid such pitfalls without resorting to merely verbal explanations?'[25]

The Directedness of Creation

The direction and, indeed, the directedness of creation is well expressed by Teilhard in this text: 'I believe the universe is an evolution. I believe evolution is striving in the direction of spirit: I believe spirit is perfected in the personal: I believe the perfection of the personal is the universal Christ'.[26]

The whole range of Teilhard's creation theology is contained here. This minuscule *Credo* embraces cosmogenesis – i.e. the universe as a cosmos or whole is developing in a precise direction. Likewise, it contains the meaning of geogenesis, biogenesis, psychogenesis, noogenesis and Christogenesis. Geogenesis speaks of the formation of matter; biogenesis, the evolution of organism; psychogenesis, the evolution towards mind; noogenesis, the progress of mind toward unity in the Omega point. Finally, there is Christogenesis, the correlation of noogenesis with the unity of the human race in Christ.

The broad development from Alpha point to Omega point is yet another Teilhardian shorthand for evolving creation. Evolving: for the upward sweep of things, despite pressures to dispersal and disintegration, is a thesis dear to Teilhard. Creation: for in his view such upward sweep is under the ever present aegis of God the Creator and Preserver. There is a life thrust animating the least of things and reaching beyond itself towards the most spiritual of beings. It ranges from extreme dispersal or multiplicity towards God, the supreme unity. For Teilhard, the energy of this thrust to unification is love. In *The Phenomenon of Man* he speaks of 'a within' to all things, operative even at the sub-atomic level. It is a force for convergence, cohesion and unity. In an early essay, Teilhard puts on the lips of creative wisdom the following words: 'I made even the atoms, infinitesimal as they are, feel that vague but irrepressible restlessness which arises from the desire to escape from the impotency of solitude. I made them want to relate to something outside of themselves'.[27] Again: 'driven by the power of love, the fragmented elements of the world seek each other out so that the world may reach its final goal. This is no mere metaphorical way of speaking and it is certainly not to be ascribed to sheer poetic fancy ... '[28] It is only at the level of spirit, however, that instinctive attraction is subsumed into perfect love. Teilhard has a lofty, not to say chivalrous, notion of sexual love. While giving it full importance, he also looks to a 'universal form of love which will bring together all the members of the noosphere'.[28] In so far as Omega point is attained, it is through the force generated by love in all its meaning.

The meaning of Omega

In fact, Teilhard offers four meanings of Omega point.[30] In each the idea of goal predominates. There is, first, the Omega of formal unity of humankind. It is to be read in the context of utopic vision, the ideal future where fulfilment is attained beyond the travails of the previous imperfect states. In common with many humanist visionaries, Teilhard sees evolution to lead to the progress of collective mind. Cosmogenesis has brought us to a crucial point. Henceforth, it is through union in thought and love (noogenesis) that development continues. A form of this development is the 'collectivist' solution along the lines of Marxist and utopian thought. Here is real development through concern and collaboration. Yet the beneficiaries are the 'race' or 'class' or 'future generations'. The individual and the personal are gravely underestimated, not to say discounted. While Teilhard showed himself anxious to understand these solutions to the human predicament, he regarded them as inadequate precisely in their blindness to personal worth and, specifically, to the problem of death. Time after time, Chardin emphasises that if the personal is ignored, or death regarded as the last word about personal existence, then creation itself is equivalently affirmed to be futile and absurd. Should conscious beings ever come to accept the ultimacy of death in any widespread way, then the forward thrust of evolution will lose momentum and human endeavour will peter out in meaninglessness and inconsequence.

Accordingly, Teilhard presents a second perspective on Omega point which takes account of a personal, transcendent centre to the creative-evolutionary process. This centre is outside and above the process or, to use more traditional language, is transcendent to it. Omega point influences the thrust of ascending life by attraction, drawing all things to itself. Its greatness is at once to support personal uniqueness in the closest unity and collaboration. This union is creative rather than assimilative. Far from swallowing up personality, Omega point causes personality to flower in full strength. Thus, Teilhard's oft-repeated adage is 'union differentiates' (*l'union differencie*). Creative union cherishes diversity. Omega point, in this second sense, is active in history not only through the provision of motive for action but principally through its own personal effectiveness. Teilhard names this active Centre of centres, God. It is the unnamed God of the sermon to the Athenians depicted in Acts 17. It is the God and Father of Jesus Christ. While the correlation of Omega point with God stems from Chardin's own commitment to religious faith, yet he holds that an adequate consideration of the presuppositions of evolution would itself indicate a theistic conclusion.

Teilhard goes further in the correlation. Not only does he interpret Omega theistically, he also understands it christologically. He feels perfectly at home with the Eastern theological stress upon Christ as Universal Ruler (*Pantocrator*) and Perfector of the world (*Consummator Mundi*). Sections of the New Testament stress the same idea: Jesus is the eternal Word of God, the image of God, the first born of all creation. In this perspective Teilhard places Christ at the centre of creation and its evolution. This centrality is not mere example or motivation. For Teilhard, Christ is the shepherd of the universe, the animator of the world. Christ is the centre of the universe, the epicentre of universal history. His cosmic action is made concrete in and through his resurrection. He does not act as a carpenter works on his materials. As we have seen, Teilhard rejects this image of God's activity on the grounds that it is both extrinsic and arbitrary. He prefers the image of attraction, as a final cause influences by its own goodness. Even this is not fully satisfactory, for it does not bring out the intimate reality of God's work through Christ. To highlight this, Teilhard speaks of quasi-formal causality. God's creative action in Christ works by attraction. The love of Christ is active as the force of cosmic convergence. All things move together in moving towards him. Even more, Christ lives in us. Just as the soul organises and unifies the body-person, so the convergence of the universe upon its centre is moulded by Christ. As the soul is the formal cause of the body-person Christ is the quasi-formal cause of continuing creation. The affinity between this and the doctrine of the mystical body will not have escaped the reader. Indeed, Teilhard himself writes: 'It is the philosophy of the universe conceived in function of the notion of the mystical body. It was in reflecting upon the mystical body that I discovered the theory of creative union ... it is by seeking to love and see Christ everywhere that one will come to understanding'.[31]

Finally, Teilhard speaks of the Church as Omega point. Implicit here is the idea of the Church as the mystical body of Christ. This fourth meaning is to be taken as an extension of the third. The Church is called to be Christ's incarnation in space and time. If love is the *fil de conduite* of evolving creation and the dynamism of creative union, then the love of Christ must be manifested in creation. The love of Christ works in another way in the Church. This love is made present in Christ's community of faithful disciples. Teilhard looks to the Church as the axis of higher evolutionary movement: ' ... at the present moment Christianity is the unique current of thought within the entire noosphere which is sufficiently audacious and sufficiently progressive to lay hold of the world at the level of effective practice in an embrace capable of indefinite perfection, where faith and hope attain their fulfilment in love'.[32] Thus, more basic than ritual, doctrine and Church order is the Church's mission to the overall work of the world. This implies that we ' ... not only bring relief but develop, not only make reparation ... but build. Love of neighbour at this point in history can signify nothing other than a total devotion to human effort'.[33] Teilhard was aware from bitter experience that this was more an ideal than a reality. He fervently wished that the Church were committed to human effort. In large measure he was vindicated at the Second Vatican Council. One of the finest documents of the Council, *Gaudium et Spes*, is deeply Teilhardian in spirit. Its coherence with a theology of creation is evidenced by Teilhard's own words: 'Nowhere is such universal love more evident than in the charity of the Christian, such as it is exemplified in the life of a contemporary believer, for whom creation has become newly meaningful in terms of evolution'.[34]

By training and practice Teilhard was an exact scientist. Yet his vision was of a world where humanity is the key and not the anomaly, the phenomenon and not the epiphenomenon. Our coming to be, hominisation, is the element of his hyperphysics which has received closest attention. Teilhard charts our roots through a past of more than a million years, Nevertheless, it was not the past which held him. He was fascinated by the human future which, for him, was partially disclosed by extrapolation from our dimmest pre-history. Our social concentration, just as much as our physical and psychic concentration led him to envisage a *sur-humanité* marked by charity of a higher order. This is expressed in Teilhard's idea of amorisation – a disposition where one grows precisely by the gift of self. It is a reformulation of the parable of the seed that lives most fruitfully of its own self-emptying. Teilhard attempts to resolve the tension of the individual and the collective along these lines. He offers the ideal of the personal where personality is defined by free association with others, and, ultimately, with the divine Other. It has been charged that he submerged the individual in the collective, the particular in the general. Yet his conception of humankind's future enables a rebuttal of such an accusation. It is a truly personalised future built upon the fruits of unselfish love and rooted in an ever-present, ever-attracting Omega point. In God, all can become all while remaining true to self. In God no suffering, no failure will remain without its vindication.

Today, when the possibility of global destruction is more spectrally real than ever and the politics of selfishness seem in the ascendant, there is a certain nostalgia to a remembrance of Teilhard's commitment to a just social order and to a science which would serve humankind rather than endanger it. Yet Teilhard de Chardin deserves more than nostalgia. His best memorial is the continuation of his programme of work, prayer and adoration. It is a demanding commitment calculated to unite those who undertake it within and without the Church. It calls for the exercise of those two virtues extolled by Teilhard himself:

attachment and detachment. And it calls for unremitting love for God and God's evolving creation.

In the previous sections of this chapter two major contributions to a 'story of creation' have been considered. However, there are other contributors to a rich tradition. A little before Aquinas, St Francis of Assisi initiated a spiritual movement with a deep appreciation of the divine presence to creation.[35] In these years, too, popular movements emerged in France and Italy aspiring to evangelical simplicity while retaining sometimes unorthodox views on the body, on matter and on marriage. Amongst these were the Waldensians, the Beguins and the Beghards. Again, the mystical insight of Eckhart (1260-1329) and Tauler (c. 1300-1361), the fresh spirituality of Hildegarde of Bingen (1098-1179), Mechtilde of Magdeburg (1210-1280), Catherine of Siena (1347-1380) and Julian of Norwich (1342-1415), offered an implicit creation theology. Apart from these streams of thought and feeling, the decline of the theological schools led to a redundant, often trivial speculation in place of the intellectual vigour of an Aquinas, a Duns Scotus or a Bonaventure. This decline influenced in no small way the breakdown of Christendom at the Reformation. The polemics of the Reform and Counter-Reform edged Christian thought into a preoccupation with a relatively narrow range of questions. Controversies on justification, on nature and grace, on free will and necessity, on reason and faith, on Scripture and tradition, obscured the earlier, freer, more experiential theology. From the Reformation onwards theology took a course that was sterile at worst, florid and abstract at best. Hence the challenges from post-Enlightenment thought found all too little response in either Catholic or Protestant tradition.

It would be unrealistic to expect from the First Vatican Council a complete or rounded theology of creation. This council – the first ecumenical council in over four hundred years – was defensive above all. In a sense, it mirrored the preoccupations of a Church retrenching before the onslaught of modernity. It tried to address intra-Church movements, some sympathetic to the spirit of the age (Hermes, Gunther) and others inimical to the advance of critical reason (traditionalists such as de Maistre and de Bonald and – in slightly different vein – Bautain and Bonetti).[36] Vatican I reacted against pantheism, emergent in European philosophy since Baruch Spinoza and exemplified by the writings of F. W. J. Schelling. On the other hand, the council tried to counter the threat of Rationalism with its spirit of positivism and evolutionary optimism. Here the diverse figures of G. W. F. Hegel and Emmanuel Kant loomed prominent. The creation theology of Vatican I is by no means negligible or insignificant. Yet it is inset to an essentially defensive response fashioned by neo-Scholastics such as Franzelin, Kluetgen and Schrader. Dominated by their neo-scholastic method (although not totally so), the council's thought categories and language seem over-formal, even arid. The defensiveness of the council precluded any attempt to explore the relation of theology to science, on the one hand, or to biblical criticism, on the other. The 'anthropological turn' of modern thought in philosophy and in politics was held at long arm's length. The increasing importance attached to experience finds little reflection in the deliberations of the council. As a result 'Catholics were not armed with the facts which would have raised them above a narrow, polemical attitude towards the scientific and biblical criticism of the day'.[37] This short-coming was to exact a high cost in the imminent 'modernist crisis'.[38]

Nevertheless, it would be unfair to reduce the work of the council to the hegemony of neo-scholasticism. At its third session Vatican I expounded the constants of Christian tradition on creation and providence.[39] In the first place, it re-affirms the 'otherness' and transcendence of God. The one, true God is 'the creator and Lord of things visible and invisible'. Canons 1-3 of the chapter 'God the Creator of All Things' (*De Deo omnium rerum Creatore*) disavow every affirmation that God and creation are one and the same.[40] Pantheism and any confusion of Creator with creation are ruled out. Similarly, Canon 4 disallows that God is any kind of world-spirit which 'by evolution of itself becomes all things'. The thrust of these four canons is to re-affirm the ancient faith in the personhood of God who can never be reduced to the measure of the universe.

In the second place, the council deals with creation albeit briefly. The fifth canon of the chapter emphasises the gratuity of creation. Creation is a divine gift freely given. It is non-necessitated. It is not required either by anything in the divine nature itself or by anything external to it. Further, creation is *ex nihilo* - an aspect recurrently underlined by St Thomas Aquinas. Its motive (*ratio propter quod fit*) is the glory of God. Lest this suggest some form of divine egoism, the chapter has it that creation is 'not for the increase or acquirement of God's own happiness but to manifest God's perfection by the blessing which he bestows on creation'.[41] This falls short of the warmth of the New Testament's proclamation of the self-giving, self-emptying (kenotic) love of God. The language of Scholasticism and the philosophical thought forms leave us closer to the nineteenth century benevolent monarch than to the God and Father of Jesus Christ. This shortcoming is addressed and, perhaps, remedied by the contributions from Pierre Teilhard de Chardin, Henri de Lubac, Karl Rahner, and Hans Urs Von Balthasar in the renewal of Catholic theology.

In its opening chapter on Revelation, the Vatican I Constitution *Dei Filius* retrieves St Paul's assertion of a knowledge of God gleaned from God's creative works. Canon One of the chapter *De Revelatione* runs: 'If anyone shall say that the one, true God, our Creator and Lord, cannot be certainly known by the natural light of reason through created things, anathema sit'.[42] A brief perusal of the proceedings of the council discloses the purpose and meaning of the canon. A reply to Mgr Gasser, one of the major figures of the council, referred to the challenges from the agnosticism of the French Encyclopaedists and the Kantian critique of reason.[43] In face of these challenges, the council affirms that we can know with certitude the existence of God and something of God as our first beginning and final goal. However, the direct object of the canon is neither Kant nor the coterie of Encyclopaedists. Vatican I, rather, addresses itself to Fideism and Traditionalism, both of which currents had enjoyed considerable vigour. Fideism is essentially a denial of the competence of reason in matters of faith on the supposition that what cannot be done by reason can be done by faith. As its title suggests, Traditionalism espouses the sole validity of tradition, primal revelation and the unalloyed obedience of faith. Vatican I opposes these positions as vigorously as it opposed the other extremes of Rationalism. Thus, the Council enters a valuable defence of human rationality in reaching the affirmation of God.

Much has been written on the precise meanings of the canon. Decades later, Karl Barth would oppose the council for what he termed its natural theology. It should be noted that the council affirms the possibility rather than the actuality of a natural knowledge of God. This possibility seems to be demanded by a biblical tradition from Wisdom 13 through Romans 1 to Acts 14 and 17. Likewise, a theological argument, well formulated by Gottlieb Söhngen, Henri Bouillard, Hans Urs Von Balthasar and others, urges that for revealed knowledge of God to strike home, the human spirit must have some prior capacity to recognize such revealed knowledge – and this presupposes an inchoate 'natural' knowledge.[44]

Theological commentators agree that the council does not teach an actual occurence of a natural knowledge of God independent of God's grace. It is also pointed out that a purely natural discovery of creation is not taught or defined by Vatican I.[45] Although the council speaks of the possibility of certitude (*certe cognosci potest*) in the knowledge of God, it does not specify the ways by which such certitude may be attained. For example, the council may not be taken to favour the proofs for the existence of God associated with St Thomas Aquinas. Nor can its terms be linked to metaphysical indications of God's existence at the expense of other indications such as conscience, the so-called natural desire for God (*desiderium naturale videndi Deum*) or the historical indications spoken of by J. H. Newman in his *Grammar of Assent.*

CONCLUSION

At the conclusion of this brief sample in Roman Catholic creation theology it is emphasised that Aquinas, Teilhard de Chardin and Vatican I do not exhaustively summate the tradition. They offer valuable approaches to a story of the earth but they do not tell the whole tale. Other aspects remain latent in their analyses. Some of these aspects are brought out by such as Augustine and Bonaventure, as well as by the mystics of both East and West. Later in this study we shall briefly advert to a major contribution from Francis of Assisi. Nevertheless, with Aquinas, Teilhard and Vatican I the following irreplaceable outlines are discerned:

1. The rejection of pantheism (Vatican I). Any divinisation of nature is not only philosophically untenable but theologically unacceptable. God is God. The creature is creature. And while there is an intimate dependence of creature upon Creator, creation is not an emanation from God in the sense of being confused with the divine. The creation has its God-given autonomy and otherness. Without prejudice to its radical dependence, the creature can stand 'before' God in its distinctiveness and self-consistency. Of great value, too, is the emphasis by Vatican I that we can know God our Creator in and through creation. This reminder, situated between the extremes of agnostic rationalism and blind faith, provides a stimulus for renewed dialogue between theology and the sciences, all of which are concerned with 'God's world in the making'.

2. With Aquinas we are reminded that the Creator and the creature are intimately related in the continued reception of being or existence. Creation institutes – indeed it is – a dynamic relationship. Creation is constant and vital. In God we live, move and have our being. Creation is now: today is the day of creation. Creation is a perduring reality, constitutive of every existent. And

yet, for all its intimacy, it is the foundation of a creature's autonomy. St Thomas would be the last to see the creature reduced to a mere puppet. For Aquinas, to denigrate the creature is to denigrate the Creator.[46] To deny the autonomy of the creature would be to deny the largesse of God. Here indeed is a generous principle. It is affirmative both of God's creative 'letting go' and of the creature's autonomy – to the point where, in the case of the human person, the creature can use his/her freedom against God's purposes. In Aquinas' view, then, God's creative touch is a supportive ground rather than a manipulative interference. Far from envisaging the Creator as a puppeteer or distant *maître du jeu*, Aquinas pushes us towards a relational concept of creation with a serene acceptance of One who grounds our freedom and empowers our activity.

3. A shortcoming of St Thomas' theological synthesis is its very completeness. It is not that the balance of freedom and necessity, of contingency and predictability, is upset. On the contrary, St Thomas' subtle treatment of transcendent and created activity can resolve the perceived tension between the creature's autonomy and the Creator's continual empowerment of all that exists. Nevertheless, the very symmetry of Aquinas' thought, its massive inner coherence, leaves us far from the existential *angst* of our own day and from the staggering complexity of the universe disclosed by contemporary physics.

This lacuna in St Thomas' theology – perfectly understandable in a thinker of the thirteenth century – is admirably addressed by Teilhard's insistence upon creation as a process. Despite the tragedies, the reverses and the absurdities commonplace in our experience, a creation perspective conversant with contemporary science will speak of a world in process or development. In fashioning this kind of perspective, Teilhard has made an outstanding contribution. Aware of the data of physics and personally involved in the science of palaeontology, he essayed a comprehensive interpretation of the directedness of all life. As mentioned earlier, his hyperphysics is an amalgam of diverse approaches to reality: science, philosophy, mysticism and theology. For some, his extrapolation from science and theology to his particularly broad canvas of history – past, present and future – represents sheer fantasy and wish fulfilment. For others, Teilhard's systematic view of an evolving creation directed to Omega point is an over-ambitious attempt to foreclose on the contingency of nature and human activity. The future, say these critics, must remain an open future, not to be subjected even to the very broad constraints of Teilhard's picture of cosmogenesis. For others yet again, his attribution of a kind of pre-life to the sub-atomic particles of matter smacks of sheer mythology. And so, on one count or another, in both science and theology Teilhard has his vigorous critics. Nevertheless, he has bravely addressed the major question of the sense or meaning of our teeming world. He has done so in loyalty to the traditional Christian faith, on the one hand, and with an intense awareness of modern cosmology, on the other hand. In regard to him the words of Werner Heisenberg have a particular application: 'In the end we do succeed in understanding this world, by representing its organisational structures in mathematical forms; but when we want to talk about them, we must be content with metaphors and analogies, almost as in religious language'.[47]

4. There is an astounding self-confidence, not untypical of the scientific mindset of the nineteenth century, to the claim made by Laplace in his *Essai sur les probabilités* (1814): 'the present state of the universe is the effect of the previous states and the cause of the states which will follow. Suppose an intelligence capable of knowing all the forces by which nature is animated and the respective situation of the beings which compose it: if any such intelligence were sufficiently vast to analyse these data, it could summate in one formula at once the movements of the greatest bodies in the universe and those of the smallest atom. Nothing would be uncertain for it: the present – as well as the past – would be disclosed to its eyes'.[48]

The assumption here is that the secrets of nature are in principle transparent to scientific rationality. This model is of the world as a mechanism where freedom and contingency are at the minimum, while necessity and predictability are at the maximum.

Twentieth century science has put severe strain on the paradigm of Laplace. The nineteenth century assumption of the eternity, stability and imperishability of matter is now less credible since the consolidation of the 'big bang' theory of origins and the acceptance of Heisenberg's 'principle of uncertainty' in physics. The dominant perception is that the universe had a beginning and may well be limited in duration. And so the perception of a universe in the making, corrorobated by the model of an expanding universe and by the hypothesis of evolution, challenges the rigid dogmatism of a closed mechanistic paradigm of the cosmos. Concepts such as freedom, contingency and finality, once outlawed from the language of scientific dogma, are again raised by physicists and biologists. These concepts take us beyond the limits of the sheerly empirical. As they are examined more closely, they are seen to require a philosophical analysis. It emerges that chance (J. Monod) and the supposed potentialities of matter (Engels, Dauvillier, Hoyle) are insufficient to account for the existence of matter or the directedness of evolution. It is manifestly insufficient to halt at a description of cosmic development while baulking at the question of the sense (meaning) of cosmic development.

In face of this context both theology and philosophy should regain nerve. It has been said that 'to the question: what existed before the "big bang", most of modern science is mute'.[49] However crude this formulation be, it represents a point of intersection for science, philosophy and theology. If science discloses the universe as a system of systems which thrive, grow and purposefully interact, extra-scientific questions inevitably arise. Amongst these are the questions about 'absolute origins' and 'ultimate finality'. Why is there being rather than nothing? Is there a pattern of meaning in the observable 'purposes' at work macrocosmically and microcosmically?

Many would argue that scientists *qua* scientists properly refuse to answer these extrascientific questions. Yet here one is at a point of intersection. From the perspective of a creation theology the possible dialogue will be facilitated by attention to the 'new cosmology' and to the recognition by many scientists of the mysteriousness of the physical manifold. Nor can a theology of creation afford to ignore the works of such as Fritjof Capra (*The Turning Point*) and of Rupert Sheldrake (*A New Science of Life*). To this dialogue the Judaeo-Christian tradition has immense riches to bring.

Aquinas' insistence on the insufficency of any being – except God – to be a total principle of explanation stands as firm as ever. His reiteration of the dependence of all being on a creative ground is a good starting point for a dialogue with modern cosmology. Doubtless, Aquinas thought in terms of a static world (when compared with the model disclosed by astrophysics). His conception predated even Copernicus' heliocentric theory and was largely the world of everyday experience wedded to Aristotelian metaphysics. On the other hand, the real world of everyday experience was his point of departure for an analysis of the structure of things. His grasp of the contingency of being made him vigorously affirm a transcendent existent who communicates being both in the aboriginal creative act and in the continuance of existence. In such a context every claim that matter is an imaginary construct or that it can provide its own principle of being is seen to be virtually meaningless. Matter is a principle of potency, not of act or perfection. The claim that it can of its own yield up life and thought is self-defeating – as if to say that of its own the less can cause the greater.

It is the task of theological analysis in the context of 'a story of the earth' to show that the materialist rejection of a transcendent 'ground of being' either introduces a hidden 'spirit' to matter or reduces life and thought to purely organic process. In this analytic task many of Aquinas' principles will be of signal help. On the other hand, the indications of purposeful development latent in the hypothesis of evolution challenge theological reflection to relate 'a story of the earth' to the Christian 'story of salvation'. No one has more consistently responded to that challenge than Teilhard de Chardin. Thus, without apology, Aquinas and Chardin are presented in our brief sample. In the relational insistence of the former and the processive thought of the latter, we are given an orientation towards a religious appreciation of creation and towards the commencement of a new dialogue with the sciences.

FOUR

Outlines for a Spirituality of Creation

Faith in creation is, like all faith, an option. By way of choice, it takes one position where there are others to take. One may choose to confess upon good, though not cogent, evidences that ' 'tis not from chance our comfort springs' or, again: 'in him we live, move and have our being'.[2] There are people who, perhaps wth good reason, hold otherwise, Albert Camus outlines a bleaker faith with stark honesty: 'to serve justice so as not to add to the injustice of the human condition, to insist on plain language so as not to increase the universal falsehood, to wager in spite of human misery for happiness'. Bertrand Russell wrote of his own stoic perception: 'Brief and powerless is man's life; on him and on his race the slow, sure doom falls, pitiless and dark. Blind to good and evil, reckless of destruction, omnipotent matter rolls on its relentless way; for man, condemned today to lose his dearest, tomorrow himself to pass through the gates of darkness, it remains only to cherish ere yet the blow falls, the lofty thoughts that ennoble his little day'.[3]

It is clear that the expansion of knowledge has led neither to happiness nor virtue. Knowledge does not necessarily bring a confident participation in being. Rarely has the disabusement of people been felt more sharply. Rarely has the precariousness of meaning been expressed more clearly. The more the universe seems comprehensible, the more it also seems pointless. Jacques Monod argues that 'man at last knows that he is alone in the indifferent immensity of the universe from which he has himself emerged by chance'. Another concern – the Oedipal fear of alienation – is expressed by Michael Bakunin's frequently cited protest: 'God is: man is a slave. Man is intelligent, just and free: God does not exist'.

Then, there is the gibe of Alan Watts that the style of Christianity empties it of all religious value. It is perhaps an understandable rejection although it applies with greater exactitude to Deism than to the great tradition of the *Credo*. The Almighty God, Father of heaven and earth, is much more than a super-artisan, a

heavenly architect. It should, however, be noted that the patriarchal image of God is increasingly rejected by those who accept
feminist theological categories.[4]

One can argue nonetheless that a creation spirituality is both
possible and desirable. Such a spirituality can be as realistic about
the threatened human condition as is Russell, and as suspicious of
alienation as is Bakunin. It starts from a more positive option than
theirs, yet thereafter it proceeds as critically as they. Its point of
departure is the primary relation to God, i.e. our dependent
finitude. The foundation of every religious stance is surely the
apprehension of contingency and the thankful acknowledgement
of the gift of existence which can arise therefrom. J. P. Mackey
reminds us: 'any man may notice the contingency of his own
existence, the un-obvious, uncertain, unconfirmed nature of it.
He may be driven – invited, inspired ... – to affirm a ground of
that existence, which ... holds its present guarantee (and) its
future prospects'.[5] This is already a kind of faith and it underlies
every subsequent doctrinal affirmation about God, Christ,
Church, moral value and hope for the future. Edward Schillebeeckx argues that the affirmation of our creaturehood is the
foundation both of prayer and mysticism. To say with thankfulness 'today is the day of creation' is an utterance of gratitude, joy
and confidence, even in the midst of adversity. It is a deep prayer
and act of worship.

It is interesting that so sober a writer as Aquinas can hint that
the creative presence of God can touch the mind and will, thus
enabling a conscious apprehension of the created relationship. In
continuity with this, Schillebeeckx can suggest: 'for human beings
... the dimension of their very being makes them open to a
conscious mutual presence between God and man ... this "being
of God" which attends man and all his works, because it is the
very ground and source of his own being-as-man is at the same
time the root and breeding place of all religious awareness ... '[6]
Creation spirituality opens us to an experience of God – mediated, indirect, yet very real. For Christian theology this leads on to
Christological and pneumatological dimensions, to the experience of Christ and of the Holy Spirit at every level of our being.
Yet it is right to linger over, to consider and perhaps to savour the
prior apprehension of the Creator-creation relationship. If
properly understood this apprehension can support and lend
depth to more explicit doctrinal forms of faith.

The apprehension of contingency reminds us that we are not
our own. The fragility of our very being makes itself disturbingly
clear. Our hold on life is indeed tenuous. We experience this in

the death of those we love. If the existentialist schools of philosophy and theatrical art are to be taken seriously, we affirm death as a personal and collective fact in all our decisions. We live with our death inscribed to every action we do and every choice we make. The fragility of life and the threat which overshadows existence lie at the root of mythic, philosophic and artistic discourses. Amongst the several functions of myth is the provision of a bulwark against the inrush of chaos and meaninglessness. The cosmogonies attempt to give respite from the panic of threatened existence. In their own way these myths evince peoples' awareness of an existential dependence which goes far beyond the network of everyday relationships. From the sciences too comes notice of the contingency of things. Sir Bernard Lovell in his book *In The Centre of Immensities* reflects that had the expansion of the universe differed even fractionally from its actual rate, human existence would have been impossible.[7] In very recent times the overarching threat of planetary destruction has obtruded a new fear into peoples' consciousness. People are aware – particularly the young – that nuclear escalation leads in one direction only, to the end of all life on this earth, thus to leave it a cursed spot, blighted by human folly.

THE RESPONSE OF FAITH AS CREATION FAITH

In face of this apprehension many responses arise. Eric Mascall pertinently remarks that 'it may well be that the doctrine of the absurdity of the world is simply what the doctrine of contingency … becomes when it is transposed from a theistic to an atheistic setting'.[8] Frequently this protestation is accompanied by apathy, rebellion or, even, the Promethean grasp for pseudo-divinity. Apathy searches for distraction from the pain of meaninglessness. Rebellion condemns reality as futile at best and malignant at worst. The ambition of Prometheus is repeated: we shall be like God: *erimus sicuti Deus*. Perhaps this is the pattern from the tower of Babel to the latest attempts to snatch at divinity through the abuse of power, money and technology, as well as through the politics of selfishness.

On the other hand, there is a countervailing affirmation that between us and nothingness there is the supportive power of God. This is not a metaphysical proof. It is, rather, an acknowledgement built upon glimpses of meaning and anticipation of fulfilling value. It is a faith, a personal stance. James Mackey rightly claims that God's existence cannot be proven in such a way that 'one could then go home, go to bed and forget as one could the conclusion of any other piece of theoretical reasoning'.[9] Yet in the experience of our own contingency we can be drawn or driven to affirm a ground of our being. At the root of all faith, forming part of its definition, is 'the acknowledgement of a power that sustains our existence in all the concrete circumstances of human living'.[10] The sense of contingency, in whatever form it strikes home to us, is really a grace – an 'invitation to see (our) world and (our) present history (as) grounded in a being (we) call God and relate to as such'.[11]

Paul of Tarsus fastened on this basic creation faith when he borrowed the memorable words, 'in him we live, move and have being' (Acts 17:28). Here is a creation spirituality in germ. It is the foundation of a serene and confident strength arising from faith in the creative presence of God. It re-echoes the psalmist's trust that the earth and its fulness belong to the Lord (Psalm 104). Far from being a private consolation, this faith can lead to devoted service to God's purpose through 'an historical enterprise involving material, emotional, purposive and communal action'.[12]

Our affirmations of God are couched in particular images and models. These images and models have consequences for the way we speak and conceive of creation. If God be thought of in purely transcendent terms, our feel for creation may well be of rule, power and law. Within the Western Christian tradition, God and creation have been envisaged frequently, though not always, in this fashion. God is the all-powerful ruler, supreme lawgiver. Creation is an artefact, a theatre in which the divine purposes are worked out through human agency. A monarchic image of God is joined to an artificial view of creation. The stress upon the total otherness and distant sovereignty of God exacts a price. It can void the world of a sense of God and, leaving the 'evil world' to its own devices, consign it to atheism. It can lead to seeing creation as something to be used up, dominated and abused. God is edged out of nature and history. Creation is deprived of its intrinsic sacramentality. It is no longer allowed to witness to God. Hence, one can sympathise with those who look to a more organic, immanent conception of creation. John McQuarrie guardedly terms it an emanationist model. Clearly, this is not without its dangers. Its most obvious danger is to confuse God and creation in a type of pantheism inimical to the thrust of Judaeo-Christianity. It can lead to a quietist approach to the world and its predicament. It can foster the negative side of contemplation by overlooking cruelty and injustice as well as by ignoring the imperative to work for change. On the other hand, its considerable merit it to facilitate an easier relation to God and a more sensitive touch in regard to creation itself.

One finds elements of this 'organic' approach in Aquinas and, again, in Teilhard. In all his writings on creation, St Thomas Aquinas emphasises the creative presence of God. Aquinas' overarching idea in regard to creaturehood is radical dependence upon the continuing creative activity of God. God 'does not leave any times, any centuries, or even hours, without his witness'.[13] It is a presence which can engender at once a basic trust in existence, a respect for the divine otherness, a reverence for all life and an awareness of the openness of the historical process. In other words, Aquinas respects the 'otherness' of God, God's nearness to all creation, and the responsibility of human freedom. Aquinas recalls that in God all things live, move and have being. We are in the palm of God's hand since, without cease, we are constituted by a creaturely relation to God. Our total dependence upon God coheres with our full autonomy as rational creatures. Any suggestion that reality is only an illusion, or human action only a mimic show, is thereby avoided. The divine action is sufficiently rich to evoke a dependent yet autonomous creation. There is an impressive balance between spirit and matter, eternity and time, necessity and freedom, in Thomas' overall view. It is true that he did not live with 'our massive and wrenching knowledge of evil'.[14] Again, the very consistency of his method suggests 'that he is looking down on the whole universe with God's eyes rather than looking up at God with the anguished suffering eyes of contemporary man'[15] Nevertheless, his view of human autonomy and of the responsibility that God gives us to use that freedom re-echoes our own aspiration to relate our faith to everyday concerns and to work for change of unjust, exploitative structures.

The confluence of relation and process lends a particular attraction to the spirituality of Teilhard de Chardin. With the Christian tradition, Teilhard affirms the transcendence of God to creation. Yet he passionately affirms also God's immanent presence to all God has made. The infinitely creative God is present to all that exists: to matter and spirit, in time and eternity. Teilhard views with considerable impatience the stock image of God, the architect of the world, the 'neolithic proprietor' of the universe. The God of creation is also the God of history. The Creator of the universe in evolution is also the Father of Jesus Christ. In Teilhard's view, evolution would be unintelligible, even intolerable, if its sustainer and animator were not a personal God. What gives warmth and light to an otherwise forbidding world is that its life is endowed with a divine, creative gift. The giver is the Alpha and the Omega, the commencement and the end of the vast movement of evolution. Teilhard prefers to speak of creative union rather than divine causality. God moves us by attraction. We seek the God who already draws us. We search for God in our aspiration and action, in our desire and love. Whether in Teilhard's scientific works or in his specifically religious writings, God is always presented in non-manipulative terms. Vitally present, God is the inspirer and giver of all development, yet ever the one who is ahead of our progress. In Teilhard's vision 'the God of the ahead has suddenly appeared athwart the traditional God of the above, so that henceforth we can no longer worship fully unless we superimpose these two images so that they form one'.[16]

The balance of contingency and necessity is maintained in the writing of Paul Tillich. The idea of the 'ground of being' is particularly associated with his work. It leads him to speak of a threefold creativity: originating, sustaining and directive. The originative creativity of God reminds us that God creates out of nothing while remaining independent of creation. Faith in God's sustenance affirms 'the continuity of the structure of reality as the basis for being and acting'. God is creative 'in every moment of temporal existence, giving the power of being to everything that has being, out of the creative ground of divine life'. Lest this be seen as an *apologia* for the *status quo*, Tillich goes on to speak of God's directive activity: 'God writes straight with crooked lines'. Providence is not interference. Rather, it underlies both freedom and destiny in bringing creation to its fulfilment. God can fulfil the destiny of creation despite the error, alienation and estrangement to which the recurrent misuse of freedom leads.[17]

The common emphasis in these strands is upon God's creative activity as trustworthy and faithful. It corresponds to the Old Testament *emeth* (faithfulness) and the New Testament *aletheia* (loyal truth). It is an approach which, without minimising the reality of evil, sin and apparently malign fate, affirms hope in God's purpose and the triumph of God's justice. It moves towards a theology of liberation. It is only when one regards creation as a positive gift and a project entrusted to human action that one can assimilate the call of the Creator who is also the Liberator. The God who gives us being is with us in every liberative impulse. Indeed, God gives that impulse and calls us to act in transformative purpose. The experiences of God as creator of the universe and as liberator of oppressed people nourish each other. God's liberative action evokes a deeper faith in a creative divine presence, while faith in God's benevolence to creation sustains the hope of a definitive overcoming of suffering and oppression. A creation spirituality, therefore, thrusts towards a vibrant spirituality of liberation.

A religious stance which fails to estimate the conflictive elements of life, or which cannot recognise the outrage of unmerited suffering, does not deserve its name. Unfortunately, theology 'for centuries did not seriously challenge the plunder of continents, and even the extermination of whole peoples and civilisations. The meaning of the message of Jesus Christ was so blunted as not to be sensitive to the agony of whole races'.[18] Today, when the protest against oppression has become part of a secular faith, it would be a scandal were religious people to shirk an option for the poor and suffering. A creation/liberation spirituality will not seek out the cross as a private asceticism. Rather, it will protest wherever crosses are raised by the unjust establishments which bestride our world. It will enter solidarity with those who carry the cross. Such protest and solidarity should be based on analysis of the social situation, but its hope will be stimulated by a vision of how things might be. In this prospect, an awareness of Christ's Easter triumph must surely play a part. Nevertheless, the human future cannot be easily read-off or programmed. Contingency and freedom cannot be fore-closed upon in some master vision of a planned future. Ready-made Utopias are untrue to reality. They do not fit the human situation. In attempting to manipulate reality they can cause immeasurable suffering. On the other hand, the critical vision of hope and the utopic thrust of action for justice find many guidelines in the creation spirituality implicit to a radical Christian witness.

In summary, a creation spirituality can arise from the experience of the fragility of being. It is an unspoken response in faith, a choice for meaningfulness rather than meaninglessness. Hence it is a fragile growth – subject to the pressure of despair in the face of evil, suffering and death. Perhaps the most sensitive people will feel that pressure at its sharpest. Creation faith of this kind requires constant renewal – hence, it cannot be subtracted from the operation of God's grace. Under that grace, it enables us to overcome 'the original generic sin ... radical mistrust of our creator'. In a remarkable essay, Donal Dorr writes: 'the awareness that I am in the hands of God is a gift: one of his greatest graces'. The same author impressively sketches a balanced spirituality: 'love tenderly', 'act justly', 'walk humbly with your God'.[19] This fusion of a personal and political dimension is timely. It enables a realistic self love as well as a search for justice for one's fellows and one's world.

THE PROBLEM OF DUALISM

A recurrent witness of the Bible is that God in creating gave us a good creation: 'God saw that it was good ... very good' (Gen 1:31). The climax of this avowal is the 'image of God' paean. Evil emerges; but it is not God's doing. It is a paradox that despite the insistence upon the goodness of creation there is a symbolism of evil – the serpent which precipitates the misuse of human freedom. Thereafter evil insinuates itself in such diffusive fashion that Ben Sirach will lament that the heart of man is desperately corrupt. Even then, however, it is 'the devil's envy', not God, which is deemed responsible for the debacle. The remarkable feature of the biblical faith is that it holds to the dominance of God's beneficent rule. Even the book of Job, surely outstanding in its 'wintry experience' of God, refused to lay blame at God's feet for the woes and ills that seem to constitute the human condition. All through the Old Testament there is a firm hope in the triumph of God's good purposes and a determined refusal to posit either the autonomy or victory of evil.

There is, however, another assessment of the balance of good and ill, and of the origins of evil itself. In the threatening circumstances of today's precarious scale of terror, we can perhaps better understand that many cultures see good and evil as warring powers, with the sway tilting now to one, now to the other, and with the ultimate outcome deeply uncertain. One can perhaps understand that the aetiology of good and evil might posit independent 'gods' originative severally of good and evil, of spirit and matter, of heaven and earth. This is the age-old tendency to dualism, a tendency almost innate in humankind.

Historically dualism takes a number of forms. One form makes a clear distinction between two principles, one of good, one of evil, equal in power, manipulative of human endeavour, ruling separately the spiritual and material in human beings. An attenuated form of this dualism affirms not so much an independent principle of evil as an evil endemic to creation itself. Thus, matter and body are considered evil while spirit and the soul are regarded as the only good. The hallmark of this perception is the identification of finitude with evil and sin. Salvation is achieved only by transcending one's creaturehood for a higher reality out of the body. The Gnostic escapes the illusory world through ritual practice and arcane knowledge. Or else he/she practises nostalgia for a lost world, a paradise, a golden age. Again, the Gnostic looks to the destruction of the present age in a divine apocalyptic intervention. It is perhaps a very understandable reaction in face of suffering, evil and death, which seem incoherent with God's infinite goodness and omnipotence.

It is significant that the chief argument used by the Church Fathers against Gnostics was the universal fatherhood of God, shown in the goodness of creation. The first article of the Christian creeds dwells upon this fatherhood: I believe in God, the Father almighty, maker of heaven and earth: *Credo in Deum, Patrem omnipotentem. factorem caeli et terrae.* It is said that creation was the earliest dogma the Christian community established against Gnosticism. St Irenaeus' accusation that Gnosticism is a blasphemy is even more clearly anti-dualist. One cannot reject the material, the bodily and the worldly, without impugning the God who created these dimensions of existence. Hence, the teaching of Marcion and of the impressively fearless Tertullian was repudiated. There is, however, an acceptance of Tertullian's insistence: 'We must not consider by whom things were made but by whom they have been perverted ... between the created and the corrupted state there is a vast difference'. This distinction between the goodness of God's creation and its deterioration due to human malfeasance is important to maintain. Creatureliness and sinfulness are not mutually implicative. Nature is the presupposition of grace, not the contradiction of it. Only if it is seen as God's good gift which has been disordered due to the misuse of freedom, can it also be regarded as in deep need of healing, and yet as the place where God's loving purposes can be effected. One finds this framework in *Gaudium et Spes* of the Second Vatican Council: 'far from thinking that works produced by man's own talent and energy are in opposition to God's power, and that the rational creature exists as a kind of rival to the Creator, Christians are convinced that the triumphs of the human race are a sign of God's grace'.[20]

There is an intimate relation between creation and the incarnation of Jesus Christ. Likewise, the construction of the kingdom of God and the liberation of the earth go hand in hand. We may not spiritualise away the bodiliness of Christ. He whom we have heard, and seen, and touched, has entered our history. He has become one of us. In assuming our flesh he declared it redeemable. Through his ministry, passion, death and resurrection, he sanctified our humanity. Thus the classical adage takes a new meaning: *nihil humanum mihi alienum puto.* There is nothing human, nothing material, which is alien to God's redemptive power and concern. If we have learned anything from Teilhard's Christology, we shall affirm that same message. By accepting creation as a God-given, God-accompanied process evocative of our commitment to its humane development, we best serve God's design. Clearly, one has to take account of the mystery of evil, *mysterium iniquitatis*. Even here, there is danger of a kind of dualism which ascribes evil to the inner heart but not to the structures which affect us even before we come to moral self-disposition. It is all too easy to castigate the sins of the weak. It is less easy to analyse, identify, and work against the sins of the great – the inhumane, exploitative social structures; the oppression of the poor, of minorities, of women; the rape of nature and the courting of planetary destruction. Yet, if we take creation spirituality at all seriously, we will consider anew the radical challenge of Christ. He gave the kingdom of God bodily form and set in motion the subversive challenge to liberate the earth and its inhabitants.

A creation faith in the light of the Gospel must surely preclude flight from the world through an evasive spirituality. Such flight would be an abdication of responsibility, a dereliction of the model set by Christ himself. Hence the readiness to cooperate in shaping a better future is coherent with the acceptance of creation and the service of the kingdom of God. This, however, must be accompanied by a critical realism – critical of oneself, one's society and of the structures established by fallible, sinful, human beings. It has been said that the Second Vatican Council was excessively optimistic – not so much in its assessment of creation as in its eagerness to come to terms with the achievements of liberal post-modern society. It would be unfair and ungenerous to ignore that achievement of the council. Yet the objection precipitates a closer analysis of the powers, structures and systems which affect our lives. There are political powers of states and governments which often are oppressive. There are economic structures which cause poverty, hunger and margination. There are social systems which all too frequently serve elites and narrow vested interests. The appropriate critical analysis finds motivation in a search for justice and in a love of God's creation. Where such an analysis is attempted, the contemplative model of spirituality is enlarged to embrace a transformative, innovative dimension. Contemplation of the goodness of God's creation is then accompanied by a realistic assessment of evil and sin. At the minumum it impels us towards a radical commitment to change personal and social patterns. It is interesting that many of those who have best developed a creation theology have more recently offered a social critique as well. Jürgen Moltmann, Edward Schillebeeckx and the growing body of liberation theologians present the exigencies of Christian praxis in regard to nature, human rights and social justice. Faith in creation can motivate us to work for a more just, more humane order in a cosmos regarded as sacramental of God's presence. This commitment to a just and sustainable way of living is both nourished by and nourishes a commitment to the God who entrusts creation to us.

There is a remarkable impact to the words of Julian of Norwich: 'God never began to love us; we have been known and loved from the beginning'.[22] In this sense, Matthew Fox's insistence upon original blessing rather than original sin has much to say to a creation spirituality. The foundational insight of creation spirituality is that God, the abundantly creative God, loves us deeply and continually. All too seldom we savour the presence of that love manifest in the goods of creation. It is time to restore the symbol of creative blessing, given with the communication of being and perduring while existence lasts. And God never repents of God's gifts. There is much value in the argument, adduced by Fox, that the most liberative paradigm is that of original and continuing blessing. Within this paradigm we can realistically – perhaps even more realistically – take account of the irrationality of sin. For sin is the denial and defacement of our creaturely relation to God. It twists and spoils original blessing. On the other hand, when original sin, rather than original blessing, becomes the dominant paradigm for the understanding of faith then 'flight from nature, creation and the God of creation' sets in. Can one say more or better than Fox's reminder: 'An exaggerated doctrine of original sin, one that is employed as a starting point for spirituality, plays kindly into the hands of empire builders, slave-masters and patriarchal society in general. It divides and thereby conquers, pitting one's thoughts against one's feelings, one's body against one's spirit, one's political vocation against one's personal needs, people against earth, animals and nature in general. By doing this it so convolutes people, so confuses them and preoccupies them, that deeper questions about community, justice and celebration, never come to the fore'.[23]

EVIL

Evil is a monumental reality. It 'bestrides our existence like a conqueror'. It assumes many shapes: ungovernable pain, natural catastrophe, human malevolence and the unforeseen, even unintended, destruction wreaked by fate or sheer 'bad luck'. A spirituality of creation which ignored this would be unreal and false. Of those who overlook evil, or prematurely spiritualise it, it can be said: 'for the very reason these men do not weep, there is something unsatisfactory about their rejoicing'.[23] If all true religion arises from protest at inhumane suffering, then theological reflection on evil must start by contesting it, by commitment to its reversal. And yet it is important to approach the question correctly. Sentiment blurs the vision. A facile piety is infantile if not worse. To bemoan evil, to wring one's hands and say 'things will be ever thus' has been a besetting fault of certain strands of religion and philosophy. To do this and no more is unhelpful. Merely to regret the world is either morbidity or an affectation. Nor can one endorse the Karamazovian decision to accept God while rejecting God's creation. This is part of the great refusal of Existentialism. Taken at face value – as perhaps it should not be taken – it appears an untimely retreat from the field of battle.

In theological reflection one discerns a number of strategies. There are those who forego a rigorous examination of the problem in favour of a pragmatic response in combatting evil of every kind. Yet this position is open to the objection that it evades the question of God's responsibility for evil. And so one finds that there are other somewhat tortuous yet impressive attempts to integrate the surd of evil into an overall explanation. These stretch from Augustine through Aquinas to worthwhile writings in our own day. What they lack in anger they gain in intellectual application. Not the least of their merits is to face the challenge sharply put by Anthony Flew: 'Someone tells us that God loves us as a father loves his children. We are reassured. But then we see a child dying of inoperable cancer. His earthly father is driven frantic in his efforts to help, but his heavenly Father shows no obvious sign of concern. Some qualification is made – God's love is not "a merely human love" or it is "an inscrutable love" ... we are reassured again. But then perhaps we ask: what is this assurance of God's (appropriately qualified) love worth, what is this apparent guarantee really a guarantee against'.[24]

CLASSICAL RESPONSE

And so one might start with Augustine: 'You ask me from where comes evil, and in my turn I ask you, 'What is evil?'[25] With Augustine, too, we might face his well phrased dilemma: 'either God cannot abolish evil or he will not. If he cannot, then he is not all powerful; if he will not, then he is not all good'. What, then, is evil? There is the classical response: evil is a privation. It is the absence of something which ought to be there: *privatio boni debiti*. It is not any kind of lack whatever. It is the absence of a due perfection such as lack of vision in a human being. Inability of a stone to see is not an evil.

Yet evil is more than an empty space. It is neither illusion nor unreality. It is a real disorder at the heart of being. Hence, it is to be understood against the backdrop of good. The classical tradition consistently maintains the essential goodness of all being: *ens et bonum convertuntur.* By the fact that a thing *is,* it is good. Independent, subsistent evil in this perspective is an impossibility. It is, rather, parasitic on good. An Aquinas would not deny that the effects of cruel actions, of wasting disease, of the accidents of nature, are evil. However, in his view, the evil lies in the perversion of good. Every act, every process, every event, precisely as being, is good. In this fashion, the classical tradition attempts to 'exculpate' God of the creation of evil. God has given being. And all being, as being, is good. The perversion is from elsewhere. It arises either in the misuse of freedom or in some other malfeasance. Thence stem the pain, suffering, unhappiness and death which stalk our world. At a stroke, the classical tradition appears to have 'exculpated' God and likewise to have closed the avenue trodden by the Gnostics towards another 'god' originative of evil.[26]

This is not quite all – nor taken on its own would such an answer be remotely adequate. In facing the question of the authorship of evil, Aquinas – representing the classical tradition – draws upon Augustine's insistence that God is not its cause. Indeed, the whole thrust of the religious perception is to deny that God could be the originator of evil. Were that to be the case, there must be evil in God. God could not be all-good. The repeated insistence of the classical tradition is that the action of God is ever positive of being: it never tends to non-being. However, the same tradition – well represented by St Thomas – admits that divine creativity allows things to go wrong and fail. Deficiencies and failures manifestly occur. There remains, therefore, a difficulty. One cannot claim that God creates the agents which, either through their own legitimate operation or through abuse of a God-given power, cause corruption or decline to occur, and at the same time totally separate God from these effects, some of which are real evils. At the very least, one has to say that God permits evil in creating the kind of world we know. How then can God be 'exculpated' of implication in evil? The classical tradition does in fact admit that God can be said to be the cause, albeit indirect (*per consequentiam*) of evil. Aquinas makes the point that God – and nature – acts for the best on the whole (*quod melius est in toto*), not for what is best in every single instance. Thus, in God's disposition – and in nature's – the good of the whole comes before the good of each part.[27] F. C. Copleston rightly observes: 'this picture of God as a kind of artist and the universe as a work of art, requiring shadows as well as lights, is apt, in spite of its traditional character, to appear disconcerting and unhelpful to many minds. It certainly is not an anthropocentric view of the matter'.[28]

Implicit to Aquinas' argument is that our world could not be without the possibility, even the actuality, of evil. Taken as a whole, the universe is such that it is better that there be the possibility of a defection from the good.[29] Aquinas argues that, where beings can fall short of the good, some of them will in fact do so. Alien as it sounds to our ears, he can say that much good would be precluded if evil were not permitted. If no evil could occur, neither the patience of the sufferer nor the vindication of justice could be celebrated. And so, for Aquinas, God both permits the moral evil inset to the misuse of freedom, and, in creating the kind of physical manifold we inhabit, indirectly causes physical evil. It is clear, then, that the classical tradition does not entertain the existential refusal of a Sartre, a Camus or a Beckett. There are a number of reasons for this. One reason, not to its credit, is that it does not seem to have that keen sense of injustice which represents the best of the modern age. Thus, its consciousness of the *status quo* was less troubled than perhaps is ours today. In addition, there was a strong conviction that God's existence and goodness could be affirmed despite – even independently of – the fact of evil. One finds, for example, in Aquinas the paradoxical claim that if evil is, God *is* (*si malum est, Deus est*). This is surely an audacious claim, the very reversal of the modern statement: since evil is, God is not. St Thomas' argument can be stated thus: 'if there were no God, there could be no good; if there were no good, there could be no evil. But there is evil. Therefore, there exist both good and God'.[30]

THE MODERN ANALYSIS OF EVIL

The modern analyses of evil, even at their most philosophical, tend to be concrete and existential. They take explicit notice of the scandal of evil and of the grave shadow it casts over the affirmation of God's goodness. While they draw on classical answers, they surpass tham in offering guidelines for confronting suffering and evil.[31] Claude Tresmontant makes the interesting suggestion that evil first emerges with consciousness. Deterioration and entropy at the preconscious level cannot be termed evil. Evil is whatever diminishes individual or personal existence . Physical evil is illness, injury and death. Moral evil is oppression, injustice and exploitation. It is the corrosion of minds and emotions through the deprivation of stability, of hope, of personal integrity. It is mental illness, neuroses of all kinds. It is hunger and imprisonment. Finally, there is sin – the abuse of freedom whereby God's love is dismissed in favour of an idol. Together these constitute the negative side of existence and effectively place a miasma over countless lives.

Like all other evil, sin is parasitic on good. It is a perversion in the human search for good whereby a creature is enthroned in place of God. The deordination is shown even in the Genesis story. There, one reads of the rapid spread of sin and the miserable effects it brings about. Sin and the effects of sin coalesce in a nexus of misery, a legacy of suffering and injustice. Sin is an area of absurdity at the heart of being. In this sense, Bernard Lonergan's remark is apt: 'basic sin is not an event; it is not something that positively occurs ... it consists in a failure of occurrence, in the absence in the will of a reasonable response to an obligatory motive'.[32] It is the root of the irrational in our self consciousness. Lonergan is thus recasting the traditional insistence that sin, like evil, is an excrescence or corruption of the good. It is the disorder 'constituted by what could be and ought to be, but is not'. It is neither caused nor uncaused but permitted by God: 'besides the actual good that God wills and the unrealised good that God does not will, there are the basic sins that he neither wills nor does not will but forbids'.[33] If sin is an aberrant failure to choose the good or to reject the morally reprehensible, it is pregnant of a multitude of effects – suffering, injustice, exploitation, death. Sinful decisions and their effects feed each other so that an ambient of unjust situations, bad example and the innate disorder that tradition calls original sin form a situation, a sin of the world. The Adamic myth underlines the view that sin and moral evil are not a necessity, as the philosophers of existential pessimism would have it. Rather, it is a perversion: evils 'are not created, they are incurred'.[34] The great merit of the original sin doctrine is to remind us that our major ills are not predicable of God but of human stupidity, greed and sin. Before we take up the question of God's responsibility we should perhaps advert to our own responsibility for the world we have made. Thus we may avoid the academic indignation of certain forms of Existentialism and be moved to work for change rather than bewail an evil world and an uncaring God.

Yet the question remains: can God be exculpated from responsibility in the evil we experience? After all, God made us as we are, foresaw the accumulation of basic sin and moral evil, and yet permits it. The arguments for and against have been amply rehearsed. It is argued that God permits evil that good may come of it, that first level evils of injustice and oppression have their sting drawn in the triumph over them by the practice of justice and love. Thus our liturgy of the Easter Vigil proclaims, 'O happy fault ... which gained for us so great a Redeemer' (*O felix culpa ... quae tantum ac talem meruit habere Redemptorem*). Again, it is argued that if God makes people free, God has to permit the misuse of freedom. Some would say that it is a nonsense to speak of creatures free to choose good or evil who were nonetheless precluded from the choice of evil. Further, it is said that God writes straight with crooked lines. While in the specifically Christian perspective this makes considerable sense, in the context of purely rational argument it is not helpful. It is open to the acerbic comment of Professor Flew: 'to call such a being, ruthlessly paying an enormous price in evil means to attain his own good ends, himself good is mere flattery'.[35] And to the argument that from first level evils come higher level goods, there is the answer that within that fine-sounding principle rests great injustice. It is not very convincing to say that the evil of the Holocaust is drawn in some retrospective vindication. To argue that the age-old oppression of the poor is a trial ground for virtue – for forbearance rather than action on the part of the poor, and or charity rather than justice on the part of the rich – is now perceived to be callous to the point of scandal.

The argument from free will is not so open to attack. It is that the value of a world wherein freedom exists – and can be abused – outweighs the evil of the abuse. The abuse, – being an abuse of freedom – is not attributable to God . That God allows such an abuse evidences God's forbearance, powerfulness and love rather than unconcern. This argument is strongest when combined with a commitment to act for humane development as an injunction laid upon us by the Creator. Creation is a project entrusted to us for stewardship and development. Neither Judaism nor Christianity has ever claimed that we have the best of all possible worlds. That claim was the fruit of rationalist speculation. In the Christian view, man and woman have been called to combat evil, in themselves, in their structures, in their creation of history.

We are called to make our world a more humane and fraternal place. This is not to evade the difficulty raised against the goodness and omnipotence of God. It is rather to argue that God's omnipotence is best seen in God's respect for our freedom, God's love best seen in God's ever present grace and help. Our world is surely one in which evil is rampant. In large part the evil is attributable to human malfeasance. All the more urgent, therefore, is the call to practical love in combatting sin, injustice and oppression whether these come from ourselves or from others.

There remains, however, the evil which cannot be combatted

directly. There is animal and human pain. It has been argued that the agony undergone by animals is irreconcilable with God's loving providence. The random strike of disease is no respecter of innocence or virtue. The awesome impersonality of natural catastrophes dashes into shreds every easy explanation whether theological or philosophical. The wantonness of nature causes millions of aborted lives to come to nothing. These instances are not traceable to human malice, carelessness or self-destruction. And yet the question remains. Can there be a physical, developmental manifold in which pain does not exist? After all, pain is an integral part of life itself. It compels us to avoid threat and to take the necessary action to protect life and well-being. Pain, writes Austin Farrer, 'is a natural inclination which stands in no need of special justification. Pain, being the grip of a harm the creature has failed to shun, enforces the heed that was lacking, or evokes the effort that was unexerted'.[36]

However, pain and suffering do not always bear this benign form. All but the most callous will protest that there is a surplus of pain in nature and in human experience. Nature, runs the adage, is red in tooth and claw. The law of the jungle is hard and cruel. People suffer abominably, cruelly, inexplicably. An unsentimental analysis will point out that there is an attrition to all physical interaction leading to both decline and development. There is a mutual interference of systems 'which is at once the cause of the diversity and the richness of our world and the occasion of decline, suffering and corruption'.[37] There would be no generation, writes St Thomas, if there wee no corruption in natural affairs. Systems of physical organization feed upon other systems. The very process of nourishment exacts a toll in the vegetative and animal domain. Even the cancer which may eat our flesh is the operation of a self contained system. One might argue with a Creator that this or that ill should never have been allowed to issue, a kind of dialogue which the book of Job would dissuade us from entering. However, if we are in solidarity with an evolving world, we cannot hope to avoid the setback and the shock from that world's processes. It may be as irrational to demand a world like ours without susceptibility to suffering, pain and death as it is to reject reality in the name of scepticism. Austin Farrer reminds us that 'God is the God of hawks no less than of sparrows, of microbes no less than men. He saves his creatures by creating in them the power to meet the ever-changing hostilities of their environment. And so, though individuals perish and species die out, there is a world of life'.[38]

The Christian answer goes further. It sees the providence of

God as the vindicator of all who suffer. At its best, this answer holds together the divine forbearance, which permits the autonomy of the natural processes, and the divine solicitude, which extends to the least of things. God is no less concerned for the individual than for the future of every species. Yet that individual concern, in the ordinary run of things, works through conservational and evolutionary forces. It is God who creatively enables the discoveries for 'the relief of man's estate'. Above all, it is God who entered into the agony of a suffering world and died with it on the Cross. Inset to this perspective, evil is not disprobative of God. As we have seen, Aquinas is sufficiently audacious to claim that it can corroborate the affirmation of God. Thereafter, the modern analysis calls us to resist physical and moral evil with all the strength available to us. The political imperative to use the vast resources of technology and science in confronting both disease and want pushes us beyond mere *angst* to action for change. The most humane, most realistic thing is to face our mottled reality and to transform what is susceptible to transformation. The Christian paradigm – drawn between the Mosaic exodus and the second exodus in Christ's death and resurrection – assures us that in this effort God is very much with us. Indeed, God has entrusted us with the challenge and is present to us in its execution.

MAN AND WOMAN AS IMAGE OF GOD

When one considers the sorrier side of human history – the oppression, the repression, the cruelty of man to man, animal and nature – one is perhaps reluctant to eulogise humanity as reflective of the divine in any way. Again, when one adverts to the crassness of consumerism, the greed of capital expansion, the destructiveness of nuclear and conventional armaments, one is perhaps less eager superlatively to press the excellence of men who gave rise to these incubi. This darker realisation marks the sensitivity of an Augustine, a Luther, a Kierkegaard. It is noticeable that the tradition to which Augustine gave rise, and which Luther and Kierkegaard invoked, places little emphasis on man as we know him/her as a theophany or revelation of God. In that same tradition, E. Lehmann has written: 'the strongest argument against "creation in God's image" is the complete silence of the rest of the New Testament on this subject, which, if it had been a prevalent idea, might have been expected to be very frequently used … in the constantly recurring treatment of the relation between God and man'.[39]

Nevertheless, it is precisely this that Genesis posits: 'in the image of God he created him, male and female he created them'

(Gen 1:27). Only humankind is made after the likeness and according to the image of God. It is suggested that the passage is best read in the context of the Jewish repudiation of idolatry (cf. Ex 20:4). Man and woman are God's only idol: 'we must not make images and likenesses of God ... and we have no need to, because God has made his own images and likenesses – us'.[40] Some take a twofold critique from the careful balance *be selem* (according to the image) and *ke demut* (after the likeness). They read here a critique of the Egyptian cult of theriomorphic idols. Genesis seems to say: 'only man and woman, not animals or inanimate things, are in God's image'. In addition, the cautionary rider – 'after our likeness' – calls in question the Iranian myths of a 'heavenly man '. Genesis thus avers that man/woman is only after the likeness of God. He/She is in no sense equal to God or a demi-God. Yet, man/woman *is* created in the image of God. Not just man, not simply woman, but both together are made in the divine image. Both man and woman are constituted in their very humanity by the breath of God. As image, they have special rights vested in their very sacredness – the terrible punishment for murder is rooted in the heinousness of desecrating the image of God.[41] As image, man and woman have the special duty to be vicegerents in a creation entrusted to them, not delivered for their wanton domination. As image of God, they have the capacity for dialogic word. The Promethean madness, the pretension to be as God, is identified as the major temptation. It was the false promise held out by the tempter – *eritis sicuti Deus*. Genesis repudiates such arrogance and calls people to a programme less exalted but more demanding – *eritis imagines Dei*.

Already there is a hint that the appropriate question is not 'in what does the image consist?' One can indeed ask about 'a certain something' which marks out humankind. In the Christian tradition this question has been frequently asked. Many answers have been given, many valuable understandings attained. These range through somewhat paradoxical stress upon physical shape to aspects of personality – reason, immortality, self-consciousness and self-disposition. Augustine makes much of memory, understanding and willing as analogies of the inner Trinity. The Second Vatican Council recalls attention to the nobility of conscience and meets the Protestant tradition in underlining the centrality of conscience to an understanding of the image of God in humankind. Conscience mediates an awareness of our vocation to communion with God. In turn, the reference to communion reminds us that imaging God is a dynamic project even more than it is an achieved 'something'. Michael Schmaus argues: 'being the image of God is to be understood functionally, not ontologically. Genesis sees the image of God not in the being of man but in a definite activity of man'.[42] In Genesis the image doctrine is not presented as a means for the knowledge of God. Rather, it presupposes such knowledge. In pressing an image-teaching, Genesis tries to foster a mutual address, a dialogue, between Israel and God, and hence between persons and God. Buber's remark is surely apt: 'the great achievement of Israel is not to have taught the one true God ... it is to have shown that it was possible in reality to speak to Him, to say "Thou" to Him, to stand upright before His face'.[43] It is this more personal framework of understanding that relates the image doctrine to stewardship, merciful dominion and vice-regency of creation in contemporary exegesis.

The New Testament does not attempt to develop the image doctrine of Genesis. Instead, it speaks almost exclusively of Jesus Christ as the image of God (1 Cor 11:7; 2 Cor 4:4; Col 1:15). Paul's affirmation is part of a cumulative argument. Christ is both the recapitulation of all creation and the definitive revelation of God's purpose. In him, the rupture of creation from Creator has been healed. Paul does not speak much about our being the image of God. He prefers to speak of our being 'conformed' to the image of the Son of God (Rom 8:29), of 'bearing the image of the man of heaven' (1 Cor 15:49), of being changed 'from one degree of glory to another' (1 Cor 3:18), of 'putting on the new nature which is being renewed in knowledge after the image of its creator' (Col 3:10).

The image of God in us is not confined to the static boundary of upright posture or reason or will. From the Eastern theological tradition this is well expressed by Vladimir Lossky: 'man ... is the person capable of manifesting God in the extent to which his nature allows itself to be penetrated by deifying grace'.[44] We are, then, more than mere individuals with a pre-determined nature and rigidly channelled potential. We are persons with free self-disposition. The image of God is maintained and fostered by the responsible, loving exercise of such freedom. For the Christian, there is the added motivation to be conformed to Christ, the image and likeness of God. This is a recurrent exhortation made by Paul in his epistles. Yet it is important to show the continuity of such conformity with the gift of human nature itself. The image of God in us is given with our very humanity. It is the strongest rationale we have for a theological defence of the human rights, civil and political, social and economic, which the Churches have come to espouse. The same tenet of the image of God in human-

kind is an effective motivation for upholding the dignity of every
man and woman precisely as human. Hence, the image doctrine
has a humanist value which should be neither diluted nor devalued. Human dignity is not a pragmatic concession. Human rights
are not in the grant of any person or body. They exercise a prior
claim which is not an optional extra. The image of God is inherent
to each person in virtue of God's creative disposition. Short of
that, no other reason will prove sufficiently strong to persevere in
demanding respect for foe as well as for friend, for stranger as well
as for kin.

It is all the more difficult to understand how the deliberate
evenhandedness of the Scriptures in ascribing the image of God to
man and woman has frequently been ignored. Man *and* woman
are the image of God. Some exegetes discern androgynous overtones in the Genesis text – the supersession of sexual difference
towards a full humanity in which the masculine and the feminine
are both realised and cherished. If this is so, it is neither masculin-
ity nor feminity which mirrors God but rather the integral exercise of human and social responsibility. Undoubtedly, the Bible
urges the complementarity of the sexes, but this is not the same as
the subsidiarity of either to the other. On the contrary, if the early
chapters of the Bible are clear on anything, it is that male and
female are equal before God, that both male and female are in the
image and after the likeness of God.

Without derogation from the biological and psychological differences in male and female, it must be stressed that it is as persons
we relate to God and exercise our freedom. The doctrine of the
image of God in humankind raises the challenging question of
whether cultural and ideological factors have been used to keep
women from the historical project to which they have so much to
contribute as of right. Further, while one has to be careful about
deriving a natural theology or theodicy from the image doctrine,
yet there is a clue to the nature of God in regarding God's image.
True, the image doctrine itself derives from a particular apprehension of God. Nevertheless, the doctrine offers further principles for an understanding of our models of thinking and speaking of God. We are brought to recognize the feminine dimension
to the metaphors of God which perforce we employ. To a degree,
the Bible has anticipated us in this: God is referred to a 'mother'
several times through the Old Testament (Is 42:14; 46:13; 49:15;
66:13; Psalm 131:2). Although the metaphorical usage in female
terms is rarer than the accumulation of male metaphors, yet it is
sufficient to found a serious consideration of the feminine experience of God.

Part Two

FIVE

Original Sin

A tradition of fifteen hundred years attached great importance to the theme of original sin. There is an irreplaceable value in this long standing emphasis but there is also a problem. The problem is at once of name, of description and of effect.

THE PROBLEM

To say 'original sin' directs attention to origins – either to the dawn of the race when sin is said first to have eventuated or to the conception of each new individual who thereby contracts it. In this way a short-circuit arises which evacuates meaning and credibility from the theme. For 'original sin' is not simply about what is supposed to have happened at a time unavailable to the tools of historical research. Nor yet should it be associated with the physical generation of each new person. It has much more to do with the weight of alienation pressing upon the human condition and exercising a more damaging effect than either of the other two understandings is likely to suggest.

To say original 'sin' evokes the objection that sin can never be other than the personally assumed free act of an individual. The ideas of a 'sin of the race' or 'inherited sin' are at first hearing likely to call forth disbelief and even hostility. People have become rightly suspicious of vicarious culpability. As J. P. Mackey put it: 'one man's guilt simply cannot be transferred to another, even if he is moral head of a moral body, and not even a divine decree can make men guilty of something which they could do nothing to prevent'.[1] It is true that theological reflection emphasises that 'sin' is an analogous term. In original sin there is comparison but not identity with personal sin. Nevertheless, it remains that the very term original sin evokes difficulties which the teacher and the preacher would do well to note. One may agree with Karl Rahner that in preaching and teaching 'we should not begin immediately with this word, which then has to be modified with a great deal of effort. We should rather acquire enough theology so that, starting with experience and with a description ... of the human situation, we can talk about the matter itself without using this word. Only at the end would we have to indicate that this very actual reality of one's own life and one's own situation is called "original sin" '.[2]

The tradition on original sin is expressed through an extended metaphor or, better, model. The dominant mode of expression – with its own inner logic and set of concepts – is cognate to the field of genetics. Thus, original sin is traced down from a single ancestor (or an original couple). It is said to be transmitted by a propagation often interpreted as physical generation. It is viewed as inherited guilt intrinsic to the subject at a depth mere bad example could never reach. At times the term 'stain' or *maculum* is used. The model carries overtones of censure on the act of conceiving a child. It bears the somewhat negative view of sexual intercourse which prevailed when the model was initially fashioned. This in itself is out of joint with our own times. Why should guilt be associated with one of the most intimate and creative moments of human life? Within the genetic model there is yet another tension. It arises from the ascription to Adam of the so-called praeternatural gifts: freedom from concupiscence, ignorance, suffering and death. If one takes at all seriously the evidence of biogenetics it is difficult to accept that the progenitors of the race could be free from suffering. Both concupiscence (understood as the sensitive movement towards the good of food, drink, rest and sex) and death are part of the nature of things in the kind of world we inhabit. The genetic model of original sin assumes that there was a momentary flash of brilliance at the emergence of humanity upon which supervened a 'fall'. Thereafter commences a slow climb to physical refinement and some degree of culture, much as might be anticipated in an evolutionary perspective had there never been a fall. For some, this 'fall' from 'original justice' is no more than the mythic nostalgia for a golden age. They would argue that the time has come to search for a newer, more satisfactory model.

These, then, are some of the internal difficulties of this model of understanding. In addition, there is the external difficulty of lack of relevance and, perhaps, of credibility. Many who fervently agree with St Paul that there is a moral fissure in our life-experience nevertheless judge the traditional presentation of original sin jejune, even trivial. C. G. Jung remarks that 'the evil that comes to light in man, and undoubtedly dwells within him, is of gigantic proportions so that for the Church to talk of original sin and to trace it back to Adam's relatively innocent slip-up with Eve is almost a euphemism. The case is far greater and is grossly understated'.[3] Is it sufficient to describe this profound truth in terms of a *maculum animae,* transmitted by physical generation or in connection with it? Is it not reductive of the mystery of evil to focus attention on an original misdemeanour thus to implicate people in an act which was none of their doing and the circumstances of which are shrouded in a nimbus of mythic detail? At the very least it seems that our notions of sin and grace, of personal responsibility and collective solidarity stand in need of re-examination.

Karl Marx claimed that 'the principles of Christianity explain all the vile actions to which the oppressed are subjected by their oppressors either as the just chastismernt for original sin or as tests imposed by God on the elect'.[4] Clearly this is not Church teaching but a caricature of it. Nevertheless it carries an element of truth. A particular view of original sin has located 'paradise' before the 'fall' and aspired to its retrieval beyond history. Thus the urgency to fashion history is seriously diminished: 'history loses its content, it is turned into a test of each individual's existence'.[5] Even more, the concept of sin becomes excessively private – rooted in the individual from his very conception, it is countered by individual effort under grace, an effort chiefly directed to overcoming concupiscence. It is not unfair to argue that in traditional catechesis concupiscence was regarded in large measure as a tendency to sexual inordinateness. Thereby the proclivity to injustice of all kinds was frequently overlooked.

And so, if people were ever content with the 'Adam and Eve' story they can scarcely be so any longer. If preachers and teachers continue to insist upon the genetic model of interpretation they may well do themselves an injustice. They most certainly will incur the incredulity of their congregations and pupils in large measure. Understandably, therefore, Edward Yarnold writes: 'either the doctrine of original sin should be altogether rejected or the "traditional explanation" of it should be discarded and another substituted'.[6] For Catholic theology the first option is not feasible. The Church has clarified its own consciousness in such a way that theology cannot rest content with a general notion of sin as if inherited or original sin had never arisen. And so one must tread the path of re-interpreting the doctrine with the difficulties arising from its traditional formulation in mind. One must look again at original sin, aware of the distinction to be made between the way of signifying (*modus significandi*) and the thing signified (*res significata*). One can profitably utilise the distinction drawn by Pope John XXIII: 'the substance of the ancient doctrine of the deposit of faith is one thing, and the way it is presented is another'.[7]

A FLAWED WORLD

There is a deep truth in the doctrine of original sin. That truth relates intimately to our experience of self, of others and of human affairs generally. Gabriel Daly has suggested that there is 'probably no other subject, if honestly and skilfully deployed, more compulsive of attention than the human phenomenon traditionally referred to as original sin'.[8] J. H. Newman argues in his *Apologia Pro Vita Sua*: 'if there be a God, since there is a God, the human race is implicated in some terrible aboriginal calamity'. It is worth adverting to Arthur Koestler's conviction: 'the evidence seems to indicate that at some point during the last explosive stages of the evolution of homo sapiens something has gone wrong, that there is a flaw, some subtle engineering mistake built into our native equipment, which would account for the paranoid streak running through our history'.[9]

It is foolhardy to ignore these data of common conviction. To return to Jung, inattention to the 'imagination of evil' adds stupidity to iniquity. Ignorance of the beam in our own eye magnifies the speck in the eyes of others. It makes us tolerate our own dark deeds while projecting them onto scapegoats. Thus are deepened the fissures which have so riddled our history. This blind spot deprives us of the capacity to overcome evil. Karl Rahner reminds us that the Church's historical pessimism has served well: 'it is the best service to improving the world here and now, because the utopian idea that a world functioning in perfect harmony which can be created by man himself only leads to greater violence and greater cruelty than those which man wants to eradicate from the world'.[10] Modern theological writing is not only sensitive to the impact of evolutionary perspectives and psychological insight on the notion of sin – it also pays extended attention to the history of sin which has dogged humanity. There is a relation between personal sin and the sin which is said to be our inheritance. And there are many forces at work besides whatever affects us congenitally: education, environment, social structures. Louis Mondin sums it up very well: 'original sin is not some kind of juridical imputation of a past event, but a structure which continues to exert its effects, and to be accepted and continued by personal sin'.[11]

Yet Christianity is positive through and through. It proclaims that we are liberated, reconciled, redeemed. Far from beating us about the ears with denunciation, the Easter message proclaims that God is glorified not at our expense but in and through our fulfilment. All too frequently, versions of Christianity have gravitated to the sinfulness of man thus to bemoan the 'human all too human'. While sinfulness is an evident fact and the 'human all too human' a part of our everyday fallibility, nevertheless they are but one side of a two-facetted reality. In the true Christian perspective it is the redeemed dimension which is primary. The many soteriological images of the New Testament must be given their rightful place. God, says Saint Paul, was in Christ reconciling the world to himself, and we are entrusted with the good news that this reconciliation has taken place.[12] There is a splendid optimism to Paul's own doxology: 'thanks be to God who gave us the victory in Christ Jesus, our Lord' (1 Cor 15:57). The Eastern Church would appear to have fastened upon this more securely than the Western in asserting the divinisation (*theosis*) of humankind. The Eastern tradition lauds the 'exchange' (*admirabile commercium*) whereby Christ became one of us in order that we might become sharers in the divine life.

However, there is a concomitant awareness that Christ's grace is healing grace. The New Testament speaks of liberation from sin. It speaks of redemption, reconciliation, restoration. We are thereby reminded of the state from which we have been rescued and from which we constantly need rescue. Forgetfulness of this would diminish the estimation both of the gift and the need. *Soteria* (redemption) and *apoleia* (need of redemption) are linked so that one cannot be known without the other. The due order is best set out by Paul: where sin abounded, grace did more abound. Even though we are aware of our own sinfulness we believe that grace is the dominant reality. Evangelical theology holds that we best know the reality of sin in the light of our redemption in Christ. Hence, our first response should be not the wringing of hands but the grateful celebration of redemption. Thus we are led to something more profound and closer to experience than an aboriginal misdeed in which willy-nilly we are all made to share. Paul's teaching takes account of an inheritance of sin but it also reminds us that we add to that legacy.

ELEMENTS TOWARDS A THEOLOGY OF ORIGINAL SIN

1. The word 'Adam' is used some five hundred and thirty nine times in the Bible. In the majority of instances it is to be translated 'man' or 'men'. Not until late in the Old Testament tradition was 'Adam' understood as a proper name referring to a particular individual. The use of 'Adam' as a proper name is a feature of late Judaism. It is certainly a post-exilic usage. The usage passed to St Paul who speaks of Adam as a single individual. The classic texts are Romans 5:12-21 and 1 Cor 15:22. There is much discussion of the background from which Paul drew his Adam-model. Exeget-

ical opinion has variously placed the model in Jewish apocalyptic, rabbinic theology, even in Jewish-Gnostic speculation on the 'first' and the 'last' man. It is evident that Paul thought of Adam as one man. However, it is far from clear that he wished to teach this in any definitive way. In counterpointing the roles of Adam and Christ, he strongly appeals to their individual efficacy for good and ill. Yet the role assigned to 'Adam', while more than a mere literary foil, in no sense commits Paul to any doctrine of Adam's personal unicity.

2. 'Original sin' is not a biblical term. The Bible knows of personal sin at all points of its development. As well, it knows of an antecedent situation which affects people in virtue of their very humanity. Personal sin, alienation from God through wilful transgression of God's law, is amply documented. Genesis portrays it vividly – the temptation and fall of Adam and Eve, the murder of Abel, the *hubris* at Babel. The spread of evil is depicted through the individuals who add to a growing 'deposit'. This amounts to an antecedent situation affecting people from their birth: 'behold I was brought forth in iniquity and in sin did my mother conceive me' (Ps 51:5); 'the wicked go astray from the womb, they err from birth, speaking lies' (Ps 58:3). The prophetic books document a patterned injustice calling forth the wrath of God upon an errant nation. Israel attains a new level of awareness of its own collective responsibility and of its shortcoming in meeting such responsibility. Thus personal sin and the situation it causes are highlighted. In addition, there is the idea that prior to personal sin a fractured moral situation is operative 'from the womb'. The Johannine reference to 'the sin of the world' is an interesting example of this. It stems from the theological model so well worked out by John: of light and darkness, of sinful flesh, of 'kingdom' and of 'world'. This cannot be directly identified as original sin: but it raises the question of redemption from a darkened, broken world by one who, taking upon himself the sin of the world, removes it.

3. For over a millenium and a half Paul has been taken to argue for our solidarity in the sin of Adam. At Romans 5:12 he counterpoints Adam and Christ. Adam is the foil for Christ. He is the one whose delict and its effects are the backcloth against which salvation in Christ shines the more brilliantly. While the wider commentary on Romans 5:12 cannot be represented here, yet a few systematic points are in order. A particular understanding of the Greek *eph ho* as 'in whom' (all have sinned) has led to the misconception that Paul urges an inclusion in the sin of Adam. Augustine is sometimes blamed for this erroneous translation. Yet one finds a similar construction in Ambrosiaster's earlier

commentary on Romans 5. Even in the third century, patristic literature interprets Romans 7: 9-10 and 1 Cor 15:22 in a similarly inclusive way. Irenaeus of Lyons can directly refer the 'forgive us our trespasses' of the Our Father to our inclusion in Adam. However, exegetes today prefer to translate *eph ho* not by 'in whom' but by 'because' or 'so that'. If the version 'because all men have sinned' is selected then the meaning of the whole text is broadened. It can be understood to say that death spread because all sinned either by imitation of Adam or by inheritance of his guilt. On the other hand, one may wish to accept with S. Lyonnet the translation 'so that all men sinned ... ' This carries the nuance that Adam introduced sinfulness into the world and it spread to all so that they now choose to sin because of an inherited tendency.

Thus there are three possible interpretations of the text: (a) that Adam, being the first, influences us by example; (b) that Adam's sin leaves us with an 'evil heart', an inherited tendency to sin; (c) that Adam's sin makes us all sinners whether we choose to sin or not. There are many careful authors who prefer the last of these understandings. While example or inherited tendency cohere more closely to Old Testament thought patterns, the logic of the passage seems to suggest that it is Adam's disobedience, not our choice, which makes us sinners. As Edward Yarnold writes: 'our sinfulness and our righteousness both derive from another'.[13] It is true that the latter interpretation brings Paul beyond rabbinic thought. The rabbinic teaching does not say that Adam 'made sinners of others'. Paul makes this extra step, thus strengthening the connotation of Adam's influence for the worse. Nevertheless, it would stretch the Pauline text to read into it a full-blown doctrine of original sin. For Paul, the sin of Adam has a real influence on our moral and physical situation. Yet if we ask of this text: does Adam's influence eventuate in us independently of personal sin? or, again, is personal sin a condition of our 'original' sin? – we shall not find an answer. Later doctrine may answer these questions more clearly, but in Paul's text one discovers neither a Yes nor a No.[14]

There appears to be a kind of hierarchy of affirmation in Romans 5:12 and ff. The primary affirmation is that superabundant redemption has been given in Jesus himself. Only in the second place does Paul depict the parlous state in which all have been plunged by the sin of Adam. There are reputable commentators who would deny that Paul teaches anything about this sin apart from its factuality. Nevertheless, there is much to recommend Lyonnet's careful view that Paul insinuates a situation of sin due not to our personal fault but antecedent to our choice and traceable to the delict of another. The major thrust of Paul's argument is that we are saved from the power of sin and death by Christ. The explanation of how that sin and its effects eventuated is not offered.[15]

4. The Scriptures, both Old and New Testaments, constantly repeat that we all need the justifying grace of God. By that grace we are brought from death to life, from sin to sanctification. Yet there remains in us a dimension that of itself will lead us to sin. Here is a valid understanding of Luther's dictum: 'We are at once both justified and sinful' (*simul iusti et peccatores sumus*). Both Testaments know of a universal and virtually irresistible impulsion to sin from which we cannot free ourselves: the human heart is desperately corrupt. Yet it took a slow development culminating in Paul to affirm that the perversity from which we need constant rescue is due not simply to our own sins but also to a fault affecting us prior even to our conscious decisions. The explanation of how this fault occurred is a separate matter. It pertains to the form, not to the core, of truth contained in the Bible. In Genesis alone we find several aetiologies: the fall of Adam and Eve, the mating of the sons of God with the daughters of men (Gen 6), the tower of Babel (Gen 11). These are pitched to different contexts and trace the progression of our alienation from God. Inset to the main biblical story of God's graciousness and human need, they present us with a valuable witness to the depth of that need. But as to the narrative circumstances and the pedagogical devices they use, these cannot be said to belong to the binding affirmations of faith.

THE GREEK FATHERS

In the seventeenth century, the riches of Christian antiquity became available to theological scholarshilp more widely than hithertofore. As a result, systematic theologians could approach the literature of the Greek and Latin Fathers in a way which dimly presaged the methodic interpretations of the nineteenth and twentieth centuries. Petavius, with some astonishment, discovered that the Greek Fathers rarely mention an 'original sin'. While they adduce elements of that doctrine they come far short of the clear formulations of the Council of Trent. Petavius wrote: 'In their writings they advert to the topic of original sin but rarely and never at length' (*originalis fere criminis raram nec disertam mentionem scriptis suis attingunt*).[16] The Greek Fathers show a considerable optimism about the human condition when compared with the post-Augustinian writings in the Western Church. On the topic of an original fall, on its effects upon subsequent generations, on the situation of infants who die without baptism, there is a brighter hue in the canvas they depict. J. N. D. Kelly remarks that there is barely a hint in the Greek Fathers that humankind as a whole shares in Adam's guilt.[17] The view of Irenaeus of Lyons (140 - 202 A.D.) anticipates this relatively optimistic emphasis of the Greeks. For Irenaeus, we all die in Adam. He derives this conviction from Paul, not indeed from Romans 5:12 but from Romans 5:19 – 'for as by the disobedience of one man, many were made sinners; so also by the obedience of one, many shall be made just'. Adam and Eve are childlike creatures, destined to grow in wisdom and grace. By nature mortal, they were to attain immortality as pure gift. In addition they were endowed with the presence of the Holy Spirit. All this was lost by sin. For the descendants of Adam and Eve those gifts were squandered away. In common with many of the early Church Fathers, Irenaeus believed that subsequent generations could retrieve their loss. People could attain an even greater share of the Spirit and at the end of time might recover all that was originally lost.

The optimism of the later Greek Fathers, such as Athanasius, Basil, the two Gregories and John Chrysostom, is frequently traced to the characteristics of the Hellenic mind. More convincing is the argument that their lighter stress on original sin is connected to their sustained polemic with Manichaeism. Whereas the Manichaeans inculcated an entirely pessimistic view of the body, of human nature and of the world, all creatures of an evil God, the Fathers of the Church who entered conflict with the heresy pointed up the freedom of the will, the abuse of which leads to actual or personal sin. Thus, to refer to J. N. D. Kelly once more: 'it is easy to collect passages from their works which ... appear to rule out any doctrine of original sin'.[18]

Athanasius and, indeed, all the Greek Fathers know of a Fall. It brings about a defacement of the image of God in humankind. Or, to change the metaphor, the Fall effects a progressive overlaying of that image through the dynamic of sin it unleashes. One finds, for example, in Gregory Nazianzen an impressively realistic detail of these effects: death, pain, sickness, ignorance, weakness of will. It is of interest to note that Nazianzen links social evils such as violence, poverty and slavery to the sorry history originated by the Fall. Given their strong conception of recapitulation (*encephalaiosis*) it is easier for these Fathers to speak of our association with Adam's misdemeanour and of its effect upon us through a 'mystical' inclusion in him. Basil can write that we were once in glory when we lived in paradise but we became inglorious and lowly because of the Fall.[19] On the other hand, the Greek

Fathers do not make much of participation in Adam's guilt. Athanasius envisages that certain figures such as Jeremiah and John the Baptist lived free from all sin. And they show a most pleasing optimism about children who die without baptism. Gregory of Nyssa and John Chrysostom explicitly mention that newly born children are without sin. According to Gregory Nazianzen, children dying without baptism are not punished. They are not wicked. They have suffered harm rather than done it.

The Eastern Fathers work within a different theological schema to those of the West. Their dominant concept is divinisation (*theosis*): 'the Son of God became Son of Man so that the sons of men ... might become sons of God ... partakers of the life of God ... He is Son of God by nature and we by grace'.[20] Their key themes are not Fall and sin, although these are not neglected. Rather the themes are participation in God's nature, rebirth in the Holy Spirit, adoption as sons of God, new creation in Jesus Christ.

One may conclude, therefore, that while the pre-Augustinian Fathers, particularly those of the East, acknowledge a hereditary corruption and link this to a transgression of Adam, nevertheless the idea of a hereditary sin does not cohere with their doctrinal presuppositions – in particular the presupposition that sin is always a free decision, an abuse of the noble faculty of will.

INFANT BAPTISM IN THE EARLY CHURCH

It is beyond doubt that the baptism of infants was practised in the early Church by mid-second century.[21] Towards the year 200 A.D. it was fairly well established. By the early sixth century it was prevalent, especially in the Western Church. Certainly there were those such as Tertullian who continued to argue for baptism at a later age. Yet their argument was not that the baptism of infants was invalid or unnecessary but rather that it was better to participate in the rite freely and consciously. Some argued against infant baptism as increasing the chances of a later fall from baptismal grace. However, it is indisputable that the wide spread of infant baptism argues to an awareness that all have need of it. Death without baptism was an evil to avoid. Thus one finds evidence of the provision of baptism in case of necessity outside the stated times for conferral of the sacrament.

In any reference to optimism on inherited sin, the penitential, sanative aspects of baptism should not be forgotten. The retention of exorcisms and allusions to the forgiveness of sin in early infant baptism is of significance. Albeit implicitly, there is predicated to infants the need for liberation from an ancient servitude.

One finds this most clearly stated in the African Fathers even as early as Cyprian. Cyprian speaks of the baptism of infants as a passing from perdition to salvation while yet he regards the infant as less guilty than the adult: 'the newly born infant has not sinned except for what, as a descendant of Adam, he has contracted at birth, of the contagion of the ancient death. These infants are forgiven not their own sins but those of another'.[22]

The Greek Fathers assess the reasons for the baptism of infants. Gregory Nazianzen and Basil mention several effects of baptism as a sufficient reason for the practice: immersion in the paschal mystery, consecration and sanctification of life, reception of the seal of baptism. They ascribe many dynamic effects to baptism – becoming a son of God, being placed in the protection of the Trinity, being fortified against the danger of future sins, being oriented to the glory of God's kingdom. Origen is the exception in referring to a 'sin' in the newly born infant. Yet even when he speaks of their baptism 'for the forgiveness of sins', he allows that babies carry the 'stain' rather than the 'sin' of Adam. By contrast, Gregory of Nyssa avers that innocent children do not need healing through purification. They have no malice but simply participate in human nature. The context – the title of his work is 'On Infants Who Die' – makes it most likely that Origen is speaking here of children who die without baptism. These sparse but firm indications corroborate the impression that even into the fifth century there is a considerable section of the Church which does not clearly inculcate a hereditary sin. For this stream of thought baptism serves many functions other than simply the release from hereditary sin.[23]

AUGUSTINE OF HIPPO[24]

In his work *De Diversis Quaestionibus ad Simplicianum,* written about 395 A.D., Augustine refers to an original sin. This is the earliest use of the term in Christian sources. Augustine has in mind Adam's sin, or, as later centuries would call it, *peccatum originale originans.* In a subsequent work, *De Peccatorum Meritis et Remissione,* he went on to apply the term to Adam's descendants. Thus he anticipates what the Medievals were to call *peccatum originale originatum.* However, the influence of Augustine is not limited to terminology. Both in content and structure his doctrine of original sin has fashioned subsequent writing in the Western Church and, in particular, the *dicta* of the Councils of Orange, Carthage and Trent.

Augustine's theology changed and deepened during his years as priest and principal bishop of the North African Church. The extent to which his views developed is one of the fascinating discoveries of modern Augustinian scholarship. Ever since the emergence of critical study of his work, three major lines have been explored: his seeming identification of original sin with ignorance and concupiscence; his insight that original sin is the privation of sanctifying grace; his theory of the derivation of our guilt from Adam. When the modern historico-critical method began to be applied, it emerged that his views on sin and grace developed in a more dramatic way than the mere juxtaposition of these three lines might suggest. In the first years after his conversion, say from 389-397, Augustine retained a relatively extrinsic idea of redemption. He insists more upon the example of Christ than upon the inner renewal brought about by our insertion into Christ's life. Certainly, the sin of Adam has induced an ignorance in us. Yet this is a difficulty or obstacle rather than an absolute incapacity to do good. Hence, at this period Augustine will insist upon conversion of the heart and not yet upon that inner principle given only in the grace of Christ. Arguing with the Manichaeans, he countered that there is no evil without sin, just as there is no sin without the free act of the person. Infants who die without baptism will not be punished even if they do not receive a supernatural reward. At this stage it is not clear that Augustine held there was an original sin in unbaptized infants. It is clear that he recognises the damage caused by Adam: death, ignorance and hindrances to well doing. However, it is unclear that he holds to a state of sin antecedent to free, personal decisions.

From approximately the year 395 one can trace the emergence of a new synthesis. Parallel developments seem to have taken place in Augustine's thought on evil, on redemption, on grace, on the sacraments and on original sin. What caused this shift from a relatively optimistic view of the human predicament? It was not his interpretation of Paul's *dictum* at Romans 5:13 ('in whom all sinned': *in quo omnes peccaverunt*) which brought about the change. Nor are the circumstances of the anti-Pelagian campaign sufficient to explain the shift. Augustine's views had already been moving in a new direction even before the polemic against Pelagius. In his *Ad Simplicianum* (397 A.D.) Augustine already speaks of humankind as a *massa damnata* utterly incapable of salvation if left to its own devices. An authority on Augustine, Karl Adam, identifies his deepening awareness of the absolute necessity of the grace of Christ as the key to the development. The combination of his pastoral reflection as a priest and bishop with a retrospective assessment of his own earlier life motivated the change. The outcome was a sombre estimation of the human condition and a passionate reliance on the healing grace of Christ. This is the synthesis enabling Augustine to enter controversy with Pelagius. It emerges clearly in his first anti-Pelagian work, *De Peccatorum Meritis et Remissione.* Here the dominant theme is the universal necessity of redemption. If Christ's death is not to be evacuated of meaning, all, without exception, need to be freed, redeemed and illuminated by him. Without Christ there is no salvation but only damnation.

Since it is through his opposition to Pelagius that Augustine earned his title *doctor gratiae* it is appropriate briefly to outline Pelagius' own teaching. He is taken to have been a British – some say Irish – monk who lived in Rome until the invasion of Alaric in 409 A.D. He then crossed to Africa and settled for a while in Carthage. In Africa, he would have seen and heard Augustine. Thence he went to Jerusalem where he successfully defended his orthodoxy against Orosius, sent by Augustine to counter him. Augustine's opposition was already pursued with such persistence that one suspects it amounted to a personal crusade. Through Augustine's efforts, two local councils condemned Pelagius and sought the endorsement of Innocent I. On news of that approval, Augustine's *dictum* was uttered: Rome has spoken, the case is finished (*Roma locuta est, causa finita est*). Pelagius sent his own protestation of faith to Innocent's successor, Zozimus. Zozimus' reaction was to absolve Pelagius from taint of heresy. Augustine's next move was to have convened the famous Synod of Carthage in 418. Attended by papal legates and subsequently ratified by Zozimus, it condemned some of the major tenets of Pelagius. At this stage Pelagius seems to leave the scene. His teaching was carried on by Julian of Eclanium (Italy) who himself went into exile under the protection of Theodore of Mopsuestia. Thus a current of thought which originally stemmed from the East and through Pelagius spread to the West, came to rest once more in the East. The doctrine of Pelagius was definitively condemned at the Council of Ephesus (431 A.D.) and went into oblivion for centuries.

Pelagius was essentially a moral reformer, even a rigorist, who rejected pessimistic views of human nature as conducive to quietism. The *leitmotiv* of his teaching is the freedom of the will, with the concomitant responsibility such freedom bears. Humankind is made to accomplish the divine purpose in the exercise of free choice. Contrary to a commonly held impression, Pelagius does not oppose human autonomy to God's sovereignty. Human free-

dom is always God's gift and is solicited by the divine law which
sets forth what to do. Pelagius calls for the fulfilment of that law:
'A Christian is he who is one not in word but in deed, who imitates
and follows Christ in everything, who is holy, innocent, unsoiled,
blameless, in whose heart there is no malice, but only piety and
goodness, who refuses to injure or hurt anyone, but brings succour to all'.[25] He details three aspects of human action: the power,
the will and the realisation. God alone gives the power. To us God
leaves the willing and the realising. In setting forth this schema,
Pelagius re-emphasises human freedom. He sees it as a nonsense
to say that there is an inherited sin which affects us even at birth:
'before man begins exercising his will there is only in him what
God has created'. In so far as Adam has affected us, it is by the
habit of disobedience which affects us by custom and example. To
speak of an inherited sin is an affront to God. Since God is willing
to forgive personal sins, God will surely not blame us for the sin of
another. It is not surprising that Pelagius, while he accepted that
baptism is a healing sacrament for adults, saw its effect for infants
to be adoption and sanctification, but not the remission of sin.

The point at which Pelagius conflicts with tradition is his theology of grace. He affirms the necessity of grace. However, he
appears to limit it to a set of exterior aids enabling the free will to
decide between good and evil. This falls short even of the optimistic Eastern tradition which accents inner renewal or divinisation.
However, one leaves Pelagius with a certain admiration for his
religious spirit, for his appreciation of the loving-kindness of God
who refuses to indict us for what we have not done, and for his
insistence that God does not predestine some to eternal life while
leaving others to perdition.

Augustine's reply is affected by his own experience of conversion as well as his pastoral realism. He is convinced of the absolute
necessity of the grace of Christ. Further, he holds that grace is a
principle of action which transforms us through and through.
These two convictions lead him to a rigidity on predestination and
free will which re-emerged much later in Luther's 'enslaved will'
(*servum arbitrium*) and in Calvin's double predestination. Yet in
the context of his day Augustine provided the required counter-
weight to Pelagius. The Bishop of Hippo proclaimed that from
the first impulse to conversion through to the gift of final perse-
verance salvation comes only from God in Christ. Whereas the
Eastern Fathers express this truth in mystical terms, Augustine
does so in moral, psychological and existential terms. He shows
clearly that grace reaches to the depths of our being. It transforms
and heals us. Augustine depicts ever more sharply the situation

from which we require to be rescued. It is radical absence of grace leading to existential disorder, selfishness, denial of higher values, and sexual inordinateness. It is a state of sin prior to an individual's choice and it affects all without exception. In effect, Augustine has moved from his early admission of an inherited misery to the predication of a universal fault or culpability.

He made this transition in the light of two inter-related convictions. In the first place, Jesus Christ is the sole redeemer. His grace is healing, saving grace. If all – even the baby newly born – stand in need of Christ's grace, then all must already be sinners. And if the new born baby dies in this state, he or she goes not to heaven, not to limbo – a hypothesis which had not yet emerged – but to hell. The other conviction grows out of Augustine's view of concupiscence. Concupiscence is both the parent and child of sin. It is the parent of sin for it impels us to personal sin. It is the child of sin for it is inseparable from the act of generation which thereby becomes guilty. In the act of our generation we become guilty by inclusion in the guilt of Adam. Augustine is reinforced in this conviction by his belief that we have a biological pre-existence in Adam and that the individual is somehow participative in the universal man.

It has been argued recently that Augustine's principal stress is christological. His teaching on sin is said to belong to the expression rather than the essence of his teaching.[26] However, it is difficult to make so sharp a distinction in his theology of grace. How can we separate what for him seem to be two facets of the one reality? It is perhaps more feasible to approach his writings with the principle of a hierarchy of truths in mind. This is a relatively modern principle although it has roots in Augustine and Aquinas. It can enable us to propose that the christological affirmation of the necessity and inner reality of grace is Augustine's main achievement. Derivative from that is his insight to our deep rooted deprivation of grace. In terms of the hierarchical principle, his use of the Adam/Eve story and the genetic model of original sin may be regarded as the least important part of his synthesis and, for our purposes, detachable from it.[27]

TRENT[28]

The fifth session of the Council of Trent devoted its attention to the question of original sin from May 24 to June 17, 1546. From this session emerged pastoral, theological and dogmatic teaching which shaped Catholic thought until the middle years of our own century. The council approved an introductory chapter (*proemium*), five canons, and several *excursus* by way of scriptural/

theological reinforcement. It is not an arrogance to claim that this century is the first to have the resources for a thorough understanding of the council's treatment of the major issues it addressed. On grace and justification, on sacraments, on Church order and ministry, on Scripture and tradition, Trent deliberated much and achieved a great deal. It did so in reaction to the apparently destructive pronouncements of the Reformation. The council sought not so much to cast new formulations of doctrine as to agree to *minima* by which the ancient faith could be expressed integrally while legitimate theological pluralism could still be maintained. Through the magnificent work of the *Gorresgescellschaft* the acts of the council, the diary of Severoli and six tracts on original sin contemporary with the council have become available in a series of publications since 1901. As a result, the theology of original sin has been enriched by the possibility of going behind the texts in a way hitherto most difficult if not impossible.

Recent decades have seen the application of the historico-critical method not only to the Bible but also to conciliar texts. This method enjoins attention to the dynamic of all linguistic expression. To understand a text there are many elements other than the purely philological. In understanding a conciliar text, one must ask about its context and the challenges it tries to meet. Of any conciliar document one must ask what is its direct teaching and where that teaching is located. One should distinguish direct teaching from implicit presuppositions thus to discern which elements are binding on our assent (*de fide*) and which, being merely explanatory, are not thus binding. It is generally agreed that the five canons of the decree on original sin contain the essence of the council's teaching. Thus the *proemium* and the explanatory asides are reinforcements rather than part of the direct teaching. Again, in attempting to understand Trent, one can distinguish the canons from the implicit suppositions to which they are inset. The acceptance of these presuppositions is necessary only insofar as without them the teaching itself could no longer stand.

The first canon deals with what classical theology calls *peccatum originale originans* (original sin in its origin).[29] It asserts that Adam sinned and thus lost the holiness and justice in which he was constituted. As a further result he was changed for the worse in both body and soul. He incurred God's anger, became subject to death, and fell under the power of the devil. The second canon links Adam's sin to the human situation. It deals with *peccatum originale originatum* (original sin in us). It condemns every assertion that Adam's sin harmed only himself and not those who came after him. Further, it condemns any assertion that the holiness and justice with which Adam was endowed were lost only to him and not to us. And it condemns the view that Adam transmitted to us only death and physical suffering, and not sin, which the council terms 'death of the soul'. Canon three describes the sin of Adam not as originating act but as inherited state. It makes three assertions: that original sin is one in origin, that it is passed on by propagation and not by imitation, that it inheres to each person as his/her own. Perhaps the major thrust of the canon is its assertion that original sin cannot be removed by our own efforts but only through the merits of Jesus Christ, our one Mediator and Redeemer. These merits, avers the canon, are applied to infants and adults alike by baptism.

The fourth canon deals with the baptism of infants. The validity of infant baptism had been controverted by the Anabaptists of Bohemia. As well, Luther's sacramental theory seemed to deny the validity of the baptism of those who could not elicit a personal act of faith. To counter Luther and perhaps the Anabaptists, Trent retrieves Augustine's emphasis by linking the theology of grace even to the baptism of infants. Against this background the council insists: (a) that for babies to attain eternal life they must be baptized even if their parents have been baptized, and (b) that, even in infants, baptism remits the sin inherited from Adam.

The fifth canon is perhaps the most significant. It culminates the argument of the other four. It repudiates every denial that the grace of Christ really remits sin. Sin is taken away and not simply not-imputed. Whereas Pighius, a Dutch Catholic theologian, seemed to imply that baptism results in the non-imputation of original sin to the baptized, and whereas Luther seemed to deny the inner reality of the forgiveness of sin, Trent insists upon the interior effect of baptism. The thrust of this canon is to emphasise the reality of the healing grace of Christ. The recipient becomes totally pleasing to God, fully reconstituted a child of God, even if concupiscence remains both as a challenge and an occasion for further grace.

In a list of adversaries distributed at the council one finds Pelagius, Erasmus of Rotterdam, Pighius and Luther. It becomes clear that canons three to five are, so to speak, reactive to current error as perceived by the Catholic official side. These canons counteract the Reformers on the effect of grace, on the necessity and efficacy of baptism, and on the disparity of sin and concupiscence. Canons one and two, however, are not directed against any opponents. With some verbal changes, they are a *reprise* of the councils of Carthage and Orange. The question arises of why they are inset here. Two possible answers arise. First, they are a point of departure for opposition to the Reformers. They signify an agreement with Luther on the necessity of the forgiveness of sin. This necessity, the council seems to say, is universal. The point of issue is how sin is forgiven and to what effect. The statements from Carthage and Orange suitably delineate the human condition from which we need redemption. Rather than formulate this anew, Trent employs with a few terminological changes the statements of Carthage and Orange. These two canons have a strategic use. They exculpate the council from any leaning towards Pelagianism. It is interesting that Calvin discerned the strategy, although he interpreted it otherwise. These canons, in his view, represented a mischievous attempt to foist upon the Reformers positions which they did not hold.[30] It would seem that Trent is not offering here a systematic formulation of original sin. In canons one and two it is simply setting out a position with which the major stances on grace, forgiveness and the efficacy of baptism could be developed in the second part of canon three as well as in canons four and five.

DOCTRINAL ANALYSIS OF THE CANONS

The simple repetition of the words of Trent – coined for another day and with specific counterpositions in view – is insufficient. Such repetition cannot meet the insistent objections from the natural sciences, from social studies and, even, from biblical exegesis. For the reflective Catholic there must be a position between 'modernism' and 'veterism', between disregarding both the spirit and the letter of Trent, and maximising its letter at great cost to a deeper understanding. Catholic tradition rightly insists upon the permanence of the meaning of doctrine. Yet it allows the distinction between the substance of a doctrinal synthesis and the way the synthesis is expressed. However, the distinction can only be grasped when a shift from the intellectual presuppositions of one epoch towards those of another has occurred. Due to the advances of the natural sciences and of historical criticism, such a shift has taken place from the cosmic, cultural and anthropological presuppositions accepted in the sixteenth century.

Our own assumptions render it difficult for us to enter a community of meaning with Trent unless the distinction between meaning and its form of expression is kept in mind. If that distinction is allowed, we can approach Trent critically yet humbly. We can shed considerable light on the question of original sin. The process of re-interpreation is not a denial of the council's teaching. Rather it is an attempt to effect the necessary transitions in the difficult process of understanding the voice of another time and another culture.

In the past two decades the interpretation of Trent has taken account of the logic of conciliar statements. Even blunt and unambiguous statements can contain several dimensions of meaning. It is argued that the foundational dimension to the decree on original sin is christological. Above all else,the council affirms the necessity of the grace of Christ. With Luther, Trent calls upon all Christians to avow that need. However, the council goes further than Luther. It affirms that even those who have never sinned personally need Christ's grace. As against Luther, Trent affirms that under the grace of Christ all become pleasing to God really and interiorly. By baptism the Christian, whether infant or adult, is made pleasing to God intrinsically, not simply by imputation or by judicial decree. This is the principal affirmation of the canons. The second level of meaning is ecclesio-sacramental. Trent says that the salvific work of Jesus Christ is applied to us through the Church in the sacrament of baptism. The Church has a mediational role secondary to Christ's. The sacraments, baptism in particular, are truly efficacious in applying Christ's saving work to each individual whether adult or infant. Baptism is necessary for all and is really for the forgiveness of sins.

The third level of meaning to Trent's canons on original sin is anthropological. Given the necessity of Christ's grace, and the necessity of baptism for everyone, it follows that prior to baptism all are affected by that lack of grace which Trent calls 'sin'. Clearly this is not actual or personal sin. By analogy it can be called sin, original sin. From this stems the insistence that the human condition is wounded, despoiled, afflicted by suffering and death. With the fourth level of meaning, we move from diagnosis to explanation. More precisely, Trent offers an aetiology of original sin. In order to explain the origin of the human misery which Christ's saving work addresses, Trent reached for an explanatory model already available to it. As mentioned earlier in this chapter, this model is from genetics, shaped by centuries of understanding of Adam/Eve, their fall and the transmission of the fall's effects.

It is not suggested that any of these levels of meaning is unimportant. However, one can argue that, just as Augustine's work is best appreciated in the light of a hierarchy of truths, so also here. A truth remains always a truth. Nevertheless, in the case of Trent each element is to be placed in the overall structure of affirmation. Many theologians argue that Trent's major commitment lies in its teaching about the structure of our redemption in Christ. Its diagnosis of our radical need of Christ's grace is valuable, even irreplaceable. Its affirmation of the profoundly transformative effect of baptism remains an essential element of Catholic doctrine. There is a substantial body of theological opinion which would hold that the aetiology or model of original sin offered by Trent is furthest from the core of faith and in greatest need of re-interpretation.[31]

A NOTE ON THREE MAJOR EMPHASES OF THE TRIDENTINE CANONS

1. *Unicuique inest uti proprium.* Canon three urges that original sin inheres to each of us 'as his/her own'. We are intrinsically affected by it. It affects us prior to our first moral act. It is more than mere example. Bad example is external and will influence us only gradually. Trent emphasises that our need of grace is with us from the first moment of our existence. Thus we are directed to something much more significant than a 'stain on the soul'. We are pointed to a deprivation which can only be remedied by the transforming action of Christ.

2. *Origine unum.* This phrase 'one in origin' is ancillary to that just analysed. It does not claim that original sin originated in one individual. Rather it urges that original sin is neither multiplied with the number of human individuals nor simply imputed to each new person. Is this unity inseparable from a physical unity of origin? It would seem not. Karl Rahner's argument is impressive: 'it is by no means clear that a moral unity (as distinct from a physical unicity) in origin of original sin has been excluded by the Tridentine canon. It is indisputable that the conciliar fathers presupposed a single individual as the originator of our troubles. It is not clear that this presupposition has been raised in any sense to a definition of faith'. However, Karl Rahner also reminds us that there must be a degree of unity in the first sin(s) sufficient to cause the universality and inescapability of the subsequent history of guilt.[32]

3. *Propagatione non imitatione.* In *Christ and Original Sin,* Peter de Rosa streses the contrast 'by propagation' and not 'by imitation'. With Pelagianism in mind Trent denies that original sin is merely the imitation of bad example. If it were simply imitation, then original sin would be an extrinsic matter. And so the primary assertion is the insufficiency of 'imitation' as an explanation of how original sin is transmitted or 'transfused'. Trent appeals to 'propagation' as the better concept. What is meant by 'propagation'? Is it the same as 'conception'? Does it mean 'physical generation'? It is likely that practically everyone was convinced, without giving it a thought, that original sin was transmitted through natural generation.[33] Yet the council reject-

ed the formulation: 'if anyone denies that the taint of original sin is transmitted to the children of the faithful by means of generation, let him be anathema'. Similarly, the proposition offered by the Bishop of Accia, Benedictus dei Nobilis, was rejected: 'original sin implies a taint and a corruption of generation, which every man acquires from his parents and which are inherent to his flesh'.[34] The reason for this is probably the council's decision not to enter matters of dispute amongst the medieval schools. Two of these questions were the nature of original sin and the means of its spread. At any rate, the council did not equiparate propagation with generation. Nevertheless, it underlined that we are all born into a graceless situation. There is a broad connection between original sin and our coming to be as members of the human race. Many theologians, while retaining the notion of propagation, invite us to move away from overtones of bodily generation towards social and psychological influences. Piet Smulders puts it: 'when the Council of Trent teaches the transmission of original sin 'by propagation not by imitation', it indicates that man incurs original sin by entrance within fallen mankind. Procreation can include not only the strict biological aspects, but also all the factors by which mankind makes someone its member, including education, environment, and example'.[35]

It emerges from our study of a tradition from Irenaeus to Trent that the theology of salvation and grace is the proper context for considering original sin. We are in a situation of sin and grace, of perdition and redemption. The dominant motif is that in Christ we are made alive and called to follow him as disciples. As a necessary counterpoint there is the stress that in every generation we need God's grace and our own unremitting effort to overcome the alienation which remains a constant of our experience. This alienation is prior to our moral choices and is a co-determinant of our moral stance.

CONTEMPORARY THEOLOGY OF ORIGINAL SIN

Contemporary theologians offer many descriptions of original sin. In the main they work within a developmental perspective. They endeavour to accomodate the thrust of Church tradition while attempting to avoid unnecessary tension with the natural and social sciences. There is a more realistic assessment of our divided, alienated situation than was possible in the classic presentation of original sin. There is a more subtle analysis of the human condition, co-determined as it is by both sin and grace. Today one finds a more extended attention to evil and sin which wreak havoc not only on individuals but also on society. Sin is a social reality as well as an individual tragedy. In this section, we shall retain the classical distinction of *peccatum originale originans* and *peccatum originale originatum*. It reminds us that original sin is never merely an individual reality. It is more than *la condition humaine*. Rather, there is a confluence of extrinsic and intrinsic, of historic and personal, of collective and individual factors.

Peccatum originale originans[36]

Original sin (as originating) reminds us that in making moral choices we are objects as well as subjects. As subjects, we make a more or less free disposition of ourselves. As objects, we find that our freedom is affected by our very situation as human beings. Contemporary theology tends to lighten the emphasis on the aetiological element of the questions offered by the councils of Carthage, Orange and Trent. These councils re-echo the scriptural insistence that the fractured human condition is not attributable to God's incompetence or carelessness. Much misery is due to the misuse of human freedom. Behind the reference to Adam/Eve is the affirmation that God's dealing with us is healing and redemptive. Many recent theologians argue that the Fall-narrative is to be seen as a backdrop rather than a main principle. Thus, they move away from literalism about Adam/Eve and the Fall. While there must have been a 'first sin' – and while it must have some significance precisely as first – we can know virtually nothing about its nature and circumstances. How could we? Folk memories do not go back to the dawn of the race. Residual archetypes in the human psyche cannot explain the matter either. And the Bible does not offer otherwise unavailable historical data.

It was noticed earlier that Trent does not have a specific adversary in mind when it details the sin of Adam and its effects. The council rather sets the scene for its teaching on the remission of sin first attained in baptism. Even conservative theologians now agree that the special status of the first sin is not *de fide*.[37] It is not *de fide* that human alienation was caused by one act rather than by many. After all, Christ has redeemed us from a whole history of sin. Yet the question remains of whether sin is a *malum catastrophicum* or a *malum evolutivum*. Is it the result of a colossal moral derangement or is it a natural component of things as they are? The mythic and religious answers tend to an aboriginal moral catastrophe. The philosophic analyses frequently but not universally prefer the evolutionary model. In either case the conclusion cannot be empirical.

The religious answer arises from the use of myth or aetiology. The philosophical response derives from a general world-view. The advantages of an aetiological explanation are highest when mythic discourse is well understood. The disadvantage is that today myth has broken. Stories of origins have been relegated to the lumber room of useless superstition. The philosophical analysis of sin and evil has a greater purchase on the moderm critical mind. On the other hand, there is the danger that talk about a *malum evolutivum* could lead to bland acceptance of an 'acceptable level' of evil and a naive expectation of progress without effort to reverse the alienation which is all.too real. At first hearing it might even seem to involve God as the author of evil as well as good.

Some theologians retain the aetiology of original sin while passing up its details. Thus Z. Alzeghy and M. Flick postulate a sin when first a moral decision became possible. The first humans may have been in a situation analogous to infants. It was only when people were capable of opting for or against God that 'sin' occured. The state of original justice perhaps did not coincide with hominisation. Original justice in the sense of perfect communion with God, untroubled by human fallibility, is a potential which has not yet been realised. Not that grace was withheld. It was – and is – given in a dispensation marked by moral refusal and fault. Original justice is prospective rather than retrospective. It lies ahead of us and is attained in a redemptive context. There are several merits to this approach. It takes account of the main outlines of the Christian 'story'. It respects the proportionality of faith in regard to sin and grace. It places the moral fault and its consequences to the account of humankind not of God. Finally, it makes ample room for human freedom in accepting or rejecting God's address. On the other hand, as a theological explanation it is strongly hypothetical. It appears contrived in its endeavour to fit the essential core of the Adamic account to the data of evolution theory.

There is a more radical tendency, associated with Teilhard de Chardin, which places the origin of evil and sin in the context of cosmogenesis. Sin, both personal and 'original', is the closure upon self against the call of God 'to be more and to be better'. At the human level sin corresponds to the regression and blind alleys marking the pattern of sub-human evolution. Sin can be viewed as entropy, the downward path towards isolation and disintegration which is countered by grace. Teilhard did not minimise the evil that is part of experience. But he saw both physical and moral evil as part of the development to Omega point. They are part of a world in evolution. To be part of a physical manifold is to be exposed to pain, disease and apparently absurd death. To be human is to be liable to sin. Thus we have always lived with the possibility of causing suffering for ourselves and for others. It would be unfair to Teilhard to leave the matter without further addition. With even greater vehemence he speaks of the call to overcome these shortfalls. The thrust of his writing is to sketch the development of the universe through consistent human effort under God's grace. In this perspective, original sin precisely as 'first' is a limit concept. It has a significance, indeed, but it is extra-empirical and does not deserve prolonged attention.

Teilhard's view is developed with considerable skill by the German editor of his works, K. Schmitz-Moorman.[38] More independently, P. Lengsfeld has written in the same orientation. Lengsfeld starts from the duality of our experience of sin and grace. We experience ourselves to be under God's grace and yet in the pull of a downward force which is more than psychological or physical disability. In Lengsfled's view there are many ways of validly expressing this dual experience. Paul's Adam/Christ diptych is a most striking formulation of it. Paul splendidly expresses the complex structure of grace, forgiveness, justification and the struggle to live as a Christian. Yet, argues Lengsfeld, the Adam/Christ diptych is influenced by the challenge Paul met in the care of his communities. Paul counters the desire for the harmony of opposites – evidenced in many of the early Churches – by presenting an example of disharmony overcome. In Romans 5:12 and Colossians 1:19, Paul addresses the tendency towards syncretism in these communities. When Augustine and other Church Fathers take up the Adam/Christ comparison they do so to teach a new lesson in new circumstances. It is sometimes said that Augustine, Ambrosiaster and Jerome deformed Paul's image. Not so, argues Lengsfeld. Against new adversaries and in a neo-Platonic framework, Augustine expressed the same truth which Paul inculcated. Against Pelagius, Augustine emphasised the inner effect of both sin and grace.

Lengsfeld holds that with modernity's insistence upon the historicity of the human condition, the most useful re-expression of the age-old experience of sin and grace is through historical categories.[39] Thus, Lengsfeld regards original sin as the expression of the negative side of our moral experience. It is a major element in the interplay bewtween movement towards integration in Christ and the tragically real thrust towards personal moral and societal disintegration. There is an associative historicity and a dissociative historicity. The former is a principle of growth, of integration, of neg-entropy. The latter is of diminishment, of disintegration, of entropy. Just as the fashioning of an associative historicity does not lie within our powers but transcends them as grace transcends nature, so too the force of dissociative historicity is larger and more potent than personal sin. Insofar as it stems from the abuse of human freedom, it has to be understood against the background of Genesis' clear exculpation of God. God neither causes evil nor makes us sin. Yet, just as pain and suffering occur with statistical inevitability in an evolving universe, so human alienation and dissociation emerge freely yet also with a statistical inevitability. The Christian assurance is that we can allow God's grace to work through us. The Christian task is to construct under grace the associative history marked out by the person and work of Christ. In the countervailing nimbus of alienation, the first sin is of no special significance and is in no sense open to identification or retrieval.

What emerges from this brief consideration is a lessening emphasis upon a sin 'back there' and its circumstances. While one must admit that there was a 'first', unique significance is no longer accorded 'Adam's sin'. At most, it has a relative significance as a limit concept, the primal link in a tragic history. G. Daly appositely remarks: 'if instead of concentrating on a primal sin, committed at the dawn of history, we pan our attention across the entire course of human history, we can view the problem of sin in a different and more realistic perspective'.[40] We can move away from the genetic model of original sin to attempt a properly theological analysis of sin and forgiveness. That we are free to make this move is clear from our brief study of Scripture, patristics and conciliar teaching. However, it is important to retain a number of clarifications. First, the Genesis account is a singularly impressive attempt to make sense of moral and physical evil, sin and death. With subtlety and force it brings before us the reality of the *mysterium iniquitatis,* the irrational fact of evil and sin. Second, when viewed in the integral Christian tradition the story of the Fall is part of the backcloth for the depiction of our radical need and its remedy in Christ. Third, while a backcloth is an aid to a clearer view, it must remain an auxiliary. It should neither rival nor displace the main scene. That scene is the salvific work of Christ continued by his people in their endeavour to live by truth.

Peccatum originale originatum

What is original sin is us? This is perhaps the more interesting question. It is also the more important one. Original sin forms part of the dual reality of our lives: guilt and forgiveness, perdition and grace. It is a co-determinant of our situation rather than a sole determinant. It is the reality which explains the moral schizophrenia so well described by Paul. The major thrust of the Catholic tradition is that original sin while very much part of ourselves (*unicuique inest uti proprium*), is nonetheless something antecedent to our free decisions (*propagatione non imitatione transfunditur*). While the vehicle for these emphases has traditionally been a model borrowed from genetics, contemporary theology tries to express the matter in newer ways.

Original sin is termed sin by analogy. Sin is a multivalent concept. One speaks of mortal sin, venial sin, original sin. The root meaning is alienation from God, from self, and from one's fellows. Thus, traditional theology speaks of aversion from God and conversion to an idol. An inevitable presupposition of sin is voluntariety. One cannot sin against one's will. Here arises the first clue that with original sin we are not using 'sin' in quite the normal way. Whereas in mortal and venial sin there must be some personal investment, quite clearly that is not the case with original sin. Artificial explanations have been offered. Corporate responsibility, inclusion in Adam as the *homo universalis* are attempts – one new, one old – to introduce the element of voluntariety. But, as argued earlier, 'not even a divine decree could make men guilty of something which they could do nothing to prevent'.[41] Corporate responsibility is a dangerous concept needing strict interpretation. We can speak of a corporate responsibility for an act performed by a section of a community or nation. Yet this can apply strictly only insofar as there was either positive involvement or negative facilitation of the act in question. People can have a corporate responsibility for an offence only insofar as they positively took part in it or omitted something they could have done to prevent it. This cannot apply in the case of a moral delict occurring before one was born. And so it must be said that original sin is not sin in the ordinarily accepted sense. It is called sin by analogy – with some similarities to personal sin and even greater dissimilarities from it. One might suggest therefore that the word 'original sin' be used sparingly given the hostility and sense of injustice to which its use facile can give rise.

And yet there is the stark reality referred to in the doctrine of original sin. There are the difficulties in our personal relationship to God. There is a de-ordination in our relationships with each other and with nature. These constitute the darker side of our moral experience. While Paul does not talk of original sin, he was keenly aware of the pull away from moral effort and from friendship with God. Again, Augustine provides a valuable insight in speaking of concupiscence as both the parent and child of sin. He rightly identifies our difficulty in reaching and maintaining moral decisions. There is an unconnectedness, a sluggishness in doing good and avoiding evil. If Karl Rahner is correct, concupsicence diminishes every commitment we make so that human beings find it as difficult to be fully satanic as to sustain full commitment to good.

It is argued that original sin is a situational reality. As free beings called to exercise our freedom for God and for each other we find ourselves in a network of factors which both help and hinder freedom's proper exercise. There is an interlocking context of social, cultural and ethical values. There is the residuum of consolidated patterns of action: of domination and exploitation, as well as of liberation and facilitation. There are love and hate, conflict and collaboration. There is religious tradition – the way people believe, hope and worship. There is the *traditio,* the handing on, of these patterns to each subsequent generation, always with some gain, but also with some loss. There is, perhaps, an objective spirit, an ambience which affects a person before the first moment of his or her free choice. Our situation carries 'the stamp of the history of the freedom of all other men'. Those who develop the situational aspect of original sin emphasise that 'the guilt of others is a permanent factor in the situation ... of the individual's freedom'. To quote Rahner once more, 'this co-determination of the situation of every person by the guilt of others is something universal, permanent and therefore also original'.[42] It affects us all. It is a fact of our history from the start. In terms of what we are called to be, there is a lack of something which ought to be present. Not an absolute loss: for the grace of Christ is also a determinant of our freedom. Nevertheless, our situation is a diminishment of our possibilities and bears the mark of something which ought not be so.

Thereafter, one essays a descriptive theory, of which there are many. Teilhard de Chardin places original sin within the purview of a world in evolution. A world in which fulfilment is reached only by hard fought stages must include partial failure, pain and suffering. Just as in physics there is talk of entropy and negentropy, in Teilhard's hyperphysics there is the same duality. Sin and evil exist. So do charity, human effort and God's grace. From their interplay comes a new and higher achievement. Where there is freedom, there with statistical inevitability will be moral fault and, even, sin. Thus Teilhard would view original sin as an element within evolution. It is the cumulative effect of human waywardness – itself the outgrowth of freedom's abuse – which impedes God's will for humankind and for the universe. At the level of the human, sin is the refusal to enter fully into the thrust towards Omega point in its full theistic sense. Original sin may be seen as the entropy induced by the human shortfall from what we are called to be. As it affects the individual, it is the pre-moral force exerted by the downward thrust of human activity which soon becomes the personal sin each one so readily makes his/her own.

Contemporary theological literature reminds us of the importance of tradition in the making and unmaking of people. Tradition is the network of factors, ethics, values, feelings, artefacts, corpus of teaching, modes of education, social provisions – which help to make people the kind they are. Religious tradition includes all the avenues by which the address of God reaches us. In Judaism and Christianity these are the word of truth and the sacraments of life. Both word and sacrament are offered in a community of faith. Yet the grace of God, though linked in a special way with the community gathered by the *memoria Jesu*, is not limited to these means. The human community is itself both the bearer of, and the impediment to, God's grace. The theologians who urge situation as a major explicative element of original sin regard tradition as also grace-impeding. They do so with the proviso that the same tradition mediates the grace of God. So, both tradition and the individual's freedom as co-determined by the tradition enter constitutively into the contemporary theological understanding of original sin.

J. P. Mackey argues that we are born into 'a tradition of the race ... which relegates God's invitation to (us) and (we) must sooner or later decide to accept that invitation or not to accept it'. The tradition which helps to make us what we are also 'jeopardises (our) prospects of opting for God'.[43] Our objective situation is marked by the 'sin of the world' (Schoonenberg) as well as by the grace of Christ. The 'sin of the world' is the cumulating history of sin, starting with the primal abuse of freedom and added to in every dereliction of the good. It is a situation which affects each new individual and which he/she in turn affects whenever he/she refuses to love God and puts idols in God's place. The fractured tradition, the sin of the world, marks out a context wherein it is impossible to make a decision for God and neighbour. It affects us before any moral decision we take so that unless some other grace-bearing initiative supervenes, personal sin will inevitably grow out of our damaged liberty. Henri Rondet speaks of the cumulation of personal sin from the dawn of history and of its effects upon the moral situation of each individual. This is more than the trite announcement that every man/woman is his/her own Adam. The sin of the race has an originating effect upon the general moral ambient. Today, as we become more keenly aware of the reality of social sin and of the consolidation of injustice in so many of our societal structures, we see more clearly the relevance of original sin as 'situation' or as 'sin of the world'.[44]

In what sense is this 'sin'? Insofar as no voluntariety is involved it cannot be personal sin. Yet, as a moral co-determinant, it is deeply coloured by antecedent personal sin and, in Piet Schoonenberg's view, by the great sin of the rejection of Christ on Calvary. Thus it lays the ground for further personal sin. Are contexts, then, variously sinful? Do tradition and situation affect our prospects of opting for God in greater or less degree according to our time and place of birth. Are there degrees of original sin? It can be replied that 'the sin of the world' effects an absolute inability to opt for God unless we are touched by gratuitous and healing grace. There are no degrees of inability, no degrees of disablement. Thereafter one can only ask: How can one measure or quantify sin and grace? How can one measure an individual's openness to God's grace or the insistence of God's offer?

We should not, then, suppress the story of Adam and Eve, of fall, of promise. These remembrances articulate human misery and hope more effectively than many a solemn admonition of liberal humanism. However, the Adamic story has to be carefully linked to the real experience of sin and grace. Otherwise it will become trivial and even alienating. If the connection between life experience, sin and grace is correctly made, the Fall and 'original sin' can speak to us still. There is a need to rethink the doctrine critically and with a careful hermeneutic. While things cannot be the same thereafter, yet the truth of the Church's teaching can emerge more strongly and clearly. By relating original sin critically to the data of experience and to the canons of doctrinal interpretation, we can recover a new level of realism. It is true that none of the several attempts to rethink original sin can claim definitive success. Yet the majority of them represent valuable contributions to a deeper understanding of sin and grace, even of creation and redemption. They enable us to retell the story of Adam/Eve, now critically assessed, in such a way that its power is renewed rather than diminished. Ultimately, their relative success must be measured by the degree to which they direct us to our need for God's enabling grace and to the surpassing answer to that need.

SIX

Evolution and Hominisation

THE QUESTION OF EVOLUTION

A theological reflection on creation cannot ignore the questions raised by evolution theory. One must ask: is there coherence or contradiction between the Christian understanding of continuing creation and the perspective thrust upon us by the theory of evolution? More is involved than a merely verbal reconciliation. The problem is not to compare words and concepts. Nor is it merely whether the magisterium permits or disallows the acceptance of evolution by Christians. For evolution theory is more than a verbal matter. It is a perspective which discloses further issues about origins, as well as about truth and value, spirit and matter, personality, and finally the responsibility of humankind to fashion history. Both in philosophy and religion the adjustment required is considerable. An evolutionary perspective entails a closer genetic link between all that exists. This already demands a major shift of outlook. It dislodges the presentation whereby humankind occupied the focus of attention, the very centre of the stage to the exclusion of all other players. Anscar Hulsbosch writes: 'if we put the age of the universe at five milliard years and then represent this time by one year ... the million years to the Quaternary, in which man appears, begins at 22.40 on the 31st December ... the birth of Christ takes place twelve seconds before the end of our imaginary year.[1]

For some, the evolutionary perspective is an unmitigated threat. This leads them to reject, or at least to be highly suspicious of, any compromise with the theory. Doubtless, echoes linger of 'old unhappy far off things and battles long ago'. Evolution was hailed by some of its propagandists as the advance signal for the welcome demise of religion. It was sometimes propounded with an arrogance which overplayed its strength and with an hostility to religion which told more about prejudice than about evolution. There was also – and perhaps there still is – a certain clash of cultures. Others welcome evolution theory as a most useful instrument of explanation. Teilhard de Chardin wrote: 'from the moment when men have woken to an explicit consciousness of the evolution that carries them along, and begin to fix their eyes, as one man, upon one same thing ahead of them, by that very fact they must surely begin to love one another'.[2] Claude Tresmontant argues that evolutionary perspective corresponds to Jewish and Christian tenets on creation more evidently than the ancient representation of the world which flourished into the nineteenth century.[3]

It is important to clarify the relationship between a Christian view upon creation and evolution theory. Otherwise we remain condemned to a sterile opposition between two extremes: fixist immobilism in regard to truth, value and religion and, on the other hand, the over-optimistic assumption of progress endemic to facile evolutionism. On the one side, people make an absolute of the *status quo*. This raises a barrier against all advance. It canonises existing imperfection, mediocrity and injustice. It is salutary to remember that ' ... the same kind of public opinion (hostile to evolution theory) opposed social justice reform: such reform seemed to be against God's intended plan of affording occasion for the practice of charity'.[4] On the other side, an uncritical acceptance of evolution is equally wrong-headed. Its faith in the upward thrust of life can easily ignore, and therefore fail to counteract, the downward thrust to dispersal and dissolution. Suffering, injustice and evil are naively overlooked, not to say tolerated. Both extremes can strangely meet in a common abdication of responsibility to technocracy. From different starting points both fixism and evolutionism arrive at a capitulation to the 'new right', the men in the white coats who serve money and power.

Hence our question about creation and evolution is not just about orthodoxy or unorthodoxy. It a question to be faced and answered for its own sake. Every answer bears us on to other questions. It leads to what Teilhard called 'hyper-physics' – where philosophy, theology, the experimental and the social sciences meet. In that common area new concerns and questions arise, not least for theology: about bioethics, about the inviolability of the person, about the just use of the earth's resources. It is argued here that if correct analyses are made, Christian orthodoxy and evolution theory can indeed co-exist. Further, a certain coherence – not, however, a forced concordism – between the Christian idea of continuing creation and the evolutionary insistence upon a world in the making, emerges more clearly. One understands better Henri Bergson's remark that evolution is creation unfolding. And Teilhard's claim takes on a new clarity: 'evolution is the expression in terms of our own experience of creation as it unfolds in space and time'.[5]

EVOLUTION: WHAT IS IT?

The scientific description is markedly different from the more popular conception. A good definition of the theory of evolution proposes 'that all life is shot through with a vital principle which enables it to grow not only in individuals but also in species so that the individual and also the species adapt to the demands of the environment thus bringing about new forms of life which may be specifically different from the old'. It is said that 'the theory of evolution is ... that all living organisms are descended from one, or a very few, original forms which are themselves presumed to have arisen ultimately from non-living matter'.[6] A little pungently John McKenzie puts it: 'evolution does not mean that the monkey became the man, but that monkey and man and all forms of life go back to a common ancestor'. In one way or other, the theory had been mooted since Buffon (1707-1788). Likewise, it is foreshadowed by Erasmus Darwin (1751-1802) and Lamarck (1744-1829).

Evolution cannot be reduced to any one of the factors which play a part in it. Charles Darwin repeatedly emphasised that evolution theory is not based on natural selection alone. The conceptual pillars of the theory are the principle of inheritance and the principle of natural selection. In his introduction to *The Origin of Species* (1859) Darwin writes: 'if any being vary however slightly in any manner profitable to itself, under the complex and sometimes varying conditions of life, it will have a better chance of survival and thus be naturally selected. From the strong principle of inheritance any selected variety will tend to propagate itself in new and modified form'. In other words, at a certain point an organism acquires a new structural variation. This variation enables it to exploit an existing environment in a new and better way, or perhaps to colonise a new environment. A variation of this beneficial kind tends to self-propagation and consolidation. More recently there has been an emphasis on genetic mutation rather than the vague postulation of chance adaptation. Th. Dobzhansky argues: (a) that modifications of gene frequency bring about structural variation; (b) that such modifications occur in response to environmental demands; (c) that they can effect a change in a species or even broader grouping, particularly when transmitted in reproductive isolation. And so the theory goes. When the potentialities of an environment have been exploited fully, the rate of evolution decelerates. There are scientists who accept evolution theory yet argue that the evolutionary thrust has now ceased. There will be no further crossing of specific or generic boundaries. Somewhat ominously, Julian Huxley has argued that further evolutionary advance on any major scale will be through social engineering and genetic control.

THE STATUS OF EVOLUTION THEORY

Evolution is not a proven law and perhaps never will be. Rather it is an hypothesis which has been shown to lead to worthwhile scientific results. It accounts well for certain data in biology, embryology, zoology and palaeontology which would otherwise remain enigmatic. Due to the hypothesis, predictions have been made and anticipations formulated which have been verified subsequently. It has facilitated the prediction of fossil organisms structurally intermediate to man and the apes. It has enabled cross-disciplinary collaboration of geology, anatomy, embryology, genetics and natural history. The hypothesis explains why the members of a phylum share a similar structure, why 'each bone of any vertebrate animal corresponds to some particular bone in every other ... ',[7] or why there are vestigial organs which no longer perform any function; or why there are forms of life intermediate to fishes and amphibians disclosed by fossil evidence. The hypothesis explains why there is an evident progression in functional specialisation and structural complexity as the observer passes from earlier to later rock deposits.

On the other hand, there are large gaps in the evidence. These are particularly noticeable where evidence would be most valuable, i.e., those transition points between species, genus and class. There is 'the law of the disappearance of pedicels' – the beginnings of new life tend not to be preserved and and therefore not to be discovered, precisely because of their paucity and their frailty. Hence, direct evidence of these crucial mutations is unlikely to be unearthed. For some observers, therefore, evolution remains an extrapolation weak in its factual base.[8] Even those sympathetic to Darwinian evolution will allow that Darwin made too much of natural selection. It has been pointed out that natural selection of itself does not produce anything. It only eliminates, or tends to eliminate, whatever is unfit or tardy in dealing with environmental demands. Rather than the gradual ascent suggested by *The Origin of Species,* many geneticists postulate short episodic thrusts of development occurring in response to environmental challenge. Even here, it is argued, competition for survival does not necessarily evoke development.

Yet, despite powerful attacks on the conventional wisdom, the hypothesis stands or falls by verification. In particular, if a test falsifies it, it must be discarded. Should it prove successful it is thereby strengthened. On these criteria, evolution remains an hypothesis, no more but no less. If it is to yield, it will be to a more fruitful, more comprehensive, more simple rival. Wilfrid Harrington summates it well: 'evolution has not been proved in the strict sense; yet ever since the theory was first proposed, it has shown its worth as a working hypothesis and that over a wide field. It still remains to be further clarified, but as a general principle it is now, in scientific circles at least, accepted without question'.[9] Erwin Nemesszeghy and John Russell hold: 'it (is) virtually certain that micro-evolution has occurred in the past and is still occurring. Although its operation can only be positively identified in relatively few cases, there is no difficulty in supposing that it has operated successfully ... in producing new species and genera within the limits of each family. The occurrence of macro-evolution is less easily established'.[10]

THEOLOGICAL ASSESSMENT

Initial reaction among Catholics to Darwin's theory was relatively mild. Sternest opposition came from the fundamentalist groups. Yet the Council of Cologne declared in 1860: 'our first parents were immediately made by God. Thus we declare plainly opposed to the Holy Scripture and to faith the opinion of those who go so far as to say that man, even so far as his body is concerned, was produced by spontaneous transformation of the less perfect into the more perfect, successively, ultimately ending in the human'.[11] The council reacted to the view that evolution had somehow come up with a cogent rebuttal of divine creative activity. Certainly this latter view is an exorbitance of scientific hypothesis. At Cologne, however, it met an equally unsubtle rebuttal. It should be noted, too, that the council is local, not universal or ecumenical, and should not be taken to represent unequivocally the Catholic position. J. H. Newman wrote in 1863: 'there is as much want of simplicity in the idea of creation of distinct species as in that ... of fossils with rocks in them ... it is as strange that monkeys should be so like men, with no historical connection between them, as that there should be an historical connection between them ... '.[12] St George Mivart's book *The Genesis of Species* – critical of Darwin but not unfavourable to evolution – was praised by reviews in *The Tablet*, *The Month* and *The Dublin Review*. Newman wrote to Mivart: 'I shall be abundantly satisfied if my Essays do a quarter of the good which I hear your volume is doing ... it is pleasant to find that the first real exposition of the logical insufficiency of Mr Darwin's comes from a Catholic ... you must not suppose that I have personally any great dislike or dread of his theory but many good people are much troubled at it'.[13]

Leo XIII's *Providentissimus Deus* (1893) reminds Catholics that no real discord need exist between the theologian and the scientist provided each keeps to his own limits and, following the injunction of Augustine, 'refrains from affirming anything rashly and the unknown as known'. Yet from the onset of the anti-Modernist reaction one can discern a new hostility to evolution theory among Church officials. The climate of suspicion fostered in the conflict with Modernism led to the censure of the works of Leroy and Zahn (Catholic writers open to evolution) and, very much later, to the stringent limits placed upon Teilhard de Chardin's theological publications. This climate appears to have lasted till well into the 1950s.

It is arguable that the old tension between faith and science has lessened in recent years. The warning against intellectual imperialism given in Newman's *University Discourses* has perhaps been better heeded. Gabriel Daly correctly suggests: 'trouble arises only when scientists make religious statements on scientific grounds or theologians make scientific statements on theological grounds'.[14] This kind of reminder is valuable in heading off those confrontations set up between a literal understanding of Scripture and scientific perspectives on origins. A lessening of tensions can also come from a clearer realisation that a scientific hypothesis and extra-scientific implications drawn from it are not one and the same. People have misused scientific conclusions to underpin claims inimical to religion. *Abusus non tollit usum* runs the adage. The abuse of an hypothesis does not mean that the hypothesis itself is necessarily opposed to, or destructive of, religion.

One truth cannot contradict another. People committed to a biblical faith will re-echo the words of Galileo Galilei, 'from Scripture and nature alike truth proceeds'. Many people will wish to re-echo Werner Heisenberg's remark: 'although I am convinced of the unassailability of scientific truth in its own sphere, I have never been able to dismiss the content of religious thinking'.[15] Yet it would be an impoverishment if the non-conflictual emphasis were simply because theology and science had ceased to address each other. If science and faith, or science and theology each had its own totally separate world of discourse then, as Newman argued, either 'the circle of knowledge ... is thereby mutilated or ... theology is really no science'.[16]

Neither theology nor the teaching authority of the Church has a direct competence in judging an hypothesis such as evolution. Theologians and those entrusted with Church office, if they are wise, will maintain an interest in the progress of the sciences – more for what they will learn than in pursuance of any pretension to jurisdiction. However, there is an indirect consideration which it would be wrong to overlook. The perception of its duty by the teaching authority may lead it to take a stand on the conclusions of a scientific theory or practice. A little bluntly the First Vatican Council stated: 'the Church, which together with the apostolic office of teaching has received a charge to guard the deposit of faith, derives from God the right and duty of proscribing false science'.[17] Lest this appear not simply blunt but unconscionably arrogant it should be noted that it implies a competence in regard to scientific conclusions only insofar as they bear upon tenets of faith or on the sacredness of human life. It is at such tangential points that the Church's duty to 'proclaim truth and reprobate error' may implicate a stance with an overlap on scientific theory. Between evolution theory and theology there have been two such tangential points: an apparent conflict with Scripture and the implications of evolution theory for a theology of the person.

In regard to an apparent conflict with Scripture, the longstanding tension has been mitigated notably by two admissions. The first is the need to differentiate religious and scientific truth. The second is the imperative to advert to the literary forms used in the Bible.

To distinguish between truths religious and scientific is hardly innovative today. Yet to do so consistently enables us to keep in mind that the Bible teaches central religious truths about God and humankind, death and destiny, life and the shaping of life – not the ever developing tenets of the empirical sciences. The Bible's context is not of theory or system but of transcendence in immanence. Bernard Lonergan reminds us of the difference between the theoretic exigence of science and the transcendent exigence of religion. These several levels or realms of meaning co-exist in the one conscious subject. Their apparent differences can be resolved by adverting to their different thrust and intention. The Bible does not rival the 'theory of evolution' as an explanation of origins. In Genesis 'neither the antiquity of man, nor his possible descent from the animal world, nor the number of first men is explicitly treated much less solved'.[18] Neither, however, should the hypothesis of evolution be understood to shoulder the task of proving/disproving God or fashioning moral values. In summary, therefore, 'the possibility of evolution is outside the ambit of scriptural consideration. What is affirmed is (our) origin from the earth, our special relationship to God, and the equality of the sexes'.[19]

It is more readily admitted today that the Bible is extremely complex in its modes of expression, its literary genres. In communicating religious truths, ideals and values, in presenting its sacred history, the Bible employs various thought forms, metaphors and literary devices. It works within the cosmic assumptions of its times and places of composition. However, these thought forms, metaphors, literary devices, and cosmic assumptions should not bind us overmuch. We read the Bible most correctly when we seek out the 'core' of meaning in each of its contexts. This core is not recoverable 'neat' from the shell of its presentation. Meaning is constituted by its expression, at least in part. And so there is no facile way of shredding off 'form ' from 'content'. Yet it is part of the exegete's task 'to separate the content of revelation from the obsolete human views attached to it, and represent it in terms of present day views and opinions'.[20] The literary forms used in the Bible run a wide gamut of allegory, myth, poetry, drama, satire. These are the means of expression of the biblical message. It is common experience that the deeper our meaning, the less literal will be our style. Plain words break and fail in the effort to express what is beyond them. Then we fall back upon gesture, action, and new combinations of words more powerful than simple prose.

Pius XII draws our attention to this in *Divino Afflante Spiritu* (1943): 'The question of literary forms in the first chapters of Genesis is very complicated and obscure. These literary forms do not correspond to any of our classic categories and cannot be judged in the light of Graeco-Latin or modern literary forms ... they relate in a simple and colourful language suitable to the mentality of a not very developed mankind the basic truths underlying the economy of salvation and the popular description of the origins of the human race and the chosen people'.[21] In *Dei Verbum,* the Second Vatican Council encourages the biblical scholar 'to investigate what meaning the sacred writer intended to express and actually expressed in particular circumstances as he used contemporary literary forms in accordance with the situation of his own time and culture'.[22] *Humani Generis* pointed out that while the first eleven chapters of Genesis come under the heading of history yet 'in what sense this is so it is for the further labours of the exegete to determine'.[23] In effect, it is difficult to identify with exactitude the nature of the literary form(s) used in Genesis 1 to 11. What is clear, however, is that the authors did not set out to depict 'straight history'. This being so, we may in principle conclude that the theory of evolution is not ruled out by the opening chapters of Genesis. These chapters offer neither rudimentary science nor history in the usual sense of the term. Since they do not envisage anything like a theory of evolution they cannot be

taken either to contest or confirm it. Nevertheless, they contradict 'the atheistic form of the theory of evolution which sees man
as nothing more than the natural child of mother earth, her
fertility and her creative power'.[24] This atheistic understanding is
an ideological assertion unwarranted by the evolutionary hypothesis itself.

It is on the second tangential point that evolution theory may be
suspected of cutting across the limits of Christian orthodoxy, i.e.,
in its possible implications for a Christian anthropology. As an
hypothesis, evolution applies to the full manifold of experience.
One cannot exempt humanity from the process of a world of
which it is a constituent part. Nor can the hypothesis of evolution
be limited to the anthropoid primates. And so the questions arise:
Are the implications of evolution theory inimical to the dignity of
the person, repeatedly affirmed in the Christian tradition? Are
our special call to fellowship with God and our adoption in Christ
Jesus in any way called in question? What are the implications of
evolution theory for the human soul? A first step to clarification
are the remarks of Pius XII in *Humani Generis* (1950).[25] While
relatively brief, they represent the first mention of 'the doctrine of
evolution' in a document of the Church's central magisterium. In
summary Pius XII declares: (a) that the evolution of the human
body from other living matter, already in existence, is an open
question; (b) that evolution is not proven theory; (c) that there
are reasons for caution – the spiritual nature of the human soul
and the doctrine of original sin; (d) that souls are immediately
created by God is a view which the Catholic faith imposes on us.

One might formulate this another way. First, the question of a
physical link in the line of genetic descent between humankind
and a lower form of life is 'open for discussion by competent
experts'. Second, those who profess that Adam was not genetically connected with an individual of a sub-human species may not
be deemed in theological error. Third, a theory of evolution
which affirms a genetic connection between the human body and
pre-human forms of life, without thereby pretending to have said
all about humankind, is not incompatible with the essential teaching of the Bible.

THE SPECIAL PROBLEM OF HOMINISATION

While the pope's words represent an important advance and, in
particular, a legitimation of further theological reflection on the
question, they do not afford a total answer. There is a theological
problem raised by hominisation which exceeds the limits of *Humani Generis*. The sweep of the evolutionary hypothesis is very

wide. One cannot declare limits to its scope. For, while evolution envisages the new and the discontinuous, its main stress is upon continuity. This is the pattern of Teilhard's hyperphysics: 'in the eyes of science the appearance of man followed the same mechanism as every other species'. Again, Teilhard writes: 'essentially man appeared in just the same way as every other species'.[26] The upward thrust of life traverses matter and spirit, animal and human. Whatever the difference and the discontinuity evinced by nature's variety, in the canvas drawn by evolution theory it is the homogeneity of life which is highlighted. Evolution sees humankind as new and different. Yet the novelty and the difference emerge from all that has preceded at the infra-human level. Theology, on the other hand, has brought out the special position of humankind. It places man and woman at the pinnacle of creation as vice-gerent of God. They are image of God. They are called to an eternal destiny. They rise above dependence on matter so that 'when the body of our earthly dwelling lies in death, we gain an everlasting dwelling place in heaven' (Preface, Mass for the Dead). If a compromise has to be made, if it is admitted that our body may have arisen from the process of evolution, it is nonetheless underlined that the human soul is directly created by God. Here lies the challenge to face the tension of these apparently conflicting theological and scientific models and to attempt to explore their compatibility.

In *Humani Generis* Pius XII re-iterates: 'that souls are immediately created by God is a view which the Catholic faith imposes upon us'.[27] This insistence is more than a *datum* of philosophy. The spirituality of the human soul is the basis of the intimate relation between God and the person. Upon this relation, in turn, rests Christianity's claim that each human being has an especial vocation, dignity and destiny. If human rights are to be anything more than a fragile concession, granted when it suits to do so, their foundation must be traced back to something unique to humankind in all nature. Hence, one can apply to the immediate creation of the soul the words of the Biblical Commission: it is 'one of the facts which touch upon the foundations of Christian faith'. Or, as Pius XII put it: it is 'a view which the Catholic faith imposes upon us'. It cannot be gainsaid that the pope is drawing upon a teaching expressed at least as far back as the great schoolmen. St Thomas Aquinas repeatedly affirmed the 'immediate creation of the human soul'. He distinguished between the human soul and the infra-spiritual forms of individuals lower in the hierarchy of being. Whereas Aquinas envisaged a gradual emergence of the vegetative and sensitive forms in other individuals, in the case of the human being the subsistent spirit can be created only by God. It is not mediated through natural processes.

One can set out Catholic teaching on the soul in punctual form as follows. It is Catholic teaching that God is the Creator of the human soul. It is also part of Catholic teaching that the human soul is not part of the divine essence. It is always a creature. When it is said that the human soul is created *ex nihilo,* this underlines the creaturehood of the soul, setting it off against any pretension to be a part of the divine essence. To speak of 'immediate creation' (cf *Humani Generis*) is designed to safeguard the intimate relation of humankind to God in nature and grace. Likewise, it reflects the biblical emphasis upon the human person's special place in nature. It re-echoes the tenet of the relation between spirit and matter. Finally, it may be of interest to note that the immortality of the soul, while implicit to the Catholic tradition, has never been explicitly defined.

One cannot fail to notice how well this metaphysics of the person underlines humankind's special dignity and eternal destiny. Nevertheless, some problems arise. First, there is the question of the unity of the person. To speak of the direct or immediate creation of the soul (while the body, it is said, may have evolved through material processes) seems to raise the old spectre of dualism. Dualism is inherent to every philosophy where the soul is viewed as imprisoned in the body (Platonism) or parallel to it (Cartesianism). The soul is, as it were, 'the ghost in the machine'.[28] Aquinas repeatedly warned against this dualism even when he insisted most strongly on the immediate creation of the human soul. A second problem lies in the postulation of a recurrent 'intervention' of God. Is it appropriate to visualise an 'intervention' of God each time a human being comes to be? Does it not make of God a *deus ex machina*? These are difficulties attendant upon the traditional stress upon 'the immediate creation of the human soul'.

ANOTHER VIEW: TEILHARD AND HOMINISATION

According to Teilhard, humankind came into the world at the heart of a process that had been in train for billions of years. On the tree of life, growing imperceptibly but ever upwards, humankind is the newest bud in which the leading shoot issues.[29] Again, the emergence of *homo sapiens* is like an arrow shot out of a tensile movement of virtually incalculable duration. These images illustrate yet another Teilhardian image – the 'within' and the 'without' of things. In all life – indeed in all pre-life – there is an inner thrust towards development which is at once masked and unveiled by external characteristics. This correspondence of a dynamic 'within' to an evolving 'without' means that the story of life is a 'movement of consciousness veiled by morphology'.[30] Consciousness develops as physical structure becomes ever more differentiated.

This story is also the story of humankind. There is a long prehistory to the gestation of consciousness. In *The Phenomenon of Man* Teilhard puts it bluntly: 'It is true that ... from the organic point of view, the whole metamorphosis leading to man depends on the question of a better brain ... But how was this cerebral perfectioning to be carried out – how could it have worked – if there had not been a whole series of other conditions realised at just the same time ... If the creature from which man issued had not been a biped, his hands would not have been free in time to release the jaws from their prehensile function, and the thick band of maxilliary muscles which had imprisoned the cranium could not have been relaxed. It is thanks to two-footedness freeing the hand that the brain was able to grow; and thanks to this, too, that the eyes, brought closer together on the diminished face, were able to converge and fix on what the hands held and brought before them – the very gesture which formed the external counterpart of reflection ... '[31]

Implicit here is the long evolutionary path towards hominisation. The primates, amongst which humankind emerged, avoided any excessive physical specialisation. An openness to a more general development was retained. This was altogether beneficial since 'specialisation paralyses, overspecialisation kills'.[32] Whereas the very achievements of many species led them into evolutionary *culs-de-sac,* in the case of the primates evolutionary possibilities remained intact: 'interminate and interminable, straight ahead'.[33] The upward thrust of life – mirrored in the deepening of the 'within' and the increasing refinement of the 'without' – proceeds through cephalisation: 'in the case of the primate ... evolution went straight to work on the brain, neglecting everything else, which accordingly remained malleable'.[34] It is unnecessary to examine in detail Teilhard's elaboration of this thrust. He writes: 'spiritual perfection (or conscious centreity) and material synthesis (or complexity) are but two aspects of one and the same phenomenon'.[35]

Towards the beginning of the Pliocene age (circa fourteen million years ago) there was a tropical and sub-tropical belt of the earth inhabited not by human beings but by anthropoids of many types. In Teilhard's view, this was the area of greatest cephalisation and vital pressure. At the heart of this 'patch', coexistent with many other anthropoid (but sub-human) species, humankind emerged somewhere in the African continent, hundreds of thousands of years ago. Thus the middle Pleistocene age (five hundred to two hundred thousand years ago) saw the frail emergence of *homo sapiens*. This emergence was the fruit of millions of years and can be recovered only conjecturally. Teilhard rejoins the mainstream of anthropologists in documenting the various fossil evidences to *homo habilis, homo erectus,* and *homo sapiens* of various families. Just as we can never know the first Greeks or Chinese, we shall never 'rediscover' the hominising mutation.[36] Teilhard reminds us that since palaeontology can discern species only at a distance from their point of origin 'the question of an original single couple has no scientific relevance'.[37]

The specific attainment of the new being is the capacity for reflection and self-knowledge. To kindle fire, to use tools, to practise art – these are but the expression of a deeper capability 'no longer merely to know, but to know that one knows'.[38] For the first time, past and present and future take on a consciously grasped significance. A new world has appeared deep within the old: 'abstraction, logic, reasoned choice and inventions, mathematics, art, calculation of time and space, anxieties and dreams of love – all these activities of inner life are nothing else than the effervescence of the newly formed centre as it explodes onto itself'.[39] Henceforth, virtually the whole thrust of evolution will be concentrated at this point of evolution. From now on, the sap of life running through geogenesis to biogenesis to psychogenesis will work for spiritual and psychic development. Hominisation therefore centres upon the development of consciousness. In his allusive fashion, Teilhard speaks of the raising of psychic temperature. Humankind emerges at that point of improvement where the 'next step' yields something essentially new and different. At the level of bodily configuration the step may have been small. At the level of psychic development, however, there is a qualitative leap. In *The Phenomenon of Man* Teilhard writes: 'when water is heated to boiling point ... and one goes on heating it, the first thing that follows – without a change of temperature – is a tumultuous expansion of ... vaporised molecules ... when the anthropoid ... has been brought "mentally" to boiling point some further calories were added ... outwardly almost nothing in the organs had changed. But in depth, a great revolution had taken place: consciousness was now leaping and boiling in a space of supersensory relationships and representations and simultaneously consciousness was capable of perceiving itself in the concentrated simplicity of its faculties'.[40]

Teilhard's account of hominisation has an intrinsic interest. However, the narrative is related here to exemplify the second of two ways of speaking of humankind's coming to be. These two ways seem very different. One has to ask whether the two modes of discourse – represented by Pius XII and by Teilhard de Chardin – are compatible. In a sense one can concur with J. V. Kopp in saying, 'to speak of the "introduction" of the human soul through a special act of creation is to remove all meaning from Teilhard de Chardin's theory of purposeful evolution towards man'.[41] On the other hand, many students of Teilhard feel that the two ways of speaking of human origins are not contradictory. It is all the more important to notice Teilhard's own remarks about the relation of theology to his hyperphysics. He will say: 'there is nothing, not even the human soul, the highest spiritual manifestation we know of, that does not come within this universal law [of evolution]. The soul, too, has its clearly defined place in the slow ascent of living creatures towards consciousness; and must therefore ... have grown out of the more general mobility of things'.[42] It should also be noted that Teilhard underlines that he confines himself to phenomena, to appearances. There is nothing to hinder 'the thinker who adopts a spiritual explanation from positing for spiritual reasons of a higher order and at a later stage of his dialectic ... whatever creative operation or "special intervention" he likes'.[43] It may be that this was written with ecclesiastical censorship in mind. Yet it was written in all sincerity and can serve as a challenge to show the coherence between the phenomenological account of hominisation and the theological requirement in regard to the same history.

There is something attractive in the simplicity of Teilhard's account of hominisation. It fits admirably the 'principle of parsimony' inset to the logic of science. It is coherent with Occam's Razor: 'it is void to do with more what can be done with fewer'. Again, an evolving cosmos can be seen as a greater testimony to its Creator than one where God had continually to intervene. Nevertheless, the concern of *Humani Generis* to retain the immediate and special creation of the human soul is no light matter. At the outset of his ministry as pope, Pius XII linked the origins of humankind to a renewed respect for human rights. He spoke of 'the law of human solidarity and love, dictated and imposed as much by the common origin or the uniformity of rational nature of all men, as by the redemptive sacrifice on the altar of the Cross'.[44] In exploring the possible coherence of these accounts one should not prematurely suppose that they are adversarial. Teilhard's own preoccupation was to reconcile science and religious faith. It is an irony that he encountered hostility in both the Church and the scientific community. There is a sustained mistrust of him by many Catholics. At the same time, he has come under fire from scientific critics such as Peter Medawar who tend to dismiss his thought as pseudo-science and even mythopoesis.

Much can be said in defence of Teilhard. Sympathetic commentators such as K. Rahner, P. Schoonenberg and R. North argue that Teilhard's view of hominisation is coherent with the teaching of the Church.[45] Rahner's monograph, *Hominisation*, takes the reader through several stages in a unified argument. In the first place, since creation is an intimate relation of dependence upon God the giver of being, one may say that there is an immediate creation whenever anything new comes to be. The relation of creature to Creator is always immediate. The immediacy of creation, however, does not rule out the operation of finite agents or causes. One must distinguish transcendent and immanent causality. In the creative coming-to-be, God's enabling causality and the causality of finite agents can both be at work, each in its own order. Wherever there is a self-surpassing by any existent at the level of being there too God's creative action underlies and enables the very self-surpassing.

In the second place, spirit is essentially other than matter. Spirit is not matter. Nor is matter spirit. And man/woman is aptly defined as spirit in the world. He/she is different from all creation below him/her. In the human person there is a unique openness to the infinite, the seed of eternal life. In theological language, then, 'the very question of a possible derivation of spirit from matter has no meaning'.[46] Even if hominisation is seen to take place in accord with the laws of evolution, the uniqueness of humankind is in no sense called in question.

Yet there is an orientation of spirit to matter and of matter to spirit. Teilhard spoke of a 'within' and a 'without' to every existent. Traditional philosophy and Christian anthropology have held that the soul is present in every aspect of our bodily reality. The human spirit is present to every aspect of our physical nature. There is nothing human which is purely animal. Human spirit pervades even the most banal activity. Indeed, 'from a Christian point of view finite spirit can never be thought of in such a way that in order to be thought to attain perfection it must move away from material reality, or that its perfection increases in proportion to its distance from matter ... Spirit must be thought of as seeking and finding itself through the perfection of what is material'.[47] In his *Theology of Death* Rahner spoke of the world-related dimension of the human spirit even after death. Christian theology urges that the spirit attains integral perfection only at the resurrection of the body. Spirit, then, looks to matter. In the case of the human spirit, it is related inescapably to matter.[48] Conversely, matter looks to spirit. It strives towards perfection through being 'in-formed' or perfected by a life principle. Karl Rahner argues that the removal of matter's limitation can be effected by God's creative activity without there being a miracle or a divine intervention as one cause among others. God's transcendent or creative activity can enable a secondary cause to move towards spiritual in-formation without thereby endangering God's own transcendence or 'reducing' spirit to matter.

God's transcendent activity – directed towards man and woman in Christ – can bring organised matter to the threshold where any further self-surpassing (itself under the divine transcendent causality) will educe the power to reflect, to be self-conscious. Wherever that threshold is crossed there is human personality. With the capacity for self-knowledge, for knowing others and God, the essence of personhood is given. At this stage, the new being is in the image and likeness of God. The hominised individual is an 'immediate' creation insofar as God's transcendent, creative action is involved. He/she is 'special' in relation to all that went before. As spirit in the world with the seed of immortality and a capacity for the divine (*capax Dei*), he/she is unique and irreplaceable. In *Sacramentum Mundi* Karl Rahner argues: 'where man is in question, God's rendering possible a self-transcendence of the cosmic causal antecedent in the direction of man is the same thing as what theology calls immediate creation'. Thus, we are made not partly by evolutionary forces and partly by God. We are wholly from God as special within creation; we are wholly the summit of an evolving cosmos'.[49] Piet Schoonenberg writes:

> We don't have to appeal to "an intervention on the part of God" for the creation of the human soul, either at the moment of generation from human parents or at that of hominisation. God does indeed create the soul, or rather he creates man as person. He creates the whole man and everything else. We can likewise say that God creates the soul immediately. For, to "create" refers not only to the first of a series ... but to the whole series ... The procreation by the parents and the origin of the child are likewise subject to the immediate creative causality of God ... In the production of the other and in its growth ... there is always an exceeding of self, an increase of being. This increase is also from God, and as such solely from God. But ... the expression does not refer to God's interven

tion or interference, but it is merely a special aspect of God's creation of the whole world. We have no need to postulate such an intervention, for the Creator does not stand only at the beginning. He constantly actualises the whole world with its duration and its growth ... the creation of the soul is nothing more or less than the emergence of a new person in this whole world ... the creation of the first man's soul is the coming to be of a person in the world which under God's creative causality has reached the summit of its evolution.[50]

This, then, is the approach of those who see in Teilhard's writings much that is valuable for creation theology. It is a theological exploration rather than a definitive conclusion. Theologians such as Rahner, North and Schoonenberg have come to hold that there is no contradiction between Teilhard's perspective on hominisation and the Church's teaching on humankind's special vocation and dignity. Nevertheless, certain questions remain to be faced. May there not be a fallacy in saying that matter transcends itself to become spirit-in-the-world? Effectively and often, Teilhard spoke of the 'within' and the 'without' – aspects which pertain to all levels of being. As we have seen, the 'without' refers to measurable qualities, to physical properties, to extension in time and space. The 'within' pertains to the self-perfective aspects of being. Teilhard also held that in a coherent perspective on the world, 'life inevitably assumes a "pre-life" as far back as the eye can see'. Granted the thrust to ever higher perfection and consciousness, the question still remains: Can precisely this crossing over to reflex consciousness occur, whether at the coming to be of the first people or whenever a new person comes into being? Rahner spoke of the orientation of matter towards spirit and of the removal of matter's limitations, to become spirit or, better, spiritualised matter. Yet the question remains: can matter thus cooperate with the divine causality in the case of the coming-to-be of the person. It is, after all, a unique case. Perhaps the analogy has been extended too readily from general 'self-transcendence', as we know it, to cover this coming-to-be of the human person? How far can dispositive causality stretch? Can one assume that in the case of human genesis the dispositive action of pre-existing life is capable of thrusting thus far? On the other hand, we regard the parents of a child as the co-authors of his/her life, not simply in the physical but also in the fully personal sense. Under God, the parents are fully givers of life to their child – not simply his/her body.

There is also the question of immortality. The immortality of the soul is not a defined dogma, but it is central to the Christian tradition. The doctrine connects closely to the credal confession of 'life everlasting'. How does the hypothesis of hominisation cohere with this tradition? From the scientific point of view, it is plausible to say that humankind is marked out by self-consciousness, explicit self-awarenes. The animal knows; man knows that he knows. In this way humankind is special within creation. But if humanity is defined by self-consciousness, how does one account for the survival of the 'awareness principle' when the material organism disintegrates at death? The older terminology of 'infusion' of the soul avoided this difficulty. Yet it should be noted that Teilhard returns time after time to the survival of the personal. He roots this conviction in the very nature of personhood and in the irrevocable quality of God's gift of personal being. It is perhaps opportune also to note that contemporary theology adverts to the distinction between the philosophical concept of immortality and the biblical presentation of the raising of the dead. Since Teilhard holds to a very strong position on the resurrection of Christ and its implications for the cosmos, his thought on hominisation should be interpreted in this light.

SUMMARY

From the point of view of theology, evolution remains a general scientific hypothesis. In this it is no different from the several theories on the world's origins presented by mathematical and theoretical physics. Theology cannot pretend to judge these hypotheses out of its own resources. However, it is imperative that theology take note of them. It is naive to suppose that they will have no effect upon the world-view of thinking people or that they have no relevance for the theological enterprise. Here was the great merit of Pius XII in his extensive comments upon the possible consequences of certain scientific theories for human dignity and human solidarity. Here too lay the great service of Teilhard de Chardin in attempting to integrate the achievements both of science and religious faith. An important legitimation has been given to Catholics who desire to keep an open mind on evolution. In so far as Church teaching is concerned, evolution is an open question up to and including humankind in its bodily dimension. Caution is enjoined, however, in regard to the special nature of the human soul which is affirmed as immediately created by God. An extension of evolution theory to undergird racism, apartheid or master-race ideologies, would have to be declared contradictory to the Christian understanding of our brotherhood/

sisterhood in Jesus Christ. Indeed, there is good reason also for claiming that such extension is likely to be an ideological abuse of science itself.

Since it is imperative to counteract any impression that theology is concerned with the soul, leaving the body to science, as it were, many theologians have attemped to show that one can take seriously both the evolutionary perspective and the traditional emphasis upon the spirituality, special provenance and inherent dignity of the human person. It is submitted here that these theologians have impressively done so. Not every difficulty has been resolved, as the questions raised above will show. Nevertheless, it is also submitted that evolution and Christian teaching are in principle compatible and that such compatibility should be kept in mind both in catechesis and homiletics.

SEVEN

Human Rights Observed: A Service of the Creator

A theological essay on human rights should observe due humility. The Churches, and theology as an activity of the Churches, may well be actively concerned today with the question of human rights. Yet neither the Churches nor theology initiated the concern. In the past they were hardly the prime exponent of these rights. The history of human rights is a troubled one. Even more troubled is the story of the countless people who have had their basic rights infringed through oppression and domination, those most cogent evidences of 'original sin'. If there is now a deeper sensitivity to human rights – alongside a most blatant, perverse and widespread denial of them – this awareness is not the preserve of the Churches or of religious people.

DECLARATIONS OF INTENT AND PRINCIPLE

It is a bitter irony that concern for human rights has been stimulated by 'the continued multiplication of violations of human rights'.[1] The precariousness of respect for human rights is an evident datum of experience. The difficulty in implementing such rights as have been declared is clearly expressed by Paul VI in *Octogesima Adveniens*: 'Human rights are all too often disregarded, if not derided, or else they receive only formal recognition. In many cases legislation does not keep up with real situations. Legislation is necessary, but it is not sufficient for setting up true relationships of justice and equality'.[2]

However, there are clear milestones which, although they recede into the distance, have marked the emergence of rights provisions. There are *Magna Carta* (1215), the *Habeas Corpus Act* (1679) and the English *Bill of Rights* (1688). These have facilitated invaluable procedural remedies. The major declarations are the French *Declaration of the Rights of Man* (August 27, 1789) and the American *Declaration of Independence* of 1776. The French Declaration stems from a humanist tradition as old as the Stoic emphasis on the inviolable dignity of reason. The American Declaration argues from the divine origin of man. It draws upon the natural law tradition but explicitly regards the Judaeo-

Christian witness for the values the declaration enshrines. To the American Constitution we owe the consolidation of legal guarantees for natural rights. Through constitutional embodiment these rights are given a priority over any laws or rules which conflict with them. Dennis Lloyd hails this advance: 'thus was created for the first time a machinery whereby natural rights might be brought into the fabric of the law and enjoy recognition and enforcement as legal rights'.[3]

In the French and American Declarations there is an impressive thrust to equality in rights. Yet, in practice, that thrust was stunted in a tragic way. In America, the Indians and the Blacks were not included among those 'created equal'. In France, there was a property qualification which gravely contradicted the fine rhetoric of the *Declaration of the Rights of Man and of the Citizen*. Since the 'sacred and inviolable' rights of property entered the determination of citizenship rights only a small minority of people qualified.[4] It has been argued that 'towards the end of the eighteenth century the proclamation of human rights was the embodiment of the concerns and aspirations of a social group, a sector of society'.[5] The essentially bourgeois conception in both the French and American declarations is exemplified by the following extract from the *Declaration of the Rights of Man*: 'every man is free to employ his arms, his industry and his capital as he deems fit and useful for himself, he can produce what pleases him as he likes'.

It was that 'act of the highest importance' (John XXIII), the promulgation of the *Universal Declaration of Human Rights* (1948), which made human rights an issue for international law. There had been the *Declaration of St Petersburg* (1888), the *Hague Conventions* (1899 and 1907) and the *Geneva Convention* (1925). These ascribed rights to individuals which could be invoked by states on their behalf. Yet, as Seán McBride has pointed out, 'the old concept that only states, as distinct from individuals, could invoke international law took a long time to die'.[6] It was only through the covenants following upon the *Declaration of Human Rights* - the *Covenant on Economic, Social and Cultural Rights* and the other *Covenant on Civil and Political Rights*, along with the *European Convention for the Protection of Human Rights and Fundamental Freedoms* (1950) – that the restriction to states of the protection of international law was finally set aside.

The *Universal Declaration of Human Rights* articulates several concerns. Politically it arose out of a desire to set 'a common standard of achievement for all peoples and nations'. After the Second World War there seemed to be a determination to create 'the stability and well being which are necessary for peaceful and friendly relations among nations'. As part of its programme the newly created United Nations Organisation adopted the goal of 'a universal respect for, and observance of, human rights and fundamental freedoms ... without distinction as to race, sex, language or religion'.[7] There seemed to exist a moral consensus that 'all human beings are born free and equal in dignity. They are endowed with reason and conscience and should act towards one another in a spirit of brotherhood'.[8] The Declaration is the first comprehensive statement of the values fundamental to the preservation and development of human dignity.

Behind the Declaration, however, lay considerable tension. The tension was between the liberal tradition on civil and political rights and the insistence by the Marxist states upon social and economic justice. Two compromises emerged. First, there was the distinction between the Declaration itself, which simply set standards and voiced aspirations, and the Covenants which would be legally binding as nations ratified them. Second, there was the division into two covenants: one to cover social and economic rights, and the other to cover civil and political rights. Even with these compromises the Soviet Union abstained from approving the Declaration on the grounds that it downplayed social and economic rights thus remaining no more than an eighteenth century 'liberal' document. On the other hand, both Covenants have been ratified by the U.S.S.R. while neither of these has been signed by the U.S. The troubled history of the signing of the covenants exemplifies the lack of consensus on what constitutes human rights and how they should be enshrined. The covenants received unanimous adoption by the U.N. General Assembly only in December 1966. Since they required thirty-five ratifications by individual states, the covenants did not come into force until January 3rd 1976 and March 23rd 1976.[9]

The Universal Declaration has been included in, or endorsed by, several national constitutions. Other constitutions have used it as a guideline or interpretative instrument. It has been claimed that 'by now most international lawyers of repute regard the Universal Declaration as forming part of international customary law'.[10] Egon Schwelb argues: 'in the years since 1948 the Universal Declaration has acquired a purpose different from the one that was contemplated and willed by many of the governments that brought it into being in 1948 ... It can no longer be maintained that it has "only moral force" '.[11] However, there is considerable possibility of derogation from the provisions of the covenants. Article 4 of the *Covenant on Civil and Political Rights* provides for derogation 'in times of public emergency which threatens the life

of the nation'. The derogation may be invoked under the following conditions: that it is to the extent strictly required by the
exigencies of the situation, that the measures adopted are not
inconsistent with obligations under international law, that discrimination is not practised in implementation. No derogation
may be made from the right to life, from provision against torture
or degrading treatment, from the ban on servitude and slavery,
from freedom of conscience. Even when derogation is duly notif-
ied, the Hague and Geneva conventions apply. [12]

There is, therefore, a considerable body of rights provisions
which survive even in time of national and international emergency. This is a major advance which should not be allowed to
peter out through defeatism or disillusion at the slowness of rights
machinery. It is correctly emphasised that further progress and
the maintenance of progress already achieved presuppose vigil-
ance by a free parliament and a critical press. In all realism it must
be noted that remedies for the enforcement of human rights are
much more important than their formal declaration. Declaration
is important. Yet it is fatally weakened if there be no effective
procedure for enforcement. The many proclamations of respect
for human rights by far outstrip the procedures and the willingness to enfore these rights. The machinery for seeking redress
against human rights violation is notoriously cumbersome. Due
process is endlessly protracted. A report to the twenty-fifth ordinary session of the Council of Europe's Consultative Assembly
remarked that 'the case for international machinery for the im-
partial supervision of the applications of the Conventions (on
rights) is unanswerable … it is difficult to get governments to
accept it'. The report admits that 'the more far reaching proposals
which envisage penal sanctions for violations of humanitarian law
are evidently less realistic and can perhaps be left to the next
generation'. [13]

The provisions of the *Declaration of Human Rights* and of
international law on human rights remain 'weak law'. The resistance of governments to outside intervention, the refusal to cede
sovereignty, the lack of enforceable instruments, are but three
reasons why this is so. There is a perduring unclarity about the
content of human rights. The political philosopher, Maurice
Cranston, has argued that the very comprehensiveness of the
Universal Declaration weakens its force. Writing from the liberal
tradition, Cranston believes that, whereas civil and political rights
are readily defined, social and economic rights are difficult to
define and virtually impossible to enforce. In Cranston's view the
achievement of a proper standard of living for all is a social ideal,

not a right. Indeed, Cranston appears to believe that what the U.N. Declaration and the International Covenants term economic and social rights are not rights at all. He argues that to burden the *Declaration of Human Rights* 'with affirmations of so called rights which are not rights at all is to push all talk of human rights out of the clear realms of the morally compelling into the twilight world of utopian aspiration'.[14]

It will be argued later in this chapter that civil, political, social and economic rights intermesh. Where one or other set of rights is infringed, the remainder fall into risk. Nonetheless, Cranston's objection cannot be shuffled away. If human rights language is inflated without care for its precise meaning, then the cause of human rights is itself damaged. There is a rhetoric of human rights which merely 'grounds them in humanity, and then leaves the notion undefined, so that the content of rights is indefinite and indeterminate'.[15] This should not mean, however, that claims should be restricted to those rights the formulation of which is the valuable legacy of post-Enlightenment liberalism. It is the merit of Marxist political theory that it recognised the insufficiency of an abstract tabulation of rights and insisted on the need to embody the values of social and economic justice. Marx viewed the 'rights of man', declared in the liberal tradition, as little more than ramparts built around the citadel of inequality and domination. He insisted that any system of rights be judged by the concrete social and economic conditions to which people are subjected. In practice, however, this has led Soviet theorists to limit political, civil and personal rights to whatever is consistent with the building of socialism. They assume, with grievous results for millions of victims, that the machinery of State alone implements the reconciliation of conflicting rights. As against both liberalism and Marxism, an emergent perspective on human rights, shared by major sections of the Christian Churches, insists on the necessity to define and foster rights not only on the civil and political fronts but also in the social and economic areas.

It remains a fatal shortcoming that the interdependence of the civil, political, social, economic, cultural and religious dimensions of human living is so weakly recognised. The references made in the early debates of the United Nations Organisation to 'legal rights' and 'programme rights' are still helpful. Rights which are attainable only in the long term need not be relegated to the limbo of ideals and aspirations. However, the hard fact is that neat ideological arguments mask the growing disregard of human rights in both capitalist and socialist blocs. At the level of theory some advances have been made since 1948. It is surely important that these be consolidated. Yet David Hollenbach's bleak assessment is far from overstated: 'though major advances have been made at the United Nations, the synthesis remains more of a political compromise than a genuine theoretical breakthrough'.[16]

THE CHURCH AND HUMAN RIGHTS

As mentioned earlier, the Churches have no clear record in human rights. The pre-Reformation Church was deeply implicated in the oppressive structures of feudalism. In Reformation times the Churches operated the Inquisition, on the one hand, and the theocratic repression of Calvin's Geneva, on the other. There was little to choose between Philip's Spain and Cromwell's England (or Ireland). The *Declaration of the Rights of Man,* with all its limitations, preceded by more than a hundred years the first timid mention of workers' rights by Leo XIII. The outlawing of slavery in the mid-nineteenth century was not a Church achievement. Nor was it assisted in any major way by ecclesiastical effort. The emancipation of the American Blacks took place at the same time as Pius IX was condemning 'pernicious modern freedoms'. There is substance to the admission by the Vatican Justice and Peace Commission that 'the Church's attitude to human rights during the last two centuries ... has been characterised by hesitations, objections, reservations and, on occasion, even vehement reaction on the Catholic side to any declaration of human rights from the standpoint of laicism and liberalism'.[17]

On the other hand, the Christian tradition motivated those who worked most assiduously for human rights and social justice. The tradition has a long standing insistence on the special dignity of man and woman as image of God. The same tradition carries a remembrance of the prophetic protest in the Old Testament against the yoke of oppression. Paul utters the marvellously subversive principle that in Christ there is neither Jew nor Greek, neither male nor female, neither slave nor free (cf Gal 3:28). Finally, there is the repeated insistence of the Founder of Christianity that God makes the sun rise on good people and bad, makes the rain fall on honest and dishonest, that we are sons and daughters of the same Father (cf Matt 5:45). This is a forceful reminder that every person is answerable to, and in the care of, God. Thereby, he or she is subtracted from the pretension by state or group or other persons to total control over the ineffable mystery of personality. To retrieve this strand of tradition – a strand frequently overlaid by other oppressive patterns – enables a re-appreciation of the value of religious freedom and a reaffirmation of personal inviolability. These two values are central to the contemporary theology of human rights.

THE HISTORY OF 'RELIGIOUS FREEDOM'

The insistence upon religious freedom is documented from early in the Christian story. Freedom is seen as a condition for access to religious truth. At first, people were content to appeal to positive law as the justification of their claim to religious freedom: 'each province, each city, has its god ... we are the only ones who are denied the right to have a religion', wrote Tertullian in his *Apologeticum*.[18] Soon, however, the claim sought out a more profound base. It moved from an appeal to Roman law and custom to the *ius naturae,* the law of nature. In his *Letter to Scapula* Tertullian wrote: 'it is of human and natural law that each one can adore what he wants ... religions should be spontaneously [freely] adopted, not by force, since sacrifices have no value unless they are offered willingly'.[19] While Tertullian points out that religious toleration does not threaten the state, he clearly links religious freedom to 'human and natural right'. God can be worshipped in truth only if people are free from coercion. About a century later, Lactantius reiterates that access to truth must be free, not forced. He wrote: 'true sacrifice cannot be offered under external pressure. If it is not offered freely and in good faith it is a curse. That is what occurs when it is obtained through torture, violence, prison'. And again, he argued: 'no one can be forced to adore what he does not want to adore'.[20]

A corollary of religious freedom as a natural right is that political power is incompetent in religious matters. The question posed in the Acts of the Apostles recurs: 'is it right in the sight of God to listen to you rather than to God' (Acts 5:29). Under state persecution, Christians continued to affirm that all authority is from God. Yet they also insisted that human authority cannot obtrude on the relation between God and the person. In 204 A.D. Hippolytus wrote: 'whoever believes in God cannot be a hypocrite; however, neither does this person have to fear the orders of civil power when it imposes something prohibited. Indeed, on account of faith in God, if this power obliges the person to do something against good conscience, it will be sweet to go to death and resist the command'.[21] These early apologists for religious freedom saw the Church's role as to preach and mediate the Gospel. Their unbounded confidence in the power of truth, and in the natural human desire for truth, led them to insist upon the inviolability of conscience against all comers. This is a radical doctrine, soon enough forgotten, the practice of which has made many a martyr in both Church and State.

With Constantine and the Edict of Milan (313 A.D.) Christianity left the catacombs. However, the Edict of Milan was not an unambiguous declaration of the right to religious freedom. It was a decree of toleration rather than a recognition of freedom in religious matters. Freedom of religious practice was declared. Yet it was 'granted', 'regulated', 'not denied'. This was a pragmatic move rather than an affair of principle: 'it is convenient for the tranquility which the Empire enjoys'. The supposition is that religion is still a matter for the State. It pertains to *raison d'etat*. An ominous note is sounded in the somewhat later pronouncement: 'the privileges which have been granted out of respect for religion should only favour the followers of Catholicism ... we desire that the heretics and the schismatics not only be denied these privileges but also that they be subjected to punishment'. With the Edict of Thessalonika (380 A.D.) and the Theodosian settlement, the confessional Christian State emerges. The emperor now proclaims that those who do not follow the Catholic religion should be punished not only by divine vengeance (!) but also 'by that power which the heavenly will has granted us'.[22]

Clearly, there is a new context. In this context, tragically, the erstwhile claims for freedom of religion and the declared incompetence of the civil power in matters of conscience were downplayed by the successors of those who, in other circumstances, had so well and so courageously advanced them. Augustine verbally re-echoes his predecessors' insistence upon the freedom of the act of faith. It was he who coined the aphorism: 'no one can believe against his/her will' (*credere non potest nisi volens*). This, however, is a psychological rather than a political freedom. In the case of the Donatists, Augustine is unwilling to follow through the full logic of his declaration of freedom of faith. He uses an argument which, in effect, is against the earlier claims for religious freedom: Coercion may have to be used to make a person truly free. He writes: 'to be considered when anyone is coerced, is not the mere fact of the coercion, but the nature of that to which he is coerced ... '[23] One feels a certain sadness as one reads the *doctor gratiae* employing the argument of the despot: it is good for you to be forced to be free. It is true that Augustine and his many successors would not see it thus. Rather, they would argue that freedom to be wrong is neither a right nor a true freedom. They would define freedom of conscience not by the freedom of the personal subject but by the rightness of the object of assent. It was this reasoning which legitimated the barbarities committed against dissenters in the middle ages and well thereafter. In generation after generation, civil power was invoked to punish, torture and kill those who dissented in matters of faith and discipline. Aquinas resolves the conflict between his sincere protestation of the freedom of faith and the persecution of heretics, by the affirmation: 'accepting faith is a matter of will, conserving faith is a matter of necessity'.[24] It was this logic which legitimated the excesses of Torquemada.

There were honourable exceptions which lie closer to the original perception of the freedom of faith. Tempered perhaps by his own experience at the hands of the public authorities. Athanasius argued that 'the truth is not announced with swords, lances and soldiers. It is proper to religion not to impose but to persuade'. Another such testimony is from Salvian of Lerins, in his *De Gubernatione Dei*. He urges respect not simply for the pagans, but even more impressively, for the heretics against whom fratricidal bitterness raged violently: 'For us they are heretics, but they do not believe they are. They consider themselves Catholics and give us the infamous name of heretic. What they are for us, we are for them ... they are in error, but their mistake is one of good faith ... '[25]

Much later, Bartolomeo de las Casas (1474-1566) insisted upon persuasion rather than coercion as the only means of bringing people to true religion: 'divine Providence established ... the one, same and only way to teach people the true religion, that is, the persuasion of the understanding through reasoning and through inviting them, and the gentle moving of the will ... '[26] Las Casas excoriated those who do evil in order, as they claim, to do good. He writes trenchantly: 'a live Indian, even though infidel [is better than] a dead Indian though Christian'. Thus he challenges the persecution of non-Christian Indians. He goes even further and places the freedom of faith within the broader context of the freedom of the human being: every human being is born free and has the right to have this freedom respected. The enslavement of the Indians, for allegedly Christian motives, is 'against all reason and justice'. Hence Las Casas devoted all his efforts to fighting the socio-economic tyranny of the *encomienda* – the giving in estate of the Indians to Spaniards. He would absolve only those *encomienderos* who promised to return all they had robbed from the Indians.

Yet the dominant thrust was towards collusion of Church and State. In the ages of Christendom the framework of thought was the necessary harmony of civil and religious powers. The doctrine of 'two swords' was a convenient legitimation of the rule of spiritual and temporal overlords each respecting the bailiwick of the other. It was recognised that the State had the duty to assist the Church in rooting out heresy. This worked well for both 'arms' – for it was often expedient for civil rulers to silence those whom the Church found too turbulent to bear. In every case the dissenter suffered. Within such an ambient the scandalous agreement was later fashioned: *cuius regio eius religio*. So much for the freedom of faith! So much for the incompetence of civil rulers in matters of conscience!

The Reformation, the Enlightenment and the emergence of bourgeois society are constituent parts of the one historical process. Each made its contribution to the emancipation from absolute state power and the claims of ecclesiastical hegemony. The Reformation stressed, though it did not always foster, the primacy of conscience. It mounted a critique of ecclesiastical institutions and gave rise to religious structures where the personal dimensions of religion were better cherished than hithertofore. The Enlightenment principle, 'dare to understand' (*sapere aude*) applied critical reason to absolute claims, whether civil or ecclesial. It urged the claims of reason and freedom with a vigour hitherto unrivalled. It distinguished between the citizen and the person, thus marking off where the State's claim may legitimately run and where not.

The response of central authority in the Roman Catholic Church was to denounce the freedoms claimed by modernity as 'absurd liberties'. Gregory XVI's condemnation of the Abbe de Lammenais, Pius IX's *Quanta Cura* and the appended Syllabus of Errors were virulent reactions. Pius IX's dominant motivation was that these liberties endangered people's salvation. To dismantle Catholicism as the state religion, to proclaim the right of all to choose their form of worship, in the papal view amounted to an equiparation of truth and error. It would be to declare that outside the Church there is salvation. All these considerations form the context of *Quanta Cura*. Yet it can be argued that another motivation was operative in the papal suspicion of new freedoms. This was the desire to continue a concordance of the altar and the throne. Leo XIII was later to write: 'reason and experience prove rulers defend their own cause when they defend the authority of the Church'.[27] For the greater part of the nineteenth century, then, the highest religious authority in the West aligned itself with a type of society in which it felt its own interests were best recognised. It seemed to favour the old political order: an alliance with monarchy, aristocracy and, *faute de mieux*, with the conservative *bourgeoisie*. With Leo XIII, it is true, there begins a movement away from such alignment. Nonetheless, one notes his condition that the State is bound to the public profession of the true religion. A nuanced commentator of the period writes: 'although Leo undoubtedly tempered the teaching of his predecessors and sanctioned limited reforms of toleration, his arguments were solidly rooted in Augustine's conviction that freedom of conscience was specified by its object not by its subject'.[28]

With the 'new theology' a decisive shift took place. This theology took a realistic view of the breakdown of Christendom. It abandoned the insistence on the natural alliance of altar and throne. Yves Congar, M. D. Chenu, Jacques Maritain, Karl Rahner and many others interpreted the tenet *extra ecclesiam nulla salus* in a much broader way. Inset to this approach was the argument that just as it was said that error has no rights, it might with equal validity be said that truth has no rights. For both truth and error are abstractions. Only persons have rights. Persons have the right to seek the truth and the duty to respect it. Similarly, persons have rights even when they err. It is true that the 'new theology' received a frigid welcome. Nevertheless, one finds anticipations of it in the more positive assessments by Pius XI and Pius XII of the rights of persons vis-à-vis the State. Similarly these popes are insistent on the rights of people to follow the dictates of their conscience. A good instance of this is Pius XII's Christmas message of 1944 which bases freedom of conscience in the dignity of the human person. However, it is with John XXIII that the fullest expression of the freedom of conscience is attained: '[one must distinguish] between error ... and the one who falls into error ... a man who has fallen into error does not cease to be a man... he never forfeits his personal dignity'.[29]

No single pope was responsible for retrieving this affirmation of the right to religious freedom. There were several factors at work. The 'new theology' was mentioned earlier. There were also changes in social structures which affected the Church from within: the industrial revolution, the rise of totalitarian states, the lesson of two world wars that the only foundation for justice and peace was the full recognition of the person as the subject, not the object, of politics. With *Pacem in Terris* and, in particular, the Decree on Religious Liberty of the Second Vatican Council (wherein the freedom to choose one's religion was explicitly recognised) one of the outstanding areas of contention with the emancipative thrust of post-Enlightenment thought was settled. It is ironic that this late reconciliation was achieved when the limitations of the liberal heritage were becoming apparent. Enda McDonagh appositely remarks: 'although it came late to a clear formulation of the fundamental right of religious freedom, the Catholic Church had anticipated some of the difficulties of a simple liberal interpretation of human rights'.[30] Amongst these difficulties were an uncaring individualism and an exaggeration of the principle of private property.

THE IRREDUCIBLE VALUE OF THE HUMAN PERSON

It is clear, then, that the history of Christianity is not identical with the history of human rights. The relation of these two histories is complex. On the one hand, ecclesiastical power all too frequently colluded with the civil power in denying what we now term human rights. On the other hand, there are positive connections between the history of Christianity and the history of human rights. For example, Christianity has for long urged as a principle that the human being is sacred: *res sacra homo*. This ranges through the image of God doctrine to Paul of Tarsus' insistence that every man and woman is a temple of the Holy Spirit. The book of Genesis, common to both Judaism and Christianity, rests the sacredness of human life upon the image of God in man and woman. As image of God they occupy an especial place in creation. With the emphasis on *templum Dei* and the indwelling glory of God, Paul lays the basis for reverence of the body/person in both spiritual and material dimensions. There is an implicit anthropology in the protest by the early Christians of the State's incompetence in the matters of service of God. There is a reserve, a *ne plus ultra,* which could from time to time be raised against exorbitant institutional demands. Again, this reserve roots in the doctrine of man/woman as *imago Dei.*[31]

St Thomas urges that personhood is the noblest reality in all nature. The human person must be defined as end rather than means. The human person, though oriented to community, is not totally defined by that relation: (*non ordinatur ad communitatem politicam secundum se totum et secundum omnia sua*). In other words, citizenship does not exhaust the depths of our personal and social being.[32] From this tradition stems the avowal, recurrent in modern papal teaching, that the human person is the principle, the subject, and the end or purpose of all institutions. Leo XIII had already put it: man precedes the State. In our own day, Pope John Paul II insists that capital is for human beings rather than human beings for capital. The dignity of the human person is the bulwark against the exorbitance of power vis-à-vis the individual. It forbids the individual to abdicate his/her freedom in face of institutional claims. Even more urgently, it forbids institutions to obtrude on the sphere where only the personal belongs. This reserve is always necessary to counter the arrogance of power. The dynamism of power drives it to arrogate what does not belong to it. The exercise of power in laicist context can demand a sevice not far removed from the most minutely ordered cult. Exercised in religious context, it can arrogate a claim which belongs to God alone. Hence the recurrent need to preserve the space between the personal and the collective, the private and the institutional dimensions.

And yet we are social beings. Without the possibility of co-operation, without those interlocking human relationships which are part of our social nature, we would deteriorate rapidly to savagery or worse. Hence, the personal can never be limited to the individual. This reduction is the greatest weakness of the bourgeois individualism of the eighteenth, nineteenth, and twentieth centuries. Perhaps the most positive thing one can say of the Church's nineteenth century rejection of 'absurd liberties' was that it divined such atomistic and potentially disruptive individualism. Hence, the opposing poles are not simply the collective and the individual. There are at least four terms to consider: the person, the community, society and state. The relation of person to community is perhaps the least troubled. Here one speaks of the interaction of persons and those human groups the members of which interrelate as persons. In these circumstances, one may anticipate, although far from infallibly so, that human dignity will be respected and human development fostered. The relation of person to society is more complex and has had a more troubled history. Society may be broadly defined as the totality of relationships and structures in which a particular people find themselves at any given time. In a sense, society is an aggregate of individuals in view of a common goal or good. Here the definition of common good is crucial and, notoriously, patent of several interpretations. 'The common good' is a concept susceptible to manipulation from many sides and easily becomes the plaything of ideology. In almost every case, the understanding of person within society is such that the inviolable worth of each member can drop out of sight. Finally, there is the tense relation of person and State. The State is described as the locus of political sovereignty with the attendant sanctions. On the one hand, the State and the common good are inseparably related. On the other hand, the suppression of personal and social rights inevitably follows the 'legal positivism and state absolutism [which] have disfigured the face of justice'.[33]

In the space disclosed between these spheres of community, society and State, human rights survive and flourish. Although this is more a negative principle than a positive delineation of human rights, it nonetheless provides an important guideline. Whenever community or society is fused into state, personal rights and freedoms are in jeopardy. It is to the credit of personalist theology to have insisted on the necessary balance between person, community, society and state. The Vatican Justice and Peace Commission puts it: 'Human personality ... is an ontological and psychological reality which is autonomous in the civil sphere ... its liberty and basic rights take precedence ... over social and political structures. The teaching of the magisterium stresses the primacy of the person as the goal of social institutions'.[34]

BEYOND LIBERALISM AND COLLECTIVISM

In the liberal tradition rights are essentially negative provisions. The tradition is strong on immunities from infringement on the individual pursuance of well being: 'rights are the fences around that field where individuals may act, speak, worship, associate or accumulate wealth without restriction by the positive action of either persons or the state'.[35] Although it has an impressive history, liberal rights theory may be said to sit too easily to the unlimited acquisition of wealth without social responsibility. In its pure form the theory is silent on how to institute the social rights of those who suffer deprivation of the most horrifying kind. On the other hand, the strength of Marxist analysis is its recognition of social and economic claims. Unfortunately, the political and civil rights so dearly won in the democratic tradition are downplayed not to say eliminated.

It has been argued that its difficulties with the liberal ethic as well as with totalitarian pretension have given Catholic social thought an advantage in adopting a stance on human rights which goes beyond these traditions. Leo XIII's *Rerum Novarum* was strongest in its defence of the social and economic rights of workers. It also vindicated the rights to food, shelter and clothing. It defended workers' rights to organise and to own property. Pius XI went further along the road of structural analysis in linking the concept of social justice to human rights. In speaking of the right to life, to bodily integrity, to the necessary means of existence, to freedom of worship and association, to own and use property, he refuses to speak of 'man on his own in a market economy'. Rather, he underlines that rights are mediated by social institutions and are shaped by these institutions for better or for worse. Urged by the horrors of World War II, Pius XII lifted the question of human rights from an abstract principle to an immediately urgent concern. In his Christmas address of 1942, he called for 'respect for and the practical realisation of the following fundamental personal rights: the right to maintain and develop one's corporal, intellectual and moral life ... the right to worship ... the right to marry ... the right to work ... to free choice of a state of life ... the right to the use of material goods'. Some years later the same pope called for a social and juridical system to protect such personal rights. A system of this kind would enshrine 'the right to life ... to one's good name ... to develop one's culture and national character, the right to develop oneself, the right to demand observance of international treaties ... ' (Address, 6 December, 1953).

With John XXIII such analysis comes to full flower. *Pacem in Terris* 'gives the most complex and systematic list of human rights in the modern Catholic tradition' (Hollenbach). Valuably, it traces the intricate relations of individuals and associations, on the one hand, and of national and international society towards individuals and associations, on the other. With its stress upon the dignity of the person and its thorough examination of complex social interdependencies, the encyclical goes beyond the liberal and collectivist analyses while containing the best of both traditions. In effect, *Pacem in Terris* places civil/political rights and social/cultural/economic rights in an integrated framework. Repeatedly, the encyclical underlines that basic human needs can neither be met nor safeguarded if political and social structures are unjustly ordered. By its comprehensive approach it represents an advance even on the U.N. Declaration of Human Rights.

The Second Vatican Council makes its specific contribution to the human rights question. *Dignitatis Humanae,* the Decree on Religious Liberty, affirms the right to religious freedom not simply as inherent to 'catholic truth' but to the very self-disposition of the person. What the Church had claimed for itself, it was now willing to accord to others. *Gaudium et Spes,* the Pastoral Constitution on the Church in the Modern World, adds the reminder that it is impossible to define either human dignity or human rights acontextually. There is a dynamic to human rights. Man is a developing being. Since his/her context is changing, due in large part to his/her efforts in collaboration, concern for human rights must pay attention to that moving context. A rigid definition of rights soon loses relevance. If the exigencies of new situations are ignored, equality before the law can mask discrimination, exploitation and flagrant disregard for human rights.[36]

A THEOLOGY OF HUMAN RIGHTS

Human rights have come to occupy a major place in Roman Catholic social thought. For several decades the Protestant Churches have systematically addressed the same question. More recently, an ecumenism in human rights work has come to the fore. To go beyond inter-church discussion and to present a specifically theological approach in the wider field of socio-political comment incurs a notable difficulty. The more definitive the theological perspective, the less likely it is to command wide-spread assent. One writer puts it succinctly: 'a pluralistic society that tries to make its unifying political and moral principles religious in any non-trivial sense is in for trouble ... '[37] It can be answered that a theology of human rights does not seek to impose itself as the only perspective. At its best, it offers a specific viewpoint on human rights as essential to the development of human dignity in an increasingly threatening context. It holds itself ready to protest when human dignity is subjected to attack. From this perspective splendid work has been done from South Africe to Central America and, perforce in a muted way, in Eastern Europe. A theology of human rights is most impressive when it is ready also to criticise its parent institutions in the name of human rights themselves.

In addressing 'all men of goodwill' John XXIII located the basis of human rights in people's innate freedom and intelligence. He appealed to the doctrine of the natural law as the point of departure for a consensus on human rights. Maurice Cranston comments: ' ... Pope John does not look on natural law in the orthodox Catholic way as something needing clerical interpretation, and limited by the exigencies of the Church's mission. Pope John's concept of natural law is something closer to that of the Stoic tradition: it is something discernible by the eye of reason alone, and something which pertains to humanity as a whole'. ×[8] This approach can hope for a wider consensus than one based on a 'revealed' perception. It presupposes common ground between Christian tenets on socio-political matters and other stances which hold to the importance of moral principle in those same matters.

The emergent Roman Catholic perspective goes somewhat further. It adheres to the traditional insistence on people's dignity as *imago Dei*. Here, the dominant value is the sacredness of the person. Human dignity is a given. It is an indicative rather than an imperative. It is not in the gift of anyone. It is antecedent to every attainment, performance or recognition. It is inseparable from human personhood. From it arises every right, every duty, every moral claim. On the other hand, this proclamation of human dignity will be empty if it is not related to social and political contexts. Rights have to be re-assessed and re-identified in each new social, economic and political conjuncture. As this task is taken up, one moves away from the 'safe' area of general principle and ready consensus. It has been noticed that the affirmative style of *Pacem in Terris* in treating of human rights has ceded to a more complex analysis in *Populorum Progressio* and *Octogesima Adveniens*. This is not merely a stylistic difference between two popes. It is rather that the intricate problems for human rights posed by the existing socio-political order have moved to the centre of concern.

In the Protestant tradition the emphases are distributed in a somewhat different way. Here, human nature does not merit the optimistic assessment of John XXIII. It is a wounded nature. The image of God is badly defaced. The Theological Consultation on Human Rights of the World Alliance of Reformed Churches declares: 'human rights are ultimately grounded not in human nature; nor are they conditioned by individual or collective human achievement in history. They reflect the covenant of God's faithfulness to his people and the glory of his love for the Church and the world'.[39] Human rights, duly observed, are a reflection of God's claim on humankind and of God's covenant with us. At first sight, this may appear to 'spiritualise' human rights to a vague exhortation. However, the contrary is the case. For the sharper awareness of social sin and the evangelical stress upon the sovereignty of God impel an analysis of social conflict. They also underline that human rights are not merely enablements. Human rights imply concrete personal and social duties. If they are to have any reality they must be apprehended as specific claims not only on ill-defined 'others' but also on ourselves who speak of human rights.

Since Vatican II the confluence of human rights analysis of the Catholic and Protestant traditions has become more evident. The major documents of the council and subsequent documents retain an emphasis upon the universalist thrust of natural law tenets. Similarly, they continue to draw upon social and philosophical arguments. Yet they unambiguously accept the evangelical claim that the ultimate basis of all rights is community in 'the same nature redeemed by Christ, with the same calling and intensity'.[40] The doctrinal foundations for Catholic human rights theory are creation in the image of God, the incarnation, and the redemption effected in Jesus Christ. Both Catholic and Protestant traditions move social rights to the centre of discussion without neglecting the personal rights so dear to the liberal standpoint. Both traditions seem to accept that it is not possible by philosophical analysis alone to develop a convincing rights theory. The impossibility arises from the multiplicity of ideology in contemporary culture. Hence, the two traditions converge in admitting the need for a common witness deriving from shared theological doctrines and religious symbols.

A theological perspective on human rights needs more than the enumeration of those rights already drawn up by centuries of political, legal and diplomatic work. There are two options for a method or approach to human rights analysis. The first is 'a return to the sources' where one attempts to derive from Scripture and Church tradition a set of 'absolute and inalienable' rights. Thus a Church can draw up a schedule of rights and, perhaps, mark out priorities for strategic action in defence of these rights. This is already a major advance from the time when the Churches were suspicious of talk about rights and defined them with an eye to institutional advantage. The problem with the method is that its results will be acontextual and the rights defined will be abstract. A second method is therefore preferred. It starts from the assumption that a task of religious faith is to protest in favour of the 'threatened humanum', 'to awaken pain at the inner and outer enslavement of man'. From there it moves to a realistic social analysis of how human dignity is being jeopardised by the mechanisms of oppression: hunger, illiteracy, underdevelopment, unemployment, torture, apartheid, terrorism and state violence. Correlatively, this approach takes account of human rights as a secular achievement. It asks: What rights have been declared? How are they implemented? How do they measure up to the requirements of human dignity in today's world? It reminds us that 'law is constantly developing. It is thus necessary to be involved in the search for new aspects of human rights at the same time as one works on the institution of those already acquired'.[41]

A major advantage of such an approach is that it challenges the Churches to be listeners as well as speakers. They can learn from the liberal achievement in regard to tolerance and freedom as well as from the Marxist critique of inequality, inequity and unbridled acquisitiveness. In this humbler yet more agile stance, theology can come to regard human rights as 'historical formulations of kingdom values' (E. McDonagh). The immediate consequence is that human rights become a matter for evangelical *praxis*. Human rights work challenges the Churches themselves to match theory and practice in constant interaction: 'anyone who ventures to speak to people about justice must first be just in their own eyes'

(Roman Synod 1971). Or, as the Baden consultation so well says: 'a primary responsibility ... is for Christians to look at their own institutions – Churches, schools, hospitals – to ensure that in each instance, the demand of the Gospel is faithfully given witness'[42] Thus we are forced to look at our own prejudices in what we claim and what we affirm to be human rights.

WHAT ARE HUMAN RIGHTS?

It is an irony of the rhetoric of human rights that their definition varies with location in the social, civil and ecclesiastical establishments. What one person or group regards as a human right is viewed by another person or group as subversive, indulgent, irresponsible. The protest for civil liberties has often become an *apologia* for State power when the erstwhile protesting party reached government. The freedom of religion, loudly demanded by the Churches, when disestablished, was grudgingly espoused when these same Churches were in establishment. It is all too easy for personal or group advantage to become the criterion for what one claims or disallows as human rights. It is argued here that the old definitions of right(s) are inadequate. The classical definition – an enforceable claim to do or to demand something (*ius aliquid faciendi vel exigendi*) – lacks the control of social responsibility. Where the exercise of one person's or group's right entails injustice to another person or group, the classical definition provides scant guidance. The conflict was often addressed with pragmatic axioms about the common good or public order. However, such maxims frequently concealed ambiguities about the nature of the common good or public order. So, far from fostering the rights of all, they tended to favour the dominant interests in the particular group or society.

More promising is the description of human rights as 'the conditions for the realisation of human worth in action'.[43] This lays a challenge to ascribe a more precise content to human rights. Talk about human dignity must be translated into practical consequences. Since social contexts are constantly developing, human rights analysis demands a continued reading of 'the signs of the times'. A good example of this sensitive reading is the schema of rights presented in John XXIII's *Pacem in Terris*. The encyclical details an inter-related complex of personal, social and instrumental rights. The schema is ordered around the needs, freedoms and relationships inseparable from living as a human being in society. Personal rights are based on the needs appertaining to humanness itself. They are the right to life, to self-determination, to family life, to work, to freedom of conscience, to freedom of opinion and to freedom of religion. These are native or natural rights, inviolable claims endowed by nature on everyone. Social rights give body to personal rights in concrete societal contexts. They specify economic, social and cultural claims which the individual can make on his/her society. These claims include rights to food, clothing, shelter, rest, to medical care, to political participation, to migrate and to move within one's own country, to assembly and association, to adequate working conditions and wages, to education. Social rights articulate the conditions without which participation in society is grievously truncated. Without these rights – and their implementation – people can 'neither survive nor flourish'. Their personal rights are set at nought. Their personal dignity is placed under severe attack. They are marginated and relegated to the outer borders of social living. Finally, instrumental rights detail the requisite conditions in law, education, health care and economic organisation if personal and social rights are to be more than paper truths. Instrumental rights include rights to juridical protection of personal and social rights, to social security, and to the circumstances indispensable to the well-being of family life.[44]

This ordering of rights respects the interdependencies of the conditions for human development. It takes account of the need for a continual revision of rights analysis. Thus, it invites the further explicitation of rights claims as contexts change. Above all, it highlights the need for an outline criteriology for human rights strategies.

RIGHTS IN CONFLICT

It has been argued that a recurrent weakness in Catholic rights theory is the underestimation of conflict in human interaction, especially in social and economic structures. As a result, protest from the Church in favour of human rights frequently lacked impact. The mind-set of Catholic thinking, it is said, over-rapidly called for unity of nations, peoples and classes without addressing the roots of conflict. This objection has been raised against the corporatist elements in Pius XI's writings and against the concept of social harmony in a hierarchic society favoured by Leo XIII. It could be said of traditional Catholic human rights theory that while its foundations in personalism were impressively firm, its priorities in conflict were far from clear.

The problem is that frequently the conflicts most damaging to human rights are between two or more sectors of claimed rights. Rights to family life and to health are often threatened by the counter claims of economic freedom. Fundamental freedoms are often over-ridden by the pretensions of national security. A list of human rights gives no protection against pressure for a 'trade-off' – for example, to downplay rights to family life and to health in favour of the promise of economic growth, industrialisation or even 'law and order'. Basic human rights are such, however, that their denial at one level derogates from rights at all other levels. A trade-off simply does not work. Where civil and political rights are denied, social rights are rarely respected either. Where social justice is disregarded, political and civil repression is not far away.

An emergent view, implicit in post-conciliar documents, refuses to concur with the notion of a trade-off of human rights. Instead, it presents an overall perspective which, in recognising the fact of competing claims, sets priorities in the light of the values of social justice, social love, and the dignity of the human person. Notably, it argues the primacy of social rights. This perspective discourages maximal exercise of personal and group rights when the exercise of one person's or group's rights leads to another's injury. Thus, apart from a number of inalienable natural rights, all rights are subject to some qualification from the exigiencies of the common good or from the competing rights of others. Nor can instrumental rights, as defined earlier, be deemed absolute or unqualified. Unless these rights are moderated by a social rights policy they can lead to an entrenchment of privilege rather than the establishment of justice for all. The key in this line of argument is the subsidiarity of personal and instrumental rights to those social rights crucial to the mediation of human dignity: rights to food, clothing, shelter, social participation and personal development. The implementation of these social rights will rebound beneficially to the maintenance of both personal and instrumental rights.

If a rights theory is to have any credence it must show concern for every person without exception. Any approach which places little store by the core of personal rights – to life, to shelter, to food, to clothing, to freedom from arbitrary arrest, to freedom of opinion, conscience and religion – is fatally regressive and unacceptable. These rights are imprescriptible. A theology of human rights worthy of that name must continue to afford them central importance. Thereafter, it is imperative to face the question of priority rights especially where social policy is in the course of formation. Such priority will be determined by conceptions of the 'common good' or 'public order' – these, in turn, being affected by antecedent social, political and moral stances. In recent Catholic thought the integral development of people within a given society as well as in society as a whole has become a dominant principle. More specifically, the urgency to remedy the margination of countless people has become a major concern. Here the 'cry of the poor, the victim and the oppressed' is regarded as having greater claim than the demands of those more favourably placed. In recent documents of the magisterium the increasingly stringent qualification on the rights of private ownership represents this preference. General guidelines rather than clearcut principles are as much as one can expect here. Yet there are such guidelines which have bulked large in contemporary theological perspective on human rights in conflict. First, the needs of the poor take priority over the wants of those who are not poor. Second, the freedom (liberation) of those who are oppressed takes precedence over the liberties of those who are powerful. Third, the participation of marginalised persons and groups oppressed by an unjust order takes precedence over support for any order which excludes such people or groups.[45]

It is paradoxical that the more human rights work develops the less an acontextual formulation of such rights will be seen to suffice. Apart from a very narrow core of absolute personal rights on which there cannot be qualification, there is a whole body of crucial rights which are irreducible to neat tabulation. Especially in mind here are social and instrumental rights. In regard to these, the appropriate tabulation of today may become the alibi for privilege and domination tomorrow. And so, from a theological perspective, the strategy of human rights is more tentative – not in its commitment to the full gamut of human rights but in its sensitivity to changing contexts.

THE ASCESIS OF HUMAN RIGHTS

1. Not only do rights claims identify duties, they also lay an onus on those who claim them in turn to respect these same claims as they arise from others: 'those who claim their own rights, yet altogether forget or neglect to carry out their respective duties, are people who build with one hand and destroy with the other'.[46]

2. Rights are also modified by the needs of others. Certain patterns of action (and consumption), standing within people's strict rights, taken in the context of social justice and love, ought not to be done (or claimed). The exercise of rights may lead to injustice to another or others. Without being able to offer a calculation of strict obligation, a theology of human rights can present the imperative for austerity, for simplicity, even for asceticism. 'Live simply that others may simply live' (the slogan for a Lenten fast campaign in Ireland) is as much an urgent invitation to Christian witness as a developed theory of rights.

3. As earlier mentioned, when rights conflict rules or maxims are frequently invoked to loose the impasse. It is a commonplace of the philosophy of human rights that there is no meta-principle for the theoretical resolution of such conflicts. Since Catholic ethical and social thinking has recourse to the concept of the 'common good', it is proposed here to examine the concept, albeit briefly. It is a concept which is appealed to with mixed results. Seán McBride reminds us that 'rulers – even in democracies – often tend to elevate the doctrine of the "common good" or the "public interest" to the status of a legal answer for any act which infringes the rights of a minority or of an individual'.[47]

The 'common good' is variously understood. One understanding defines it in terms of certain socio-political ideals. Since these ideals require more precise specification, there is the danger that the 'common good' will elide with the ideology of the dominant group. Someone decides what the common good is and then defines human rights in terms of what subserves that 'good'. Instead of safeguarding human rights, this procedure would incur 'real danger of sophistically redefining actual slavery to an imposed ideal as freedom to do what one ought to do'.[48] On the other hand, there is the liberal democratic understanding of the common good as 'the complex of arrangements in any society which must be established if all the citizens are to enjoy the necessary freedom to exercise their basic rights and to pursue their interests without unnecessary infringement from others'.[49] The advantages of this conception are patent in its maximising of personal freedoms and opportunities. However, there remains the awkward question of determining what constitutes a 'necessary infringement' on the exercise of rights. With what bias is this determination made? Furthermore, wherever the call for a just distribution of the goods of society and for a better opportunity to participate in the social processes becomes urgent, the liberal democratic conception of the common good has come under strain. Its transformative impetus, grown weak since the establishment of bourgeois social values, is insufficient to underpin the thrust for a just and truly participative society.

In *Mater et Magistra,* John XXIII offers a somewhat different conception of the common good. There, the common good is described as 'the sum total of those conditions of social living, whereby men are enabled more fully and more readily to achieve their own perfection'.[50] In mind here is a set of social conditions facilitative of the personal development of all who make up society. Clearly, the common good is not simply the sum of individually conceived goods. Rather, John's idea of the common good looks in two directions. With the liberal view it looks to the good of concrete individuals. With the Marxist view, it endorses the need to set defined social goals – which, in the Catholic view, must be orientated towards social justice and the cherishing of persons. The ascesis required here, apart from the discipline of rigorous social analysis, is to refrain from the premature definition of what constitutes personal and social goods in the concrete instance. There is a temptation, not always avoided, heavily to define these goods in function of what Catholic teaching holds to be values and disvalues.

EIGHT

Ecology and Creative Stewardship

Ecology is described as 'that branch of biology which deals with the relation of living organisms to their surroundings, their habits and modes of life'.[1] However, there is more to the matter than biology. Ecology opens on to the ethical, political and religious dimensions of life. In its derivation (*oikos* = house) ecology reminds us that the cosmos is a home shared by many existents. Hence, the discipline has come to embrace a sensitivity to the disposition of living and non-living resources in the interest of the whole. As *logos* (= reason or word), it entails critical thought about the steps required to make ecological sensitivity more than a vague exhortation. Thus, the ecological and the political awareness are seen to be one.

The ecological problem is relatively new. As problem, it stems from the expansion of technology in the nineteenth century to 'a progressively accelerating reality, with correspondingly accelerating social impact'.[2] As challenge to politics, social ethics and religious practice it has been taken up very recently. Although ecology was already debated in the 1960s, the Second Vatican Council did not advert to it as a major problem. However, the issue was taken up in the subsequent years. In 1968, the sixth resolution of the Lambeth Conference urged Christians 'to take all possible action to ensure man's responsible stewardship over nature; in particular in his relationships with animals, and with regard to the conservation of the soil, and the prevention of the pollution of the air, soil and ocean'.[3] In 1971 Paul VI warned that 'by unconsidered exploitation, man risks [nature's] extinction and is further in danger of becoming the victim of that degradation. Not only does the material world become a permanent menace through pollution, new illnesses and an unbridled power of destruction: the human ambient goes out of control, creating for tomorrow an environment which may very well be intolerable for humankind'.[4]

This warning is all the more impressive in that *Populorum Progressio* (1968) did not show the same sensitivity: 'Industry is a necessity for economic growth or human progress ... by persistent work and use of his intelligence man gradually wrests nature's secrets from her and finds a better application for her riches'.[5]

The Synod of Bishops at Rome (1971) pointed out: ' ... such is the demand for resources and energy by the richer nations, whether capitalist or socialist, and such are the effects of dumping by them in the atmosphere and the sea that irreparable damage would be done to the essential elements of life on earth ... if their high rates of consumption and pollution which are constantly on the increase were extended to the whole of mankind'.[6]

It is imperative for the Churches to develop a theology of nature. To acquiesce in the rape of nature derogates from our stewardship of the earth. We cannot love God and be deliberately careless of nature. Again, inattention here leaves the field open to the cruellest exercise of technological imperialism, on the one hand, and the kind of ecology which makes light of social justice, on the other hand. There is an ambiguity in certain ecological arguments. These tend to restrict the benefits of technology to those already in possession of them. There is a selfish ring to the calls of people who, jealously guarding their comforts and profits, look for a moratorium on the spread of technology. A theology of the earth must reflect more than middle-class, first-world interests. The ecological imperative must include the call to justice. Justice and sustainability must proceed together: 'it cannot be that the ecological conflict is concerned only with sustainability, and the social conflict only with justice: both conflicts are about both'. A theological reflection on ecology 'must make more urgent the requirements of just distribution, not only of consumer goods but also of the economic power of production'.[7]

THE PROBLEM STATED

What, then, is the problem? The Brandt Report outlines it sharply: 'it is clear to us that the growth and development of the world economy must in future be less destructive to natural resources and the environment so that the rights of future generations are protected. Few threats to peace and the survival of the human community are greater than those posed by the prospects of cumulative and irreversible degradation of the biosphere on which human life depends'.[8] The same urgent note is raised by the Global 2000 Report in regard to the points of high pressure *viz.* food, energy, minerals, and forest: 'there is a potential for global problems of alarming proportions by the year 2000'.[9]

Those, like Barry Commoner, who have stimulated a new popular awareness present a direct case. Since there is an immense literature setting out that case, Commoner's 'three laws' will serve as a convenient summary. First, 'everything connects to everything else'. Since all being is relational, there is a knock-on effect to any interference with nature. The use of additives and pesticides in the production of crops can have dramatic results upon human health. Deforestation leads to soil erosion, to silting of river beds, to drought and 'desertification', to the destruction of thousands of species of animals, insects and plants. Second, 'everything must go somewhere'. This applies with tragic urgency to the dumping of radio-active wastes into the ocean. The Irish Sea has been declared 'the most radio-active sea in the world'.[10] Little wonder that despite the assurances of official bodies, people are increasingly reluctant to eat fish drawn from that source. Another example is the dispersal in the atmosphere of plutonium, one of the most carcinogenic elements known. According to the National Center for Atmospheric Research (U.S.), by 1975 more than five million metric tons have been dispersed by bomb-testing, satellite re-entries, nuclear accidents and effluents from nuclear re-processing plants. Uniformly distributed, one pound of plutonium is capable of inducing lung cancer in every person on earth![11] The third 'law' follows from the other two: 'there is always a cost'. There is no 'free lunch'. Ecological irresponsibility claims its toll: at home and abroad, now and in the future. Thus, through the depletion of valuable resources, through pollution, through the threat to people's health, the attack upon the ecosphere entails a punishment not simply on the guilty but also on the innocent.[12]

Many factors intermesh in the ecological crisis: ownership, technology, the natural arrogance of technological man, certain values and visions in society. It is also clear that the fate of future generations, the good earth of now, the hundreds of millions of undernourished and starving throughout the world, depend on humane and enlightened policies in regard to the use of the earth's resources. Even yet the power blocs seem infected by a moral blindness on the problem. The Brandt Report emphasises that much more than natural catastrophe is to blame for famine and underdevelopment. There are mismanagement, callousness and corruption. Were governments sufficiently wise and sufficiently courageous to devote to these problems of structure and distribution the resources they scatter on nuclear build-up, a hope for the future might be well founded. A former director of the U.N. development programme, Sudhir Sen, gives the lop-sided application of science as the reason for the disparity between major advances in tropical medicine and minimal achievement in tropical agriculture. Sen argues that recurrent food crises are due to folly even more than to exploitation of people. Others would be harsher in their critique of science and technology. They note that only 4% of the world's research and development is conducted where 70% of the world's population live. It is remarked that 'the search for more and ever more terrible weapons is of first priority among the scientists and engineers all over the world ... no other activity absorbs a greater proportion of the total investment in research than that activity spent on the progress of science and technology for war. The number of scientists and engineers involved in military projects is estimated at a million'.[13] It is perhaps understandable that the much vaunted objectivity of the sciences is increasingly called in question. Rubem Alves reminds us that 'knowledge is always a function of practical interests'. The question that must always be raised is 'which interests is contemporary science advancing'?[14]

THE AMBIGUITY OF SCIENCE AND TECHNOLOGY

A tangle of motives and ends lies behind the apparently disinterested procedures of science and technology. Doubtless, there is an entirely positive side to their genesis and development. Both science and technology prosecute the drive to know and understand, to change the environment for the better, even to use the goods of the earth for the benefit of oneself and one's fellows. This may be clearer when one considers the work of the lonely innovator, or the invention of the wheel, or the conversion to agriculture. However, with the industrial revolution, in its emergence and aftermath, science and technology seem to enter a qualitatively new state. There appear at once new possibilities for freedom from old servitudes as well as new modes of domination and destruction. The very success of science and technology gives rise to a multiple problem. The paradox of technological advances is that the solution of one problem often leads to the creation of a new one. In terms of ecology, the disastrous thing is that the prevalent scientific world view regards the universe as a mechanism. To use Charles Birch's phrase: 'it has led to a factory view of nature, with humanity pitted against nature'.[15] And if it is true that science reflects the society in which it is practised, then in an unjust society these injustices will be reinforced, and even consolidated, through scientific expertise.

For the old image of humble, detached, individual research is grievously outmoded, if not obsolete. The research scientist is frequently an employee, working with industry or the military-industrial complex. He or she performs frequently to research contracts or consultancies. He or she is often engaged in providing an answer for use by decision makers, political, industrial or military. Science and technology increasingly serve not the commonwealth of mankind but particular institutions and interest groups: 'when we think of "science", even the research section, we do best to conceive it first as part of the white collar, bureaucratic world of work; and then to consider the special features that make it particularly interesting and valuable'.[16] It is imperative to question the assumptions that scientists are always disinterested, that they are always competent in risk management as well as honest about failure, and that science policy is above subservience to minority interests.

The definition of technology, like most definitions, presents a very positive side. It is the purposive control of the environment, the programmatic extension of our ability to harness the forces of nature for specified ends. Understood thus, technology can be seen as the stewardship of our extensive and expanding habitat. Nevertheless, in its operation there are major ambiguities. The forces of greed, *hubris* or inordinate pride, profiteering and the service of partisan interests have all played their part: 'we cannot appreciate our "developed" technology in its world context without recalling the rape of resources and cultures in South America, the genocidal slave-trade in Africa, and the barbarously intolerant destruction of sacred customs and beliefs all over. Now the third world peoples are left in a hideous mess – social, intellectual and spiritual – thanks to that European imperialism whose material benefits we have taken for granted until very recently'.[17] All too often the underlying rationale of the technological enterprise is that nature is a thing – to be used up, controlled and dominated. Labour itself and, by consequence, the human person become a commodity. In his encyclical *Laborem Exercens,* Pope John Paul II vigorously contests this reduction. From a different standpoint, Herbert Marcuse traces the quantification of nature and the banishment from it of any inherent finality. Technological 'reason' degrades nature to pure quantity or extension (*res extensa*) at the mercy (ironic word) of science and technics (*res cogitans*). Being is then seen as raw material for production. Reality is straitened to the order of the mechanical. Truth is reduced to efficaciousness. Inexorably a universe is projected where the domination of nature and the manipulation of people proceed apace. Jürgen Moltmann notes the theological rationalisation of this fatal conjuncture: man is seen as the subject who rules; all other creatures are his objects; his rule over nature becomes an evidence that he is in the image of God. Lethal argument! In this direction lies the silencing of nature, the death both of nature and humankind.[18]

We can be sure that an apparently value-free science and an unbridled technology lead to destruction rather than to genuine development. We must, therefore, 'beware lest the stone age return on the gleaming wings of science' (Winston Churchill). On the other hand, it would be blind to ignore the potential of both science and technology for the benefit of humankind and of nature. Science and science-based technology brought comfort, better health and some social equality. J. R. Ravetz, by no means uncritical of scientific ideology, argues that 'the scientific movement deserves at least as much credit on a world scale as institutionalised religion ... '[19] The same author bluntly remarks: 'we now depend on science-based technology as on air ... '[20] It would be folly to discount the achievement and potential of technology in medicine, food production and distribution, education and communications. It is not a valid option to turn back the clock to a romanticism, religious escapism, fundamentalism or unthinking piety. Whereas technology makes a bad master it could become a good servant. Assuming the possibility of the conversion, one can argue that converted technological reason could help develop and use our resources for the benefit of all. The just, humane and sustainable society is not willed into existence by good intention or fair speech. It has to be constructed. In such construction a properly directed technology can represent an opportunity for the poor of the earth. It can facilitate the emergence of a more just, more humane order. It can serve the habitat rather than destroy it. The problem is that those at the nerve centres of power seem to follow another order. Whatever we can do (for profit or power) that we should do. Many governments base their decisions on health, education, housing and energy on pragmatic grounds with considerations of available technology as the dominant criterion. It can become a vicious circle since the operation of technology reflects the conditions of the society to which it is inset. Thus the problem stands. A proper distribution of science and science-based technology presupposes a widespread conversion to justice in the economic, political and social orders. It becomes ever clearer that the call for ecological sensitivity is part of the call to social justice.

By another route we come to see the ambiguity of science and technology. Of themselves, they do not provide 'a blue-print for survival'. Indeed, it has been remarked that the really contradictory idea of our time is that of such a blueprint. There is no ready-made solution to the problem of justice and sustainability.

Certainly there is no solution independent of far-reaching social, political and economic strategies. To call for restraint in the use of energy, for alternatives more sparing of resources in the long term, is both good and necessary. To contest the ever more furious arms race, whether conventional or nuclear, seems the only decent choice in that awful context. Yet these options are but a beginning. And they are by no means assured of a successful outcome. Witness the resistance of the rich countries to the very idea of a new, international, economic order. Witness the resistance of these same countries to any thorough-going proposal for social change. Only the incurably optimistic or the patently foolhardy can minimise the range of problems inherent to making technology our servant rather than our tyrant. To speak of global control seems remote theorising. To some it is redolent of totalitarianism. Yet, arguably, anything less is ineffective. By whom is control to be exercised? Under what code of values? By which criteria? These are but the obvious questions. No less easy are the questions about the nature of work so dramatically altered by the advent of high technology, about the obsolescence of the wage as an instrument of income distribution, about the use of increased and sometimes enforced leisure. There are few clear answers. One imperative is surely clear – the injustice to people and the attack upon nature must be reversed. We cannot sustain the world as a rich world. Justice requires that the rich become poorer that the poor may survive.

THEOLOGY IN A NATURE-SENSITIVE MODE

To question and oppose modes of domination inherent even to theological reflection has become a major task of theology. In an earlier chapter, the dangers of a monarchic conception of God were noticed. In this conception, God becomes a dominative figure over and against creation. Depending upon the society and the epoch, attributes are projected upon God which speak more of the time and society than of God. While Jesus deeply respected the Jewish concept of Yahweh, he nonetheless called in question the sheer monarchic extrinsicism of parts of the Old Testament. *Abba* was his preferred address to God – My Father, Little Father. The intimate, caring quality of God's presence was expressed both in Jesus' relaxed attitude to nature and his compassionate willingness to heal. Other periods there were through the Christian millenia when the cultural influences of Roman and Teutonic law became almost inextricably woven into people's concept of God. These were of majesty and power, rule and authority, sanction and punishment. Today, however, models of domination and power are severely controverted. The process theologians – Hartshorne, Cobb, Ogden and Whitehead himself – present the idea of a God compassionate and in solidarity with a striving cosmos. Rather than stand over and against creation, God enters it, is part of it, draws it upwards and forwards. All things have their inner (conative) and their outer (quantitative) aspects. They retain their freedom and their purposiveness even in their relation to God. God is the one in whom all things cohere, God is the 'persuasive lure of their inner life'. In this view, God feels with the universe in its pain, in its failure, in its joy. Not only does God give life and love, God is responsive to that life and love.

In such a model of God's compassionate presence, nature is no longer viewed as something to be dominated, battled or exhausted. It is accorded an intrinsic value and a respect previously denied it. Nature, or rather the systems within nature, can be seen both as subject and as object. This is neither animism nor unrestrained romanticism. For process theology is careful to elucidate a hierarchy of values: from the vibrant earth to lesser creatures through mammals to human beings. Relative to humankind, the rest of nature has both an intrinsic value – for itself as it were – and an instrumental value as the support of human life and well being. Charles Birch puts the balance of value succinctly: 'in the ecological view of nature, when the interests of people and elephants and kangaroos come into conflict, the non-humans count for more than zero in the equation'.[21]

The prevalent power-constructs come under attack from the several strands of liberation theology: womens' liberation, black theology, liberation theology as practised in Latin America and Asia. Cumulatively, they challenge the stereotypes of male, racist and colonial power. They vigorously abet the demand for sensitivity to people and nature by questioning in the name of Christianity every ideology of domination. In particular, feminist theological reflection insists that stewardship of the earth is antithetical to domination of it. Rosemary Reuther and Dorothy Dinnerstein argue that the domination of nature is based upon socially dominative models of master-servant and, indeed, upon the unbalanced relation between men and women.[22] Reuther criticises the theological models redolent of male domination even when these are used within theologies of liberation. For example, while she believes that the patriarchal God of the dominant white tradition has alienated people from themselves, from each other and from nature, she also fears that the equally transcendent almighty God of liberation and black theologies, if absolutised, could lead to similarly undesirable results. Reuther calls for a balance to the 'wholly other' concept fashioned by patriarchy: 'only a regrounding of the power of the future within the power of the primordial matrix can refound the lost covenant of man with nature and use a theology for the redemption of the earth'.[23]

It is, therefore, important to broaden our concept of God's presence to creation if our theology is to give adequate consideration to the new ecological problems. God still speaks. God still is present. For the Christian, God speaks and is present in many ways: in Jesus Christ, in people, in nature. J. H. Newman's claim is perhaps the most precise: 'there are three main channels which nature furnishes for our acquiring this knowledge *viz.* our own minds, the voice of mankind, and the course of the world ... '[24] Conscience, history and nature are beacons to God, each deserving proper respect. A toll has been exacted in regard to nature as sacramental of God's presence due to the pragmatism of science, the collapse of metaphysics and the Barthian critique of natural theology. Yet 'a post-modern interest in being' has made its presence felt wherever people have begun to reject technocratic modes of domination whether in politics, religion or culture. In the Christian tradition, this re-awakening interest in the quasi-sacramentality of nature can point to Paul's conviction that the works of God (*poiemata*) show forth God's power and divinity. Nature points to God and can witness to the divine presence: 'ever since God created the world, his invisible qualities, both his eternal power and his divine nature, have been clearly seen: they are perceived in the things God has made' (Rom 1:20).

Again, the hymn to Christ in Colossians 1 must surely direct us to an appreciation of our reconciled cosmos. All things have been reconciled in Christ. In him all things hold together – the cosmic system is itself an expression of the divine Word and the divine Love. The inescapable conclusion is that nature – our habitat and the theatre of God's salvific purpose – deserves appreciation as a trace of God's threefold presence, a *vestigium Trinitatis*. It is neither facile nor sentimental to emphasise that nature must be treated with the respect and justice its creaturehood deserves.

Hence it is not an indulgent novelty when people argue towards a new cosmological myth, a new story of the earth. A theological reflection conducive to wider justice and ecological sustainability needs an overarching interpretation of life, nature and personality. A critically re-established story of creation is needed. The Judaeo-Christian tradition has supplied us with normative materials for the purpose: the Old Testament itself, and in particular the Genesis accounts critically understood; the Gospel's haunting memory of a Christ who loved people in the concreteness of their surroundings; Paul's clear relation of creation to God's wide ranging redemptive purpose. The Eastern conception of Christ's universal rule – Christ the *Pantocrator* or *Cosmocrator* – has much to offer this reconstruction. So, too, has the Franciscan estimation of nature as a graced interlocutor of humankind. Again there is the relational concept of creation dear to medieval theology and devotion. And for those who today search for an holistic view of life, of nature and of religious faith, the world view offered by Teilhard de Chardin continues to exercise a fascination. Throughout his extensive work, he presents an ample rationale for respect of our habitat and constructive work for its improvement. We should love our world in its very materiality – not simply because of its origin in the sacred, but also because at its heart, drawing it forward beyond itself, is the creative love of God. No one more clearly than Teilhard has discerned the activity of God in the microscopic and macroscopic dimensions of our world. Few have expressed the consciousness of the divine process more beautifully than he. Likewise, as we have already seen, he integrates the infinitely extended operation of evolution with the creative, providential work of God. For many Christians Teilhard re-opens the exciting prospect of seeing Christ as the Reconciler of all creation, at once its origin, its animator and its goal. Teilhard's world-story can accomodate the infinitely small and the infinitely great. The virtually infinite span of time is the backdrop for his interpretation of the outlines of history. The barely hinted possibilities of stellar exploration and space colonisation are, in his view, no longer mere fiction but matter for serious reflection in the religious context. For Teilhard all these new questions can find answers coherent with orthodox Christianity. He regarded doctrine as a framework for the expansion of thought and sensibility rather than a strait jacket for the intelligence and the feelings. Whoever imbibes the spirit of Teilhard de Chardin and endeavours to understand his 'hyperphysics' will have ample material for a 'world story'. This story is respectful of nature, reverent of man and woman, and evocative of commitment to the cause of Christ – a Christ not merely of the heavenly domain but also of a universe translucent of his presence.

Whereas the world-view of classical science and technology, mirroring the mechanistic perception of nature, stands in tension with this 'mystical' thrust, the 'new physics' evinces no such hostility. There are many clues from relativity theory and quantum physics to relatedness-in-continuity of the physical manifold. Here, perhaps, is a renewed encouragement for resuming dialogue with the sciences, this time with the interests of nature as a continuum in mind. In an optimistic view, the split between reason and sensibility, between *logos* and *eros,* can be overcome. It becomes clearer that the universe is neither a plaything of the mythic gods nor a flat, lifeless object laid bare to the severe rationality of technology. Rather, it is a vital system of interrelated systems existing in in an interdependence hitherto unsuspected. Charles Birch has called for an 'interpretation of experience that will apply up and down the line from protons to people'. This is not to deny the differences within being. It is simply to underline that 'what we superficially see as static entities are, on analysis, processes'.[25] The major contributions of Teilhard de Chardin as well as of scientist-philosophers such as Birch is to move beyond a mechanistic view of the world to propose a newer mind-set and a newer language. Along with their positive estimation of how science can be done, and technology practised, they offer important elements for a more adequate story of creation. Indeed, they fashion the language and stimulate the imagination required for a dialogue between two sundered cultures. As these thinkers see it, the new story will be continuous with the old. However, it will extend the cosmogonic-historical myth of Genesis to a new standpoint from which the dialogue can open. The new story of creation will be more effective in inculating both reverence for the earth and responsibility for social justce.

SOME CONCRETE RECOMMENDATIONS APHORISTICALLY STATED

1. 'Hurt neither the earth, neither the trees, nor the sea.' (Rev 7:3)
This injunction is a direct challenge to an ethos of despoliation. Heedless denuding of forests, uncontrolled fishing of the ocean, wanton misuse of the soil, run counter to the text just cited. Equally disconsonant with the biblical command are the spewing of radio-active waste into the seas and the emission of plutonium into the atmosphere. It is true that since the advent of humankind animal species have been hunted and forests cut back. With the discovery of agriculture direct intervention to the environment began. Poor agricultural methods and the felling of trees caused once verdant lands to become deserts. Nevertheless the scale was not such as to interfere with the regenerative capacities of the earth for the work of replenishment. Now the scale of intervention is different. Technological operations, particularly nuclear technology, are such that the whole of nature is threatened and, for the first time, the ecosphere is in danger of reduction to sterility. Short of this, the 'greenhouse effect' and the strain on

renewable resources put a huge question mark over the prodigality of consumption in the rich nations. Our energy use has been raising the atmospheric temperature and destroying protective ozone layers. Thus is incurred the risk of dramatic change in weather patterns as well as the melting of polar ices. In these circumstances, the Christian conscience is driven to call halt. An Irish missionary who is also an anthropologist has movingly argued that the Christian sensibility cannot withdraw 'from the wider story of the earth in order to concentrate attention on the uniqueness of the Christian story'.[26]

2. 'Walk lightly upon the earth'.

One would tend to agree with Teilhard's strictures on eastern religion for its proclivity to sanction passivity in the face of suffering. Teilhard criticises its apparent failure to inculcate a developmental ethic. He speaks of its lack of 'a changeful orientation to the world'.[27] Yet the Taoist maxim, 'walk lightly on the earth', evinces a reverence for nature which traditions other than Christianity have shown. Taoism enjoins on its followers to reverence nature's way while Buddhism venerates nature's Dharma. The words of Lao-Tzu express this well: 'the great Tao flows everywhere, to the left and to the right, all things depend on it to exist, and it does not abandon them. It loves and nourishes all things but does not lord it over them'.[28] The religions of the East, with their respect for organic growth, raise a question over the anthropocentrism of the West, destructive of nature and subjugative of the greater part of the human race. We are thus directed back to liberative elements within the Judaeo-Christian tradition: that all life is held in trust, that as free beings with the capacity to destroy both life and environment we have a religious duty to cherish our habitat and our co-inhabitants. In a Christian setting, to walk lightly on the earth enjoins a respect for nature, stewardship of its resources, and co-operation with its systems insofar as we know them. Practically, it means care to replenish renewable resources. It commands opposition to the profligate consumerism which has trivialised people's lives with implanted need and arid satisfactions. It is not a matter of preaching austerity to those whose stomachs are empty and whose homes are bare. It is to call in question the luxury tastes of the rich countries and the rich classes, tastes which are met at high cost to people, animals and inanimate nature.

As if to show that the ethics of justice and sustainability bring us up against socio-political issues, the question of limits to growth arises. This question requires careful handling. One must ask:

Whose growth is to be limited? Is a moratorium to be placed on the growth of countries deeply depressed by the injustices of the present economic order? And what kind of growth is being discussed? Is it growth on the coat-tails of expansionist capitalism to the benefit of the multi-national corporations? Similar questions have to be put to the call for 'steady-state' economics. Is this not to freeze into permanence the injustices of the existing order? If earlier references to the interests served by the lopsided disposition of research and development have any validity, the pronouncements of the politicians and the experts need continued criticism. Many of the options they propose, many of the programmes they set, are irreconcilable with global solidarity and social justice.

What can Christians do? One can but raise questions which, however, may open some avenues. In the first place, there is the content of teaching and preaching. How far do preaching and official Church documents even yet include the concerns of justice and sustainability? Are we reminded frequently enough of the ambiguity of technics, not simply in medicine but in the areas of food production and distribution? Are we challenged as individuals, parishes, local Churches, to practise merciful stewardship of our habitat? Do our catechetical programmes include a creation theology supportive of a just, participative and sustainable society? Do our Churches stand with those people and groups (e.g. Greenpeace, the Green Alliance) who endeavour to raise consciousness on the ecological issue and who try to 'walk lightly on the earth'?

3. A chastened anthropocentrism

In several contexts throughout this study it was noticed that the *imago Dei* doctrine assigns to man/woman a special, even supereminent, place in God's creation. The doctrine brings out the special dignity, rights and duties of humankind. It opens onto the further insight of merciful stewardship of the earth. The biblical accounts are certainly anthropocentric but only in a qualified sense. Cumulatively they argue that creation is for man/woman. They proclaim that the glory of God is humankind fully alive. Nevertheless, creation as a whole has a significant place in God's plan. It is neither a shadow nor an insubstantial backdrop against which humankind stands out as the sole worthwhile reality. Creation itself, as Paul reminds us, is destined to 'share the glorious freedom of the children of God' (Rom 8:21-22). In the infra-human, according to both Augustine and Aquinas, there is a trace of the Trinity, a *vestigium Trinitatis*. A Christian theology, sensi-

174 Ecology and Creative Stewardship

tive to the evolutionary perspective, will perceive even more
clearly the slow, silent yet impressive upsweep of life as part of
God's plan for salvation and creation.

More recently, in the context of an ethic of responsible stewardship, Bernard Häring has written of 'a chastened, sober
anthropocentrism'. He argues: 'we cannot overlook the levels of
being, the grades of significance, and above all, the position of
man in the universe. A chastened, sober anthropocentrism implies a consciousness of our belonging to the whole. In a certain
sense, we can say: "We are members of one another" also in view
of sub-human reality'.[29] A responsibility for both justice and
sustainability pin-points the imperative for restraint in the use of
God's gift of creation. If humankind abstracts from its solidarity
with nature, the sufferer is not only nature but humankind itself.
Sixty years ago, John A. Ryan S.J. wrote: 'the only life worth
living is that in which our cherished wants are few, simple and
noble'.[30] It is at once a very old and a very new principle. It is as
old as the Sermon on the Mount. It is as new as the liberative
movements which have sprung up not only in Latin America but
in Asia, North America and Western Europe. It adds point to the
invitation of the Lenten adage used by *Tróciare*, the Irish Catholic
development agency – 'live simply that others may simply live'.[31]
A change in the habits of waste, consumption and general profli-
gacy will have to come if world poverty is to be realistically
addressed.

Thus emerge repeated calls for a realistic ceiling on standards
of living in rich societies, in the interest of justice and sustainability. In mind is not the birth control ideology once opposed by both
Peking and the Vatican. Unacceptable, too, from the Christian
point of view is to freeze an unjust *status quo* with its scandalous
disparities of wealth, nutrition, and standards of living between
the northern and southern hemispheres. Since justice for humankind and justice for the earth intermesh, one has to speak of a
radical overhaul – a revolutionary change – in the social, political
and economic systems which bestride the world. One should not
expect from a creation theology the technical answers to these
challenges. One may, however, look for a prophetic impetus to
contest the despoliation of people and nature, so much a feature
of our technological age. Whereas unbridled technology assumes
that what can be done may be done, a creation theology will
enjoin a collective asceticism. In this asceticism the pretension to
play God with other human beings and with nature would be
reined back. What we can do, we sometimes ought not to do
(Moltmann). Here the Christian values of stewardship, solidar-

ity, respect, mercy and moderation come to the fore with renewed clarity. Nothing less than a chastened anthropocentrism is indicated. Humankind is not the only inhabitant of the earth. The refusal to sanction rabid self-indulgence is healing for both people and nature when given consistent effect. People are edged away from a dominative, exploitative mind-set towards a nature-sensitive, justice-oriented view. This, in turn, must lead not to romanticism but to the harder outlines of liberative action. John Carmody's call to politicians and opinion formers is daunting yet realistic: 'If the scenarios of the environmentalists are warranted … a rational politics or religion would … calculate the global levels of consumption supportable in the future, imagine how fairly to distribute the sacrifices needed to meet these levels, and set to the work of shifting the culture at large from a base in relatively gross material satisfactions to a base in spiritual satisfactions immeasurably more human'. [32]

4. *'The earth is the Lord's and everything in it' (1 Cor 10:26)*.

This Pauline text contests the taboos and superstitions of ages. It represents the smashing of idols (*gotzendammerung*) whereby the cosmic superstitions inculcated by the mystery religions were thrown aside by early Christianity. Such protestations of freedom earned for the first Christians the charge of atheism. However, Paul's intention is quite different. It is to show the legitimacy of responsible freedom and to enjoin wise stewardship of creation on the Christians at Corinth. Paul's de-divinisation of nature should not be interpreted as a licence to despoil the earth. On the contrary, the thrust of faith in the lordship of Christ is towards reverence for matter as open to spirit, even to divinity. Faith in Jesus as Lord of all joins faith in creation in a new veneration for the deepest possibilities of humankind and of nature as a whole. Whoever accepts the full reach of the incarnation can no longer deprecate creation.

Nevertheless, it has been argued with passion that Judaeo-Christianity is manipulative, artificial and reductive of nature. [33] It is claimed that Christianity is not conducive to ecological sensitivity. Those conversant with the sad history of the earth's despoliation and the collusion therein by Christians, sharply question the credentials of the Church in calling halt to the earth's domination. Perhaps their strongest argument is from reprobable performance: 'by their fruits shall you know them'. It was the 'Christian West' which spawned, and then blessed, the excesses of colonialism, the savageries of exploitative trade, the inequities of the industrial revolution. 'Increase, multiply and subjugate the earth' has been taken only too literally. Some traditions within

Christianity have been closely allied to the rise of capitalism. The 'two kingdoms' doctrine, in its separation of the kingdom of Christ from the kingdom of the world, can undergird a dominative attitude to nature. It can give rise to a type of faith which fits comfortably to capitalist economics of unlimited growth and selfish development. Witness the attack by a group of American lay people on the draft pastoral by the U.S. bishops on the American economy. The 'counter-pastoral' nakedly puts it: 'who declares for development declares for profit'.

On the other hand, by contesting the old taboos of the Semitic world, Judaism enabled people to see their role of stewardship more clearly. It facilitated the responsible husbandry of nature. No longer divine, nature could be seen as the ambient in which God was served faithfully. The New Testament did for the Hellenic world what the Old Testament did for the Semitic. It emptied the pantheon of pagan religion in proclaiming the unique lordship of Christ. Thus, argue the apologists for Christianity, a new motivation was given to view creation as the domain of God entrusted to human care. The sacramentalism of the medieval Church consolidated this positive estimation of nature as God's gift, a theatre of God's presence. The Catholic tradition consistently refuses to sunder nature from grace (although the nuance of the term 'nature' in this context should be noted). If this be coupled with St Thomas' insistence that being is God's noblest gift (with the exception of grace), the basis is laid for a religious perception of ecology.

The World Council of Churches has given an invaluable lead in its continuing application to the study of 'faith and science in an unjust age'. Particularly significant is its insistence on the mutual implication of social justice and ecological sustainability.[34] Underlying its argument is the perception that the earth is under the claim of God revealed in Jesus Christ. Side by side with this witness, worthwhile guidelines have come from Roman Catholic sources linking the work of justice to sensitivity to creation. There is the peculiar circumstance, noted by J. B. Metz, that the Catholic Church, precisely in its long hostility to the changes wrought by the Enlightenment, has the opportunity to move around and beyond the unacceptable consequences of that bourgeois revolution. It is not to its credit that Catholicism has sturdily resisted the liberal programme of freedoms: civil, political, intellectual and religious. On the other hand, the relation of Roman Catholicism to the industrial revolution has been uneasy. In an earlier chapter it was argued that that relation has become even more strained since the pontificate of John XXIII. The critique of injustice to people and to nature has been effectively articulated within the theology of the last twenty years. Few have expressed it better than Rosemary Reuther when she argues: 'the abuse of the resources of the earth becomes acute when a small ruling class ... use the labour of the vast majority of people to extract these resources, but without having to take into consideration their rights and needs as human persons'.[35] The earth does not belong to us whether we be few or many: it is the Lord's and is entrusted to our care.

5. St Francis of Assisi.

Even minimal acquaintance with St Francis of Assisi discloses his perception of a friendly communion between people, animals and the earth: all live in the same great house of God the Father.[36] In this perception Francis was not unique. Columban of Bobbio, Brendan of Clonfert, Kevin of Glendalough, Cuthbert of Lindisfarne – to mention but a few – are noted for their appreciation of all living creatures and their harmony with the habitat. Nevertheless, in an unparalleled way Francis' consentience with all living things has stimulated religious feeling and artistic imagination in the eight centuries since his death in 1226. His first biographer, Thomas of Celano, intimates Francis' 'most gentle feeling of devotion toward all things'. Celano also writes of Francis: 'he discerned the hidden things of creation with the eye of the heart, as one who had already escaped into the glorious liberty of the children of God'.[37]

Were this an easily purchased thing, a sentimental fancy or the romantic projection of an overwrought imagination, then Francis of Assisi would have little to say to us. However, Francis offers much more than facile piety. Leonardo Boff rightly senses in Francis the marriage of Eros and Agape. Eros is a life affirming movement. It enlivens, deepens and transforms both its subject and its object. At its best, it is a co-feeling, a *consentire*. It is 'compassion' – a sympathy and an entering into communion with its object. It unites subject and object 'with fellow feeling, with enthusiasm, with desire'. Agape goes further. Without crushing eros, it goes beneath it to reach 'the foundation and the fascination of all love which is God, giving himself in and through all things'.[38] The marriage of Eros and Agape enabled Francis to achieve that kind of *caritas* whereby he could recognise 'in all things beautiful the One who is beauty and in face of whatever was good to shout: the One who has made us is best'.[39]

It can be argued that 'the little poor one' (*poverello*) perfected certain traditions rather than inaugurated something entirely new. E. A. Armstrong, in his *St Francis: Nature Mystic,* adduces the influence of the Irish tradition of spirituality. The traits of this spirituality were total dedication to Christ, acceptance of poverty, flexible organisation, and a deep love of nature.[40] There is a striking coincidence of these characteristics with the thrust of Franciscanism in its earliest days. This is all the more significant in that Irish spirituality still exercised a strong influence even in the eleventh and twelfth centuries. The Irish foundation at Ratisbon (1090) was certainly influential. At Nuremburg and Vienna there was an Irish monastic presence even into the fifteenth century. Closer to Francis' own territory was Bobbio where Columban's memory remained vibrant centuries after Francis' death. Like Francis, Columban esteemed poverty and lived a deep communion with nature. Common to both men was a love of the Scriptures. Both would have been influenced by the biblical praise of God in God's handiwork. The magnificent Song of the Three Children (Dan 3:57-88,56) – with its praise of God in wind and water, birds and animals, elements and earth – would have been familiar to Francis and was particularly dear to later Irish spirituality. It is with good reason that Armstrong makes much of these coincidences and insinuates a real influence of Irish ideas and practices on the early Franciscan movement.[41]

What, then, was the inner thrust of Francis' 'nature mysticism'? It would be inappropriate to confine it to simple piety. Rather, Francis' spirituality grew out of his ability to perceive the presence of God in every being and to cherish every existent in its filial relation to God. In other words, Francis' vivid apprehension of the fatherhood of God entailed for him a fraternity with all that God had made. When Francis spoke of Brother Sun and Sister Moon, of Brother Fire and Sister Water, he had in mind 'the calm brotherhood of all beings, children of the same Father, and brothers and sisters to each other'.[42] Even more, this confraternity with earth, air, fire and water, with plants and animals and birds, with every man and every woman, represented a cosmic mysticism harmoniously blended into an evangelical mysticism rooted in love for the person of Christ.[43]

When Francesco Bernardone left his family home and his previous way of life, a multiple conversion was in train. Above all, there was a conversion to Christ, the Man from Nazareth, discerned in the countenance of every poor and suffering person. One of Francis' first works was to serve the lepers, the most abandoned of all the poor. There is ample evidence that this was no easy task for the hitherto fastidious devotee of gaiety, courtesy and refined living. At work was a movement from relationships defined by money, power and self-centred gratification to simplicity, compassion and other-regarding renunciation. Thereafter, Francis sought out woods and secluded places. This was not so much a *fuga mundi* as the adoption of a new mode of being characterised by frugality, heroic love and a refusal to dominate or exercise lordship. It was as if the Franciscan project was to exemplify a world in which equality and fraternity would be the seedground of charity.

Leonardo Boff rightly speaks of Francis' practice of a cosmic democracy. This was a mindset of 'being with' rather than 'being over': it bespoke a fraternity conceived of in all-inclusive terms. And so one finds that Francis showed an unfailing gentleness to his colleagues in the new congregation, to women, to the poor, to animals, to plants, and even to the frequently threatening elements. This cosmic fraternity/sorority is nowhere clearer than in Francis' Canticle of Brother Sun, completed as Francis drew near his own death. Again, it is said that the words 'brother/sister' were especially dear to him. The key values in this confraternity are an estimation of God's intimate presence in Christ and a consequent gentleness with persons and nature. Correspondent to these values were appropriate modes of action such as hospitality, friendship, co-operation with others. At the same time, the return to nature by Francis and his companions 'may have nurtured in [them] an independence which rendered some of them less amenable to authoritarian direction'.[44]

He whom Dante called 'the sun of Assisi' combined in one person and in one short life-time religious feeling, erotic love of creation and harmonious social relationships. Perhaps because of this very fact, his influence goes well beyond the order he founded and the Church he loved. Boff does not exaggerate when he claims that Francis is 'the purest figure ... of the dreams, the utopias and of the way of relating panfraternally that we are all searching for today'.[45] In particular, his approach to the exercise of power, to women, to the poor and to nature, contains a rich mine of inspiration and challenge. Just as the *sequela Jesu* is not a matter of direct imitation, neither are we called to emulate Francis' parables-in-action of his exemplary charity. We are not expected to preach to birds. Nor can we appeal to 'Brother Fire' to cauterise diseased parts of the body as in St Francis' day. For modern Christians, and others besides, it is Francis' mode of being which is most instructuve. It would be all too easy to dismiss him as a fascinating but utterly discountable example of childlike piety. This would be a serious underestimation of the enormous inner strength which powered his life project. For he had fashioned a new way of being human in God's presence. It was a healing, attractive, reconciling way. All too soon it was cast in another direction as institutional interests and the demands of larger power structures tamed the explosive power of Francis' own way. This, however, was not Francis' doing. He continues to provoke us to rediscover the paternity of God and the fraternity of Christ in our world and in our brethren. He challenges us to look once again at patterns of domination which exploit the poor, which alienate man from woman and woman from man, which despoliate nature, which drive a wedge between the self and God who is then fashioned in the image of the oppressor and the powerful. If universal fraternity/sorority is the result of being poor as Francis was poor, then his critique of our present day assumptions is truly radical.

NINE

Justice and the
Goods of the Earth

There is a grim realism in David Hume's comment that 'it is only
from the selfishness and confined generosity of man, along with
the scanty provision nature made for his wants that justice derives
its origin'[1] Hume identifies two factors here: in the first place, the
imperative to regulate the inhumanity of people to people and, in
the second, the responsibility to husband the goods of the earth.
Here and there in mythic or utopic writings we are reminded that
Hume's grey but accurate logic can be transcended. That is to say,
selfishness need not be taken as the abiding norm. There is
another way for human beings to relate in mutual respect and
solidarity. And the earth, if respected and cherished, is generous
in the support of life. The aspiration to a fairer, less pain-ridden
disposition of the earth's goods is well expressed by the Greek
poet Aristophanes:

> All shall be equal and equally share all wealth and enjoyment,
> nor longer endure, that one should be rich and another be
>   poor,
> that one should have acres, farstretching and wide,
> and another not even enough to provide himself with a grave:
> All this I intend to correct and amend –
> now, all of all blessings shall freely partake,
> one life and one system for all men I'll make.[2]

It has been a recurrent aspiration in many cultures that the
iniquities of great wealth and grinding poverty shall be abolished.
Similarly, the belief is evident in prophetic and utopic writings
that such disparity was not in the original scheme of things.
Injustice results from an aboriginal fault or fall.

Yet, on the whole, these sentiments did not have much cutting
edge in their respective societies. It is said that the strongest and
most enduring social criticism in the ancient world came from the
Jewish heritage. While it would be a deformation of the biblical
witness to impose upon it Proudhon's dictum 'all property is
theft', one discerns there a strong critique of unjust, inhumane
profiteering. A subversive memory haunted the best of Jewish

religious consciousness. The memory was of a time when Israel itself was subject to a harsh slavery, reversed by God's dramatic, liberative gesture in the Exodus. This memory served as a sharp criticism of the thrust to domination emergent in Israel itself: 'Do not ill-treat or oppress a foreigner; remember that you were foreigners in Egypt' (Ex 22:21. Cf. Lev 19:33-34 and Deut 10:19). Further, Leviticus admonishes: 'You do not own the land: it belongs to God and you like foreigners are allowed to make use of it' (Lev 25:23). There follows a stringent code for the just treatment of the poor. An impoverished Jew, forced to sell land, was to have it restored in the Jubilee year. It was as if God insisted upon the restoration of an original equality. Usury and profiteering were excoriated, especially when these practices battened on the poor: 'Do not make him pay interest on the money you lend him and do not make a profit on the food you sell him. This is the command of the Lord your God who brought you out of the land of Egypt ... ' (Lev 25:37-38).

This social criticism develops into the dramatic protests of Amos and Isaiah against the exploitation practiced by a ruling class totally forgetful of its origins. And so the shepherd of Tekoa (Amos) and the Jerusalem nobleman (Isaiah) bring to expression some of the most potent social protest known to religious literature. Their prophetic voice rings out to stir people even today in contestation of the miasma of oppression which darkens our world as it darkened the society of Amos and of Isaiah.

In the New Testament several parables criticise social injustice. The story of Dives and Lazarus (Lk 16:19-31) highlights a distortion of right relationship. In the riches of one and the poverty of the other 'the relationship of brotherhood and equality which we accept every time we call God Father, is being denied in practice'.[3] The parable of the rich landowner extends the critique – the single-minded pursuit of wealth is a deformation of right relation to God (Lk 12:16-21). There is a radical critique of wealth in the Gospel paradox: 'it is easier for a camel to go through the eye of a needle than for a rich man to enter the kingdom of God' (Mk 10:24). In announcing the kingdom of God, Jesus condemns the 'deceit of riches'. It is difficult to know which are the actual words, the *ipsissima verba* of Jesus in Luke's version of the Beatitudes, yet these Beatitudes clearly reflect Jesus' own critique of irresponsible wealth: 'Blessed are you poor ... hungry ... weeping ... woe to you rich ... filled ... laughing now' (Lk 6:20). Perhaps the most striking glimpse we get of the early Church's critique of inequality is the 'communism of love' (Bloch) described in Acts 4:32: 'The group of believers was one in mind and heart. No one said that any of his belongings was his own, but they all shared with one another everything they had ... There was no one in the group who was in need ...'

The Jerusalem experiment in common ownership is dominated by a strong conviction of the imminent return of Christ. This anticipation, as well as the memory of Jesus' own attitude to property, may have led to an initiative which would haunt the most generous minds of Christianity throughout the centuries. The barriers raised by possessions came down. Communal goods were for disbursal as need indicated. Some people sold their property to support their brethren. Others placed houses at the disposition of the Church. The chief activity, along with prayer and fellowship, appears to have been the preaching of the Gospel to the Jews. The expectation of the immediate return of Christ led to an almost hand-to-mouth style of living in sharp contrast to the productive industry at Qumran, the seat of the Essenes. In the early community of Christians at Jerusalem 'organisation was kept to a minimum and, in view of the extensive expectation of the imminent return of Jesus, further forward planning was completely absent'.[4] Strain was felt as the return of Jesus did not occur. Accusations were made of partiality and neglect (Acts 6:1ff). In the fifth decade of the first century the occurrence of famine placed further pressure on the Jerusalem community. Was this the community for which Paul instituted collections (Gal 2:10 and Rom 15:20)? Was it the community which was later to secede from the broader Church to become the Ebionite movement, the Church of the poor?

It would be interesting to follow the theme of the use of goods through the rest of the New Testament. While one finds a vigorous contestation of the environing values, one notices that this critique remains within the Church. The insistence of Paul that there is neither Jew nor Greek, neither male nor female, neither bond or free, is taken seriously within the community of Christians. The limitations of minority status confined social protest for practical purposes within the community. Edward Schillebeeckx points out: 'beyond question, the New Testament recognises that in addition to the inner renewal of life, the life-style of the kingdom of God includes a renewal and improvement of social structures. These New Testament Christians practised this in the sphere in which they were really able, in the structuring of their own Christian community ... '[5] As abuses occurred they were sharply rebuked by Paul and James. The class distinction at the *agapoi* in Corinth is sternly reprobated by Paul: 'would you rather despise the Church of God and put to shame the people who are in need ...' (1 Cor 11:22).

The words of James are unforgettable in their depth of emotion: 'as believers in the Lord Jesus Christ, the Lord of glory, you must never treat people in different ways according to their outward appearance ... If you show more respect to the well dressed man ... then you are guilty of creating distinctions amongst yourselves ... Who are the ones who oppress you and drag you before the judges? The rich ...' (James 2:1-6).

The ideals of freedom, equality and fraternity/sorority are clearly presented in the New Testament. It is a freedom in the Holy Spirit, a fraternity in the communion (*koinonia*) that should be the Church, and an equality of all in the one Jesus Christ. If no major critique of slavery or poverty is mounted, this is most probably because these early Christians 'had to limit themselves to the construction of a community ethic within an unfriendly, indeed hostile world ... '[6]

CHURCH FATHERS AND A CRITIQUE OF WEALTH

With the Church Fathers of the third, fourth, and fifth centuries one meets a biting social criticism which challenges the larger society. Through the fourth century, Christianity began to grip the minds and hearts of people from the most varied backgrounds. In its sense of community, its openness to all, its eagerness to help those in need, and its doctrine on the right use of goods, the new faith challenged the attention of the ancient world. It is said of early Christianity; 'even though it endured external persecutions and internal divisions, it ultimately succeeded in capturing the minds and hearts of the majority of the urban population in the Empire'.[7] These Christian communities retained the remembrance of Christ's love for the poor and outcast. Just as in the primitive communities there was an ethos of sharing, particularly at Jerusalem, in the local Churches of the third and fourth centuries there remain both a sharp criticism of exploitative greed and a worthwhile action towards eliminating deprivation amongst the brethren. A strong critique of wealth was offered. For example, in the aftermath of the Decian persecution, when many Christians had apostasised, Cyprian of Carthage examines the causes of that collapse: 'Because the long years of peace had undermined our practice inthe way of life God had given us ... each was intent on adding to his inheritance ... Forgetting what the faithful used to do under the apostles, and what they should always be doing, each one with insatiable greed was engrossed in increasing his own property'.[8]

St Basil of Caesarea (fourth century) wrote of the amnesia caused by wealth. People forgot that they were stewards, not owners, of God's creation. Thus they became unjust. They came to resemble 'a man who, in taking his seat in the theatre, would like to keep others from entering ... and be the only one to enjoy the show that all others have just as much right to see'.[9] St John Chrysostom responded to a criticism of his preaching: 'I am often reproached for continually attacking the rich. Yes, because the rich are continually attacking the poor ... those I attack are not the rich as such, only those who misuse their wealth ... '[10] Interesting from the point of view of this study is the continual re-iteration of the right of all people to the goods of the earth. In the early third century Clement of Alexandria emphasised that 'all things are common and not for the rich to appropriate an undue share. That expression, therefore, "I possess and possess in abundance; why then should I not enjoy" is suitable neither to man nor to society ... God has given us ... the liberty of use, but only in so far as necessary; and he has determined that the use should be common. And it is monstrous for one to live in luxury, while many are in want'.[11] With customary vigour, Ambrose of Milan reminded his hearers: 'God has ordained all things to be produced so that there shall be food in common for all and that the earth should be the common possession of all. Nature has produced a common right for all but greed has made it a right for a few'.[12] In this light one better understands Ambrose's denial that alms could ever be a sufficient excuse for inequity: 'you are not making a gift of your possessions to the poor person. You are handing over to him what is his'.[13] Chrysostom is even sterner: the rich, even those who have acquired their goods honestly, are in possession of the goods of the poor.[14] Under the surface of this tradition is the conviction that private property with its attendant divisions and inequalities is the result of the fall. The most accurate reflection of the patristic teaching is that the earth and its fruits are intended by God for the enjoyment and sustenance of all. This finality has precedence over any individual rights.

Many of these Fathers propose measures to resolve penury and deprivation in their communities. Tertullian speaks of a common chest the accumulation of which should be devoted to the poor, the prisoners, the orphans, and the destitute. Chrysostom's priorities for the use of resources is highly instructive: 'first fill him [Christ] when he is hungry and then set his table with lavish ornaments ... don't neglect your brother Christ in his distress while you decorate his house ... '[15] The Shepherd of Hermas offers a practical strategy for fasting: 'on the day you fast do not taste anything except bread and water. Compute the total expenses for the food you would have eaten in the day ... and give it to a widow or orphan or someone in need ... '[16] To the clergy Origen of Alexandria proposes: 'we must not keep for ourselves more than we give to our hungry or thirsty brothers ... '[17]

These are strands of an often submerged tradition. They show a radical commitment to just sharing of the goods of creation. It has been argued that the drive to eliminating poverty in the Christian communities was unique in antiquity. Unfortunately, when Christians attained social establishment the prophetic edge became blunt. It is a sad feature of subsequent centuries that reformers and prophets were frequently persecuted in the Church itself. While many worthwhile initiatives in Christian fraternity/ sorority came from within the Church, it is an unresolved enigma that more effective protest against slavery came from sources other than official Christianity.[18]

THE CHALLENGE TO THEOLOGY POSED BY POVERTY

According to Gustavo Gutierrez, the first challenge in regard to poverty is to renounce the idea we have of it. Poverty is the need of the suffering individual. Yet, if it is to be realistically confronted, it must be seen as transcending that. It must be viewed in its extent, its forms, its causes and effects. It is a fact of staggering proportion. It is underdevelopment. It is deprivation of the necessary means to live. It is hunger, homelessness, bad health. It is lack of access to the goods and services which are the right of all. It is voicelessness in the decisions which affect one's life. It is lack of participation in the social processes. It is a margination perpetuating itself from one generation to the next. It puts a question mark over easy talk about the common purpose of the goods of the earth. It rises up to mock the Genesis command to stewardship of creation. What kind of stewarding can be exercised by those who are deprived even of the means to live?

In a study such as this the cumulation of statistics is of limited help. Yet some quantification of poverty is essential if its scandal is to strike home. More than eight hundred million people live in conditions of absolute poverty. Twenty million die annually of starvation. Over five hundred million people go to bed (if they go to bed) hungry each night. The major problem of our ninth decade is food shortage – this at a time when resources, both technological and economic, are poured into arms, nuclear weaponry and so-called national security. The disparity between rich and poor becomes so evident that a major social cataclysm seems ever more likely and, even, understandable. The disparity is particularly evident between northern and southern hemi-spheres, but it flaunts itself in backwaters of poverty throughout the First World.

There is no easy innocence in the face of such massive suffering. The millions who die each year of starvation, not to speak of those whose physical and psychological development is impaired, raise a cry which cannot be ignored. Poverty, hunger and disease stalk a rich world. A clear responsibility devolves upon those who retain a relative affluence. The developed countries have prospered at the expense of the poor of the earth. To a scandalous degree, they continue to do so. The introduction to the Brandt report carries the warning: 'there is a real danger that in the year 2000 a large part of the world's population will still be living in poverty. The world may become overpopulated and will certainly be over-urbanised. Mass starvation and the dangers of destruction may be growing steadily – if a new major war has not already shaken the foundations of what we call world civilisation'.[19]

From the poor countries has come the demand for a new international economic order. Formulated for the first time at the sixth special session of the United Nations in 1974, it has passed into the received terminology of those who call for a more equitable social, economic and distributive system. It is about the transfer of appropriate technology, the creation of an international commodity market, and the provision of funds to give greater participation to poor countries. The major documents of the post-conciliar Church realistically assess the scale of poverty, calling for a discernment of its roots and strategies for its elimination. Since the pontificate of Leo XIII a totally different analysis of wealth and poverty is made. Poverty is recognised as a structural problem requiring public-political as distinct from private-ascetical responses. In the social teaching of popes since John XXIII a political demand is made for the implementation of policies to ensure access to goods and services requisite to foster human dignity. *Octogesima Adveniens* stresses the need to pass from pure economics to politics: 'in the social and economic field, both national and international, the ultimate decision rests with political power ... [20] This is a notable shift from the moralising tone of earlier analyses which merely called for charity on the part of the rich and resignation on the part of the poor.

Theological analyses of poverty cannot acquiesce in appeals to the 'will of God' and the 'natural order of things'. Disquisitions on spiritual poverty and detachment today find decreasing theological support. Poverty is an evil to be fought. It cripples people physically and psychologically. It is the result of unjust action hardening into oppressive structures. It arises from political, social and economic patterns of injustice. Whereas God has given creation to all, human negligence, greed and stupidity keep their victims starving and poor. A distinction is made between poverty and impoverishment. Poverty is material poverty: it is the result of misfortune, lack of natural resources, even the result of natural catastrophe. Impoverishment, on the other hand, is the result of unjust actions and structures. Historically these patterns were set up by the rich colonial powers. Today they are perpetuated in a more subtle way, often by these same powers, and aggravated by the stranglehold of neo-colonial classes on land and resources within the poor countries.

SOCIAL SIN

This distinction between poverty and impoverishment demonstrates that the causes of deprivation are neither supinity nor fecklessness on the part of the deprived. The culprit is rather the distortion in social structures whereby a minority prosper and the great majority of people are despoliated of the conditions of human development. One can better understand the criticism by the assembly of Latin American bishops at Puebla of inadequate housing, infant mortality, homelessness, bad health, starvation wages, unemployment and underemployment, compulsory migration – in short, the sub-continental reality of impoverishment. This impoverishment is 'a scandal and a contradiction to Christian existence', 'contrary to the plan of the Creator', 'a most devastating and humiliating kind of scourge'. The bishops go on to condemn such structures as the well-springs of injustice. They make several references to social sinfulness. The yawning gap between the rich and poor is described as 'a situation of social sinfulness'. Sin is shown to have both personal and social dimensions. Not only is there personal sin, there are sinful situations 'which cruelly affect countless human beings and diminish the freedom of all'.[21]

In *Foundations for a Social Theology*, Dermot A. Lane speaks of social sin as the 'destructive and dehumanising trends which have become built into the basic structures that organise life'. Lane continues: 'social sin is not normally planned in a deliberate or conscious way; instead, it arises directly as a consequence of human blindness or personal sin'.[22] The value of this emphasis on social sin is that it deprivatises sin and highlights its social havoc. To adapt a contribution to the Synod of Bishops (1971): it is sinful to live like Dives with Lazarus at the gate. In *The Work of Justice*, the Irish bishops state: 'unless people develop an awareness of social sin and a positive social conscience there is little hope of our achieving a just or Christian society'.[23] These emphases bring into focus the distortion of God's purposes in exploitation, inequity and injustice. There is the further implication that condonation of, or involvement with, unjust structures is social sin. It is an interesting consideration that social sin may be another, perhaps more effective, expression of original sin, the sin of the world. We are challenged by the Gospel to overcome this 'network of domination' with as much urgency as we are bidden to overcome our personal sin.

In today's circumstances the option against sin must include an option against social sin. In other words, the rejection of sin implies a firm rejection of 'embodied injustice' and an unambiguous solidarity with the victims of such injustice. The statement of the Roman Synod of 1971 becomes all the more significant: 'action on behalf of justice and participation in the transformation of the world fully appear to us as a constitutive dimension of the preaching of the Gospel'.[24] This means that Christians as individuals, and their Churches as institutions, must oppose the forces of impoverishment. In large part, these processes make up the collective dimension of sin. Where the social dimension of sin is identified realistically, when sin is not confined to the traditional bounds of sexuality, several consequences follow for theological reflection and, even more crucial, for the practice of Christians.

THE OPTION FOR THE POOR

One of the most significant concepts to emerge since the Second Vatican Council is the 'option for the poor'. It has been remarked that as a term it compares in its effect with 'justification by faith alone' (*sola fide*) of the Lutheran reformation. Like the *sola fide*, the option for the poor can appeal to good scriptural warrant. In the New Testament this includes the annunciation of Jesus' public ministry: 'the Spirit of the Lord is upon me, because he has chosen me to bring good news to the poor. He has sent me to proclaim liberty to the captives and recovery of sight to the blind; to set free the oppressed, and announce that the time has come when the Lord will save his people' (Lk 4:18-19). There are the truly subversive words of the *Magnificat*: 'He has brought down mighty kings from their thrones and lifted up the lowly. He has filled the hungry with good things and sent the rich away with empty hands' (Lk 1:52-53). And there is James' fierce denunciation of any option for the rich: 'You dishonour the poor. Who are the ones who oppress you and drag you before the judges. The rich. They are the ones who speak evil of that good name which has been given to you' (James 2:6-7). In the documents of Medellin (Conference of the Episcopates of Latin America [CELAM] 1968) both 'the option for the poor' and 'liberation' are given considerable prominence. The bishops of Latin America resolved: 'we must ... distribute our apostolic personnel and efforts so as to give preference to the poorest and the neediest ... '[25] This commitment is taken up and expanded at Puebla (1979). Here the bishops devote an entire chapter of their final document to the 'preferential option for the poor'. Service to the poor is declared to be the privileged gauge of discipleship. Although internal tension and external persecution be the result, the conversion towards 'fuller identification with the poor and our own poor' remains a priority. In his address to the Brazilian bishops at Fortaleza in 1980, the pope reiterates the option for the poor: 'it is a call to special solidarity with the humble and the weak, with all those who are suffering and weeping, who are humiliated and left on the fringes of life and society ... '[26]

What, then, is the option for the poor? The sharpest definition moves away from models of 'charity' and 'relief' towards those of 'solidarity' and 'justice'. There will always be a place in the Christian consciousness for ministry to individual victims of the misfortunes of life. We should all be the worse for the underestimation of this ministry. Yet, on its own, it is insufficient insofar as it fails to identify the remediable causes of misery or omits to contest them. All too easily it becomes a chaplaincy to the *status quo*. An option for the poor goes much further. Negatively, it condemns the extreme poverty – impoverishment – afflicting so many millions of people. Positively, it commits the Church to understand and denounce the mechanisms which generate widespread deprivation. It leads to solidarity with marginalised people and to the affirmation of the validity of their aspirations. It means working with people of goodwill in combatting injustice and oppression. It means challenging the prevalent structures in Western countries and the dominant international economic order. It is nothing less than a conversion from old alignments and narrow institutional concerns to much less comfortable solidarity with the victims of injustice. It is also a conversion to the ministry of Christ who stood beside the outcast and those of little account.

There are several suppositions which underpin the option for the poor as a theological stance. In the first place it is affirmed that the making of history is in people's own hands. History can be fashioned through concerted effort by oppressed people in contesting the forces which oppress them. People can become the active subjects of their history rather than passive objects within it. In one of his Brazilian addresses Pope John Paul II made this clear: 'you must struggle for life, do everything to improve the conditions in which you live. Do not say it is God's will that you remain in a condition of poverty, disease, unhealthy housing ... do not say it is God who wills it'.[27] In *The Power of the Poor in History* Gustavo Gutierrez can write: 'in spite of all vicissitudes, and however dramatic their setbacks, the ones hitherto "absent from history" are beginning to be present to it'.[28]

In the second place, the option for the poor demands a realistic analysis of social reality. The words of Jon Sobrino are memorable: 'the theological problem for me is simple: how do I tell the sacred story of this country? Nothing can substitute for being incarnate in your own reality'.[29] To 'tell the truth about the country', to tell it from the standpoint of the victim and the oppressed, is a relatively new project. There is a validity to Simone Weil's remark that history is the compilation of the depositions of assassins with respect to their victims and themselves. There is a suppressed story which can be retrieved only through the application of a 'hermeneutic of suspicion' to all official histories and which can be continued only with the help of a radical social analysis. This analysis interprets the operation of social, economic and political forces. It endeavours to discern who are the beneficiaries and who are the victims of these forces. Social analysis can be done at the general level of national and international politics or at the more particular level of welfare, educational, health and social policies. Good examples of social analysis from the standpoint of commitment to justice are the trenchant statement from the Brazilian Bishops, the draft document of the U.S. Conference of Bishops on the economy of the U.S. and, in a major way, the documents issuing from the Puebla conference. Clearly, social analysis puts an end to the erstwhile 'innocence' whereby the Churches endeavoured to maintain a benevolent social non-alignment. Choices are demanded in regard to a method of social analysis, in regard to the problems which are discerned as needing attention, in regard to the interpretation and use of the results of analysis.

In the third place, in issues of social justice a neutral stance is rarely what it seems. Here, strict neutrality is a chimaera. So-called neutrality has frequently a hidden agenda. It can spell acquiescence in oppression and alienation. The option for the poor is by definition partisan. It enters solidarity with those who suffer, who are humiliated, who are marginated. It entails risk not simply of disappointment or repercussion but also of appearing naive and impractical. Those who speak in solidarity with the poor 'cannot avoid a certain onesidedness and must run the risk of saying something provisional'.[30] They forego the protection of timeless concepts and nicely balanced sentiments. While they cannot evade the responsibility for correct, accurate research, those who make the option for the poor will read the social context insofar as possible through the eyes of the threatened individual and of oppressed groups.

WHO ARE THE POOR?

In *Witnessing to Justice,* Pedro Arrupe named the poor: agricultural labourers, refugees, those who suffer persecution for their faith, those deprived of basic human rights, those relegated by the powerful and the prosperous to the margins of society. Segunda Galilea spoke of those alienated on the margins of society, the lower proletariat in the cities, the unemployed and the disabled. In Ireland, the poor are the homeless, the chronically unemployed and their dependents, many of the elderly, long term prisoners – particularly those sentenced through informer evidence or as the result of forced confessions, mentally handicapped people, and others.[31] This identification of the poor is indispensable. Without it the term 'poor' can be used to divert attention from the implications of the option for the oppressed. 'Poor' can be understood in many senses. It can be applied so loosely as 'to deprive the notion of "option for the poor" of any effective meaning, since everybody can be seen as poor in some sense'.[32] The option is for those deprived of food and shelter, of participation in the social process, of access to necessary goods and services, of education, of respect for their very humanity.

THE CHURCH AS AN INSTITUTION OF SOCIAL CRITICISM

In addressing the Indian people at Oaxaca in Mexico, Pope John Paul II promised that he would be their voice. This promise should be linked with the pope's insistence at Puebla that injustice must be named clearly. This is not simply the response of an energetic pope – it touches on the idea of the Church as an institution of social criticism. J. B. Metz has spoken of the responsibility of the Church, precisely as institution, to facilitate critical awareness and bring it to expression. Such responsibility enters three areas: defence of the individual vis-à-vis institutional exorbitance, critique of totalitarianism of the right or of the left, and promotion of social justice.

A challenge is thereby presented to the Church as institution. One can speak to others of justice only if one is sensitive to one's own practice of justice. Hence, the first step must be the protection of the individual's rights within the Church: 'we must undertake an examination of the modes of acting and of the possessions and life-style found within the Church itself' (Roman Synod, 1971, III). Once more, we are re-directed to the care of the primitive Christian communities to institute amongst themselves the practice of justice, fraternity and real participation in the life of the Church. How can the Church as institution call for respect for the rights of women when women are debarred from ministry in the Church? How can the Church call for participation of all in the social processes when a model of Church is frequently imposed of rigid hierarchic structure and mandarin-like procedures of decision and policy-making?

If critical protest is to be effective, it must be well informed and intelligently formulated. Justice and Peace bodies are requisite not only at national level but at diocesan and deanery level. Their remit should be the identification and documentation of areas of injustice as well as the facilitation of initiatives to confront specific injustices. Critical protest requires certain minima without which it sows the seed of its own destruction. It must be discerning. If it is not, one jumps on every bandwagon which comes along. Father Arrupe puts it well: 'to be on the side of the poor and the oppressed is not necessarily always to be on the side of ... every movement ... that proclaims itself to be on the side of the poor ... movements whose remedies ... are simplistic, short-sighted, resulting from an emotional rather than an objective view of the concrete situation, or whose aim is power at any price'.[33] Secondly, critical protest requires clarity about what is to be achieved. It is all too easy to be self-indulgent: 'if our activity ... arises from a transferred anger ... then it will be counter-productive'.[34] One slips into serving personal or institutional interests rather than those professedly being defended. Hence, critical protest presupposes concerted planning. Its form should be decided only after reflection with those affected by any action taken. Once again, the importance of 'knowing the facts', of analysis and preparation, comes to the fore. Thirdly, critical protest will show itself in symbolic acts, passive resistance and, where indicated, civil disobedience. Such courses of action are best when they highlight injustice in specific contexts and bring pressure for its eradication. Perhaps their greatest effect is to sow seeds of change in public consciousness: 'symbolic acts ... are quite effective ... if they are not simply isolated gestures without any follow-up, but mark the beginning of a change of attitude or policy, or of a more constructive and carefully worked out solution'.[35]

It is not the competence of the Church (or of theology) to offer detailed social, political or economic blueprints. However, this should not become an excuse to withdraw – or to demand the withdrawal – of the Church (or of theology) from solidarity with those who suffer injustice. On the contrary, it is a duty – and a right – of the Church (and of theology) to work for the coming kingdom of love, justice and peace. Such work cannot be purely 'other worldly': God's kingdom is built in this rather than any other world. Neither can the work of justice be purely negative. Certainly, it means 'breaking with whatever inhibits a radical meeting with Christ in the "nobodies" of this world'.[36] Yet it must also take a positive form and have a specific content. Justice for all and true fraternity/sorority have become a major aspiration of the oppressed whether the oppression be racial, sexual, political or economic. It is a large part of the option for the poor not only to insist on the validity of this widespread aspiration but, even more, to stand in solidarity with those who work for the aspiration's fulfilment.

It has been remarked that the people 'who effectively convict the world of sin are not those who scream about other peoples' evil but those whose lives proclaim an alternative'.[37] The alternative is many-sided. There are the works of gifted individuals such as Mother Teresa of Calcutta. A particularly impressive alternative is proposed by countless unnamed individuals who serve the Gospel of justice and love in basic Christian communities. Their strength lies in their prophetic embodiment of simplicity, mutual help and the struggle for justice now. This alternative, which has cost the lives and the liberty of many who live it, deserves the support rather than the suspicion of the institutional Church. Dom Helder Camara depicts his move from close links with government and the rich towards naming injustice and promoting the liberation of oppressed people. Dom Helder speaks of working *with* rather than *for* the poor. This engages the true sense of compassion – to suffer with (*compati*). Compassion implies entering the situation of the poor and challenging the hollow prejudices against them. What is it to feel the powerlessness of ever being on the defensive? Of being inarticulate or immobile? To suffer the uncertainty of casual work? To experience the attrition of chronic unemployment? It is one thing to come from outside, with ready-made plans and projects. It is another to join people in seeking the causes of deprivation and working towards suitable remedies. To do this will perhaps require a new agenda in the Church. It will mean forsaking institutional interests, perhaps the loss of erstwhile patrons and supporters. Yet, as has already happened in part of the Church in Latin America, it could lead the Church to forego its more conservative interests thus to become the voice of the dispossessed, speaking with them in the demand for real equality and simple justice.

THE 'DOCTRINE' OF PRIVATE PROPERTY

That the right to private property is affirmed in Catholic social teaching is incontestable. Unfortunately, the 'doctrine' was frequently used to enlist the Church in defence of large vested interests in a manner calculated to give little purchase for a reform of social structures. It is therefore necessary to distinguish the intention from the use of the teaching. On the one hand, the doctrine was intended to safeguard freedom and personal initiative. On the other hand, frequently 'people have preferred to retain only the aspects of the defence of their private property, ignoring the more fundamental principles involved'.[38] Many Catholic presentations of social ethics incurred this imbalance. One encounters the claim that 'ownership as such confers a complete right of disposal', a thesis which is in tension with the biblical perspective on the use of goods. Until very recently Catholic social theory appeared to presume that a society based on private property and on an hierarchical distribution of power was the only just order.[39] There is a long-standing hostility in magisterial documents to socialism in all its forms. It has been argued that the Church was far more alert to left-wing excesses than to those of an equally exorbitant right-wing.[40] Regrettably, the teaching on private property for long appears to have served that ideological climate whereas the original perception bore upon the protection of human dignity and the opportunity for human development.

In an earlier section of this chapter, the strictures of many Church Fathers on the uncaring use of riches were noticed. These Fathers did not contest the right to ownership. However, they strongly highlighted the duties attached thereto. Even cursory reading of texts from Cyprian of Carthage to Ambrose of Milan discloses that none of these Fathers admitted an absolute or unqualified right to private property. With St Thomas Aquinas (1225-1274) we read a lucid, systematic treatment of both the rights and the duties of private ownership. Aquinas does not contest the social order of his day. Yet it is interesting how sober is his defence of the rights of property and how clear are his limitations to the appropriation of the good of the earth. He emphasises the communality of these goods (*communitas rerum*) antecedent to every appropriation or subsequent title. The earth's riches are destined primarily to meet human need. This common purpose overrides every other disposition through private arrangement or human law.[41]

St Thomas ascribes to every person a native right to own external goods. His approach reinforces the subsequent argument that 'ownership should be widely distributed through society, so that all may have their just share of the things God has given for the benefit of all'.[42] As with every natural right, the right to own and to use goods resides in human nature itself. It is to be viewed in the perspective of what is necessary for the development of human dignity. However, it seems clear that Aquinas does not accord a natural law title to any particular disposition of property. These dispositions rest upon contingent arrangements such as a pact between individuals, positive law, or common agreement. To use St Thomas' own phrase, they are *secundum humanum condictum*. Since they are contingent ways of giving effect to what is admittedly a natural right they do not carry an immediate or direct sanction from natural or divine law. It is therefore excessive to make Aquinas say: 'any ownership that was set up was set up by natural law and is binding in natural law'. Again, it is demonstrably non-Thomistic to suggest that 'nature allies herself not only with the system of private ownership in general, but with the division of property actually made amongst individual men'.[43]

Aquinas believes that private ownership is socially desirable even on pragmatic grounds. Public order – the common good is best served when the adage 'to each his/her own' (*unicuique suum*) is recognised. Things are done better when each person cares for his/her own goods. In St Thomas' view greater care is taken in the common enterprise under the incentive of private ownership. However, in regard to the use of property Aquinas lists strict conditions: goods should be used as if they were common to all; there should be an easy sharing for the relief of the necessity of others.[44] He approves of the legal provisions of the Old Testament whereby the gleanings of corn, grapes and olives were to be left for the widow, orphan and alien. Again, he mentions with approval the Jewish bounty of the Jubilee year whereby the fruits of the earth in that year were available to all. Doubtless, St Thomas writes with the ideal of common enterprise, widespread participation and social charity in mind. In such a context it is understandable that he does not offer any detailed model for the reduction to practice of his demanding exhortation to the common use of the goods of the earth.

Nevertheless, there are duties to the needy. In line with the patristic tradition St Thomas emphasises these clearly. The common purpose of the earth's riches to meet human need over-rides all legal dispositions when it comes to urgent necessity. No title or property disposition can hinder the relief of human necess-ity. Two consequences ensue. First, there is a lien on wealth in regard to the needs of the poor. Second, the person in urgent need has the right to take what he/she needs from the superfluity of others. In regard to the social lien on wealth, St Thomas appears to be more radical than his commentators. Whereas many comm-entators made much of an obligation in charity, Aquinas sees it as an obligation of justice. This is clear from his citation of Ambrose: 'it is the bread of the poor you withhold, the clothing of the naked you retain'.[45] St Thomas is equally affirmative on the right of someone in need overtly or covertly to take what is needed. It is to his principle that the Brazilian bishops currently appeal when they say: 'it is lawful for a man to succour his own needs by means of another's property by taking it either openly or secretly'.[46] This is not a licence to anarchy or despoliation. It is simply to apply Aquinas' principles where in the midst of superabundance people are excluded from the very means of subsistence. Failure to advert to such injustice and to demand change would be 'a tacit acceptance of genocide'.[47]

Notwithstanding these strands, Catholic social teaching – even in the early twentieth century – favoured the undisturbed pre-sumption enjoyed by private ownership not only of personal property but also of the means of production. While Leo XIII espoused the rights of workers to a living wage, he nevertheless supported the standing order. In his view 'inequality of rights and power proceeds from the very author of nature'.[48] Despite recurr-ent papal criticism of the harshest elements of capitalism, the first clear subordination of private ownership to another principle is in *Mater et Magistra.* Here John XXIII, in affirming the right to private ownership, subordinates it to the common good. The keynote is private ownership with social responsibility. Towards the end of John's pontificate *Pacem in Terris* (1963) describes private ownership as a means to an end, a suitable means for safeguarding the dignity of the person. In effect, this is a reversal of the earlier emphases – or, better, a recovery of a more ancient tradition. Thereafter, the universal purpose of created goods becomes the main principle while the right to private ownership is affirmed in a subsidiary way. Thus, one of the major documents of the Second Vatican Council, *Gaudium et Spes,* underlines that God intended the goods of the earth for the use of every human being. To this main purpose 'all rights whatever, including those of private property and free commerce, are to be subordinated' (*Populorum Progressio*, 22).

This universal purpose of the goods of creation is not mere verbal predication. It is a task to be accomplished in the values of social justice, human solidarity and social love. A contemporary understanding of ownership must take account of the process of industrialisation and the problems posed by advanced technology. There is a distinction between the ownership of property and the larger question of the control of the means of production. While this is not a complete distinction, nonetheless it is not a trivial one. Had the distinction been made sufficiently clearly, the intention of the tradition on private property would not have been so often obscured. This tradition endeavours to safeguard the independence of the individual and the right to personal development. It was never intended to provide an *apologia* for the capitalist system. In his encyclical *Laborem Exercens* Pope John Paul II stresses the priority of labour over capital. He speaks of the revision both in theory and practice of the right to private ownership of the means of production: 'one cannot exclude the socialisation, in suitable circumstances, of certain means of production'. To this can be linked the 'social mortgage' spoken of by the same pope at Puebla and taken up recurrently by the final document of that assembly.[49] This mortgage or lien demands not 'an *a priori* elimination of private ownership of the means of production but the satisfactory use of such means for the common good, for the benefit of the nation or the community'. It is clear that the pope does not regard state capitalism as an authentic guarantee of the responsible use of the means of production. In fact, his critique runs much deeper than a call for nationalisation. It raises fundamental questions about the ways people and groups wield disproportionate economic and political power to the exclusion of weaker groups. It contests land speculation in urban and rural contexts. It envisages the expropriation of large estates held to the detriment of landless people. Above all, it withdraws the legitimation of a false conception of the Church's teaching on private ownership. Far from legitimating ownership at all cost, that teaching insists that an exaggerated conception of property rights must not be allowed to hinder radical solutions to social injustice.

Rightly, therefore, the Irish bishops in *The Work of Justice* remind us that there is no such thing in justice as 'the absolute right to do what I like with my money, my profits, my capital or my land'.[50] No one can claim to have profited by his own unaided efforts. Because of this interdependence 'the social dimension in the generation of profits must be acknowledged in the disposal of them'.[51] The insistence on social interdependence and the social mortgage on all wealth opens a range of questions for international, national and local politics. Specifically, it impels consideration of more just distribution of the earth's goods and better access for the poor, the illiterate and the hungry to the necessities for human development. In the name of justice the rich countries are challenged to re-examine their methods and priorities in regard to food, health, education and economic development. In turn, since juster policies are costly and they require public support, we are all called upon to re-examine our position in regard to fair taxes and collaboration in action for the elimination of poverty. Appropriately, Paul VI reminds us: 'Let each one examine his conscience, a conscience that conveys a new message for our times. Is he prepared to support out of his own pocket works and undertakings organised in favour of the most destitute? Is he ready to pay higher taxes so that public authorities can intensify their efforts in favour of development?' (*Populorum Progressio*, 44).

CONCLUDING POSTSCRIPT

The implications of the above are several. In the first place, justice is as much about giving as receiving. It is as much about respecting the entitlement of others as it is the demand for oneself. In the second place, justice is a social reality. This social quality, in a sense, is paramount – although social justice requires respect for the rights and inculcates the duties of individuals. There is a cohesion without identity between the emergent theological reflection on justice and John Rawls' argument that justice is not primarily a quality of individuals and their actions but a predicate of social systems and institutions.[52] In the third place, propositions about justice have to be framed in the plural – not to say fractured – context of today's world. While claims about justice/human rights can be derived from natural law theory and Christian sources, there is a sharp realisation that diverse cultures and contexts can indicate somewhat different conclusions. This is not relativism but realism.

There is an increasing agreement that the agenda on human rights and justice exemplified by the U.N. Declaration of Human Rights has lagged behind the nexus of contemporary problems in safeguarding human dignity. The U.N. Declaration provides a minimum or baseline on the right to life, to personal freedoms from torture, arbitrary detention etc. In this it has made, and continues to make, an invaluable contribution. Since 1948, however, areas of human need and hindrances to human development have come into a prominence then only implicit. These are margination from the decisions affecting peoples' lives, effective exclusion from the social and political processes, lack of the minima for economic self-sufficiency and, now, the grave spectre of continental famine. The demands of justice can be identified in more than a preliminary way: famine in the circumstances of a world where ample means abound is an injustice which cries to heaven. The questions of political will, political strategies and moral purpose arise. These questions may not be left to the technocrats whether politicians or economists. There are moral issues here – issues of right and obligation. There are obligations for governments to respond to the priority of need rather than political self-interest. There are rights of governments to ask the support of their citizens in finding just and humane policies for the eradication of global want. And there is the right/duty of citizens to press governments to match the generosity of countless ordinary people.

Reading List

Reading List

ONE: CREATION AND ORIGINS – DIVERSE PERSPECTIVES
Mircea Eliade, *Myth and Reality*, Allen and Unwin, London, 1964.
Langdon Gilkey, *Religion and the Scientific Future*, SCM Press, London, 1970.
Andrew Greeley, *Unsecular Man: The Persistence of Religion*, Schoken, New York, 1972.
G. S. Kirk, *Myth: Its Meaning and Functions in Ancient and Other Cultures*, Cambridge University Press, 1970.
A. R. Peacocke (ed.), *The Sciences and Theology in the Twentieth Century*, Oriel Press, London, 1981.
T. F. Torrance, *The Ground and Grammar of Theology*, Christian Journals, Belfast/Dublin/Ottawa, 1981.

TWO: THE EARLY STORY: CREATION IN BIBLE AND CHURCH FATHERS
Robert Butterworth, *The Theology of Creation*, Mercier Press, Cork, 1969.
Langdon Gilkey, *Maker of Heaven and Earth*, Anchor Books, Doubleday, New York, 1965.
Zachary Hayes, *What Are They Saying about Creation?*, Paulist Press, New York, 1980.
J. N. D. Kelly, *Early Christian Doctrines*, A. and D. Black, London, 1965.
Leo Scheffczyk, *Creation and Providence*, Herder and Herder / Burns Oates, New York / London, 1970.
Michael Schmaus, *God and Creation*, Sheed and Ward, New York, 1969.
G. Von Rad, *Old Testament Theology*, Volume 1, London and New York, 1975.
Norman Young, *Creator, Creation and Faith*, Collins, London, 1976.

THREE: AN EMERGENT TRADITION
StThomas Aquinas, *Summa Theologiae*, 1a, especially q. 45, aa. 1-8.
Pierre Teilhard de Chardin, *Oeuvres de Pierre Teilhard de Chardin* (9 volumes), Paris, 1955-69.
Frederick Copelston, *Aquinas*, Penguin, Harmondsworth, 1955.
Louis Dupré, *The Other Dimension*, Doubleday, New York, 1972.
Donald Grey, *The One and the Many: Teilhard de Chardin's Vision of Unity*, Burns Oates, London, 1969.
Anthony Kenny (ed.), *Aquinas. A Collection of Critical Essays*, Macmillan, London / Melbourne, 1969.
Henri de Lubac, *The Religion of Teilhard de Chardin*, Collins, London, 1967.
E. L. Mascall, *Existence and Analogy*, Darton Longman and Todd (Libra), London, 1966.
J. A. Weisheipl, *Friar Tomasso d'Aquino*, Doubleday, New York, 1974.

FOUR: OUTLINES FOR A SPIRITUALITY OF CREATION
J. G. Donders, *Creation and Human Dynamism*, Twenty Third Publications, Mystic, Conn., 1985.

Austin Farrer, *Love Almighty and Ills Unlimited,* Collins (Fontana), London, 1966.

J. Fichtner, *Man: The Image of God,* Alba House, New York, 1978.

Matthew Fox, *Original Blessing. A Primer in Creation Spirituality,* Bear and Co., Santa Fe, 1983.

John Hick, *Evil and the God of Love,* Macmillan, London, 1966.

Edmund Hill, *Being Human,* Chapman, London, 1984.

Vladimir Lossky, *In the Image and Likeness of God,* Mowbray, Oxford, 1975.

John F. O'Grady, *Christian Anthropology. A Meaning for Human Life,* Paulist Press, New York / New Jersey / Toronto, 1976.

FIVE: ORIGINAL SIN

Z. Alzeghy and M. Flick, *Il Peccato Originale,* Queriana, Brescia, 1972.

G. Daly, 'The Problem of Original Sin' in *The Furrow,* January 1973, pp. 13-26.

do., 'Theological Models in the Doctrine of Original Sin' in *The Heythrop Journal,* XIII, April 1974, pp. 121-142.

J. P. Mackey, *Life and Grace,* Gill and Son, Dublin / Sydney, 1968.

K. Rahner, *Foundations of Christian Faith,* Seabury, New York, 1978.

do., 'Theological Reflections on Monogenism' in *Theological Investigations,* Volume 1, Darton Longman and Todd, London, 1961 and 1966, pp. 229-296.

Peter de Rosa, *Christ and Original Sin,* Chapman, London / Dublin / Melbourne, 1965.

P. Schoonenberg, *Man and Sin,* Sheed and Ward, London / New York / Melbourne, 1965.

E. Yarnold, *The Theology of Original Sin,* Mercier Press, Cork, 1971.

SIX: EVOLUTION AND HOMINISATION

A. Flew, *Darwinian Evolution,* Paladin Books, London, 1984.

J. de Fraine, *The Bible and the Origin of Man,* Desclée, New York / Tournai / Paris / Rome, 1962.

E. Nemesszeghy and J. Russell, *Theology of Evolution,* Mercier Press, Cork, 1972.

R. North, *Teilhard and the Creation of the Human Soul,* Bruce, Milwaukee, 1966.

K Rahner and P. Overhage, *Hominisation,* Herder and Herder, New York, 1965.

P. Schoonenberg, *God's World in the Making,* Gill and Macmillan, Dublin 1965.

SEVEN: HUMAN RIGHTS OBSERVED – A SERVICE OF THE CREATOR

D. M. Clarke, *Church and State. Essays in Political Philosophy,* Cork University Press, Cork, 1984.

Maurice Cranston, *What Are Human Rights?,* Taplinger, New York, 1973.

Alan Falconer, *Understanding Human Rights,* Irish School of Ecumenics, Dublin, 1980.

David Hollenbach, *Claims in Conflict. Retrieving and Renewing the Catholic Human Rights Tradition,* Woodstock Studies 4, Paulist, New York, 1979.

E. McDonagh, 'The Worth of the Person' in *Doing the Truth,* Gill and Macmillan, Dublin, 1979.

Allen O. Miller, *A Christian Declaration on Human Rights,* Grand Rapids MI, 1977.

Pontifical Commission for Justice and Peace, *The Church and Human Rights,* Vatican City, 1971.

EIGHT: ECOLOGY AND CREATIVE STEWARDSHIP

E. A. Armstrong, *St Francis. Nature Mystic,* University of California Press, Berkeley / Los Angeles / London, 1973.

Leonardo Boff, *St Francis. A Model for Human Liberation,* SCM Press, London, 1985.

John Carmody, Ecology and Religion, Paulist Press, New York, 1983.

Barry Commoner, *The Closing Circle,* Bantam Books, New York, 1971.

T. S. Derr, *Ecology and Human Liberation,* W.C.C., Geneva, 1973.

D. Dinnerstein, *The Mermaid and the Minotaur,* Harper and Row, New York, 1976.

E. McDonagh, 'Technology and Value Preference' in *Doing the Truth,* Gill and Dublin, 1979.

S. McDonagh, 'The Good Earth' in *The Furrow,* July 1984.

J. Moltmann, *The Future of Creation,* Fortress Press, Philadelphia, 1979.

do., *God in Creation. An Ecological Doctrine of Creation,* SCM Press, London, 1985.

R. Reuther, *New Woman. New Earth,* Seabury, New York, 1965.

Roger L. Shinn, *Faith and Science in an Unjust World* (especially Volume 1), W.C.C., Geneva, 1980.

The Brandt Report. North-South. A Programme for Survival, Pan Books, London and Sydney, 1980.

NINE: JUSTICE AND THE GOODS OF THE EARTH

D. Dorr, *Spirituality and Justice,* Gill and Macmillan, Dublin, 1983.

do., *Option for the Poor,* Gill and Macmillan, Dublin, 1983.

J. Eagleson and P. Scharper (eds.), *Puebla and Beyond. Documentation and Commentary,* Orbis, Maryknoll NY, 1980.

J. Gremillion (ed.), *The Gospel of Peace and Justice. Catholic Social Teaching since Pope John XXIII,* Orbis, Maryknoll NY, 1976.

G. Gutierrez, *A Theology of Liberation,* Orbis, Maryknoll NY, 1973.

do., *The Power of the Poor in History,* SCM Press, London, 1983.

J. C. Haughey (ed.), *The Faith That Does Justice,* Woodstock Studies 2, Paulist, New York, 1977.

D. A. Lane, *Foundations for a Social Theology,* Gill and Macmillan, Dublin, 1984.

J. Rawls, *A Theory of Justice,* Harvard University Press, 1971.

Between Honesty and Hope, Orbis, Maryknoll NY, 1969.

Synod of Bishops, *Justice in the World,* 1971.

Irish Bishops' Conference, *The Work of Justice,* Veritas, Dublin, 1977.

Pontifical Commission for Justice and Peace, *The Universal Purpose of Created Things,* Vatican City, 1977.

Notes

Notes

INTRODUCTION
1. E. Schillebeeckx, *Jesus an Experiment in Christology*, Collins, London, 1979, p. 630.

ONE: CREATION AND ORIGINS, DIVERSE PERSPECTIVES
1. Ernan McMullen, 'How Should Cosmology Relate to Theology?' in *The Sciences and Theology in the Twentieth Century*, Oriel Press, Henley and London, 1981, pp. 17 - 57, citation at p. 39.
2. For an excellent popular treatment cf. E. Nemesszeghy and J. Russell, *Theology of Evolution*, Theology Today Series (6), Mercier Press, Cork, 1972.
3. The several theories advanced by physicists in this area are dealt with impressively in Claude Tresmontant: *Comment se pose aujourd'hui le problème de l'existence de Dieu*, Editions de Seuil, 1966, pp. 5-49.
4. Cf. Jean Ladrière: 'Faith and Cosmology' in his *Language and Belief*, Gill and Macmillan, 1972, pp. 149-186.
5. Cited by T. F. Torrance: *The Ground and Grammar of Theology*, Christian Journals, Belfast, 1980, p. 5.
6. *ibid.*, pp. 15-43.
7. Werner Heisenberg: 'Scientific Truth and Religious Truth' in *Cross Currents*, Winter 1975, p. 466.
8. T.F. Torrance, *op. cit.*, p. 17.
9. Jean Ladriere, *Language and Belief*, Gill and Macmillan, Dublin and London, 1972, p. 161.
10. *ibid.*, p. 183.
11. B. J. Carr and M. J. Rees: 'The Anthropic Principle and the Structure of the Physical World', *Nature*, 278 (1979), pp. 605-612.
12. Ernan McMullen, *op. cit.* p. 41.
13. Ladriere, *op.cit.*, p. 184.
14. Bernard Lonergan, *Insight*, Longmans, Green and Co., London, 1957 , p. 546.
15. Van A. Harvey, *The Historian and the Believer*, S.C.M., London, 1967, p. 257.
16. E. Cassirer, *An Essay on Man*, Yale University Press, 1962. p. 84.
17. Mircea Eliade, *Myth and Reality*, World Perspectives, Allen and Unwin, 1964, p.1.
18. Cassirer, *op. cit.*, pp. 81 and 82
19. Langdon Gilkey, *Religion and the Scientific Future*, SCM Press, London, 1970, p. 103.
20. Andrew Greeley, *The Persistence of Religion*, Schocken, New York, 1972, p. 96.
21. Cf. P. Ricoeur, *The Symbolism of Evil*, Beacon Press, Boston, 1967, *passim*.
22. Ladrière: *op. cit.*, p. 173.
23. P. Ricoeur: *The Symbolism of Evil*, pp. 352-3.
24. Greeley, *op. cit.*, pp. 110-112; Gilkey, *op. cit.*, 85

25. E. Schüssler-Fiorenza, 'Feminist Theology' in *Mission Trends* (4), Paulist Press, 1979, at p. 208.

26. E. Schillebeeckx, *Christ, The Christian Experience in the Modern World*, S.C.M., London, 1980, p. 519.

27. *ibid*, p. 811.

28. R. Butterworth. *The Theology of Creation*, Theology Today Series. No. 5, Mercier Press, Cork, 1969, p. 24.

29. *eo. loco.*

TWO: THE EARLY STORY: CREATION IN BIBLE AND CHURCH FATHERS

1. Deutero-Isaiah may date after the return from captivity in 537 B.C. Nonetheless the text brings clearly to expression the ordeal of a captive people and the threat to their religious consciousness as well as to their communal identity.

2. Reply to Cardinal Suhard from the Secretary of the Biblical Commission (16 January 1945). Cf. Denzinger-Schonmetzer 3864.

3. E. Voegelin: *Order and History*, Vols. 1 to 4, Louisiana State University Press, Baton Rouge. G. VonRad: *Old Testament Theology, I,* London and New York, 1975.

4. G. Von Rad: *Old Testament Theology, 1*, p. 138.

5. Amos Wilder: *The New Voice*, Herder and Herder, New York, 1969, pp. 54 and 70. Cf. John Shea: *Stories of God*, Thomas More Press, 1978, p. 60.

6. Shea, *op. cit.*, p. 144.

7. W. Harrington: 'Little Less than a God', in *Doctrine and Life*, March 1976, p. 166.

8. E. Schillebeecks: *Christ: The Christian Experience in the Modern World*, SCM Press, London, 1980, p. 811.

9. *ibid:* p. 522.

10. *ibid.* p. 518.

11. *ibid.* p. 525.

12. *eo.loco.*

13. *ibid.* p. 185.

14. Hymn for Morning Prayer. Feast of the Exaltation of the Holy Cross.

15. E. Schillebeeckx, *Christ*, p. 191.

16. *ibid.* p. 209. Cf. Y. Congar: *Jesus Christ, Foi Vivante*, Cerf, Paris, 1966. p. 145.

17. J. Moltmann: *The Future of Creation*, Fortress Press, 1979, p. 123.

18. L. Scheffczyk: *Creation and Providence*, Herder, 1970 p. 48.

19. *ibid.* p. 51.

20. First Epistle of Clement, 19,2; 35,6; 59,3.

21. *ibid.* 1,8.

22. J. N. D. Kelly, *Early Christian Doctrines*, A. and D. Black, London, 1965, p. 26.

23. E. Schillebeeckx: *Interim Report on the Book Jesus and Christ*, SCM Press, London, 1980, p. 112.

24. Kelly, *op.cit.*, p. 173.

25. *Adversus Haereses*, 4, 20-21; 4,41.

26. Scheffczyk, *op. cit.*, p. 75.

27. *Stromata*, 4,16; 5,16.

28. *De Trinitate*, 5:13-15.

29. *De Genesi ad litteram*, 1,4,9. *De Genesi ad litteram*, 1,6,12. *De Trinitate*, 5:13-15. *Confessio*, XI, 8-10.

THREE: AN EMERGENT TRADITION ON CREATION

1. Alan Watts: *Nature, Man and Woman,* Wildwood House, London, 1973, p. 39. J.A.T. Robinson: *Honest to God,* SCM Press, London, 1963. For St Thomas' writing on creation cf. *Summa Theologiae,* Ia, qq. 45-46; *Contra Gentes,* 2, 16. For good general studies of Aquinas cf. F.C. Copleston: *Aquinas,* Penguin, 1955. J. A. Weisheipl, O.P.: *Friar Tomasso D'Aquino,* Doubleday, New York 1974.

2. Thomas offers more than one definition of creation. Creation is a relation of dependence: *'creatio ... non est nisi relatio ... ad creatorem ut ad principium sui esse ... ' Summa Theologiae,* Ia, q. 45. art. 3(c). His primary definition, however, is *'emanatio totius entis a causa universali quae est Deus'. Summa Theologiae,* Ia, q. 45, art. 1(c). *Ens per esentiam, ens per participationem* (being by essence, being by participation) is a couplet fashioned by St Thomas Aquinas himself. It dates from the relatively late *Contra Gentes.* Aquinas frequently uses it to express the relation between Creator and creature. Cf. *Summa Theologiae,* Ia, q.6, art 3(c); *ibid.,* q. 47, art. 1(c).

3. *'esse ... est illud quod est magis intimum cuilibet et quod profundis omnibus inest ... ' Summa Theologiae,* Ia, q. 8, art (c).

4. Cornelio Fabro: *Participation et Causalité sêlon S. Thomas d'Aquin,* Louvain/Paris, 1961, p.35.

5. *Summa Theologiae,* Ia, q. 45, art. 2 ad 2.

6. *La Foi de l'Église,* Cerf, 1978, p. 123. The citation is from F. Varillon: *L'humilité de Dieu,* Centurion, p. 118.

7. *Summa Theologiae,* Ia, q. 45, art. 3(c).

8. E. Mascall: *Existence and Analogy,* Darton, Longman and Todd (Libra), London, 1966, p. 146.

9. *De Potentia,* 3, 3, ad 1.

10. *Summa Theologiae,* Ia, q. 45, art 1 (c).

11. *ibid.,* Ia, q. 104, art.1(c).

12. *ibid.,* Ia, q. 8, art. 3(c).

13. *eo loco.*

14. *Summa Theologiae,* Ia, q. 8, art 1(c).

15. This Thomist position is developed by the Transcendental Thomists and most notably by Karl Rahner.

16. L. Dupré: *The Other Dimension,* Doubleday, Garden City, New York; 1972; p. 389.

17. J. H. Newman, *Parochial and Plain Sermons,* Vol. 6, Rivingtons, 1870, pp. 123-4.

18. *The Phenomenon of Man,* New York, 1967, p. 297 (or, in the Fontana paperback edition, p. 326).

19. *Oeuvres de Pierre Teilhard de Chardin* (9 Vol.), Paris. 1955-69. The citation refers to Vol. 7, p. 398.

20. H de Lubac: *The Religion of Teilhard de Chardin,* New York, 1967, p. 23.

21. *Oeuvres,* Vol. 2, pp. 80-81.

22. Cited by Donald Gray: *The One and the Many: Teilhard de Chardin's Vision of Unity,* Burns and Oates, London, 1969, p. 19.

23. *Writings in Time of War,* New York, 1968, p. 95.

24. Claude Tresmontant: *Pierre Teilhard de Chardin: His Thought,* Baltimore, 1959, p. 91.

25. *Writings in Time of War,* pp. 163-4.

26. This *Credo* recurs in Teilhard's writings in one form or other. Cf. his *The Heart of Matter,* Collins, London, 1978.

27. 'The Eternal Feminine' in *Writings in Time of War,* p. 192.

28. *The Phenomenon of Man,* pp. 264-5 (Fontana, p. 290).

28. Cf. Donald Gray: *The One and the Many,* p. 82.

30. For an excellent treatment cf. Gray, *op.cit.* pp. 95-132.
30. 'Creative Union' in *Writings in Time of War*, p. 174.
32. *The Phenomenon of Man*, p. 297 (Fontana, p. 326).
33. Cf. Gray, *op.cit.*, p. 110.
33. Oeuvres, Vol. 6, p. 192.
35. Cf. Chapter Eight.
36. Cf. J. P. Mackey: 'Christian Faith as Personal Response ' in *Faith: Its Nature and Meaning*, Gill and Macmillan, Dublin, 1972, p. 54.
37. Leo Scheffczyk: *Creation and Providence*, Burns and Oates, London and New York, 1970, p. 244.
38. G. Daly, O.S.A.: *Transcendence and Immanence*, Clarendon Press, Oxford, 1980 for an outstanding treatment of Modernism and the reactions to that movement.
38. *Constitutio Dogmatica de Fide Catholica (Dei Filius)*. Chapter I - *De Deo rerum omnium Creatore*. Chapter II - *De Revelatione*.
40. Canons 1 to 5, cf. Denzinger 3021-3025.
41. Denzinger 3002.
42. Denzinger 3026.
43. *Acta et Decreta Sacrorum Conciliorum Recentiorum*, Collectio Lacensis, VII, p. 130.
44. Henri Bouillard: *Karl Barth. Parole de Dieu et Existence Humaine*, Aubier, Paris, 1957. Hans Von Balthasar: Karl Barth. Darstellung und Deutung seiner Theologie, Hegner, Köln, 1962. Gottlieb Söhngen: 'Analogia Fidei' in *Catholica* (Paderborn) Heft 3, pp.113-136 and 176-208.
45. Cf. Scheffczyk: *Creation and Providence*, p. 243. R. Garrigou-Lagrange: *Dieu. Son Existence et Sa Nature*, (Vol. I), Beauchesne, Paris, 1950, p. 20.
45. *Summa Contra Gentes*, 3, 69.
47. W. Heisenberg: 'Naturwissenschaftliche und Religiose Wahrheit' in *Schritte Uber Grenzen. Gesammelte Reden und Aufsatze*, Munich. 1973. Cited by Hans Kung in *Does God Exist?*, Collins, London, 1980, p. 630.
48. *Essai Philosophique sur les Probabilités*, 1814. (*Oeuvres complêtes*, VII, p. 6).
49. Kung: *Does God Exist?*, p. 640.

FOUR: OUTLINES FOR A SPIRITUALITY OF CREATION
1. E. Schillebeeckx: *Interim Report on the Books Jesus and Christ*, SCM Press, London, 1980, p. 114.
2. Divine Office, Morning Prayer, Thursday Second Week of the Year, Hymn. Acts 17:26.
3. Albert Camus: *The Rebel*, Penguin, 1962, p. 249. Bertrand Russell *Mysticism and Logic*, Penguin, 1953, p. 59.
4. Alan W. Watts: *Nature, Man and Woman*, Wildwood House, London, 1977. There is by now a vast literature in feminist theology amongst which cf. Virginia Mollenkott, *Women, Men and the Bible*, Abingdon Press, 1977.
5. J. P. Mackey, 'Christian Faith as Personal Response' in *Faith: Its Nature and Meaning*, ed. Paul Surlis, Gill and Macmillan, 1972, p. 65.
6. E. Schillebeeckx: *Jesus: An Experiment in Christology*, Collins, 1979. p. 630.
7. Cited by T. F. Torrance in *The Ground and Grammar of Theology*, Christian Journals, Belfast/Dublin/Ottawa. 1980, p. 3.
8. E. Mascall: *Existence and Analogy*, Darton, Longman and Todd (Libra), 1966, p. 126.

9. J. P. Mackey: 'Christian Faith as Personal Response' in *Faith: Its Nature and Meaning*, p. 65.

10. *ibid., p. 65.*

11. *ibid.*, p. 69.

12. This point is well developed by Langdon Gilkey at Chapter Six 'Creation and the Meaning of Life' in his *Maker of Heaven and Earth*, Doubleday (Anchor), 1965.

13. E. Schillebeeckx: *God Among Us*, SCM Press, London, 1983, p. 98.

14. Colm Connellan, *Why Does Evil Exist*, Exposition Press, Hicksville, New York, 1974. In this book Fr Connellan compares Aquinas' approach to the problem of evil with those of Camus and A. Flew.

15. *ibid.*, p. 68.

16. Pierre Teilhard de Chardin, 'The Heart of Matter' in *The Heart of the Matter*, Collins, London 1978, p. 53.

17. Paul Tillich: *Systematic Theology*, Vol. I, Nisbet, London, 1953. Cf. a good study of Tillich on creation in Norman Young: *Creator, Creation and Faith*, Collins, 1976, pp. 103-127.

18. *Why Do We Need a Third World Theology*, C.I.I.R. London, 1984.

19. Donal Dorr: *Spirituality and Justice*, Gill and Macmillan, Dublin, 1984, pp. 8-18.

20. *Gaudium et Spes, 34.*

21. *Matthew Fox, O.P.: Original Blessing: A Primer of Creation Spirituality*, Bear and Co. Santa Fe, 1983, p. 48.

22. *ibid.*, p. 54.

23. H. Meynell: *Grace Versus Nature*, Sheed and Ward (Stag), London and Melbourne, 1965, p. 90.

24. A Flew: *New Essays in Philosophical Theology*, SCM Press, London, 1966. pp. 98-9.

25. *De Moribus Ecclesiasticis*, II,II,2-3.

26. 'Quid sit malum opportet et ratione boni accipere' in *Summa Theologiae*, Ia, q. 48, art. 1 (c). And again: 'Malum non agit secundum quod est privatio quaedam sed secundum quod ei bonum adiungitur' *ibid.*, ad 4.

27. 'Melius et perfectius est (in universitate creaturarum) si in eo sint quaedam quae a bono deficere possunt,......quae deficere possint, quandoque deficient' *ibid.*, art. 2 ad 3; cf. *Contra Gentes* III, 71.

28. F. C. Copleston: *Aquinas*, p. 147.

29. Cf. our footnote 27 above.

30. *Contra Gentes*, III 71; cf. Boethius: *De Consolatione Philosophiae*, P.L. (Migne). 63,25.

31. Bernard Lonergan, *Insight*, Longmans, (Student Edition), 1968. p. 667.

32. *ibid.*, p. 667.

33. *ibid.*, p. 668.

34. Austin Farrer: *Saving Belief*, Hodder and Stoughton, 1967, p. 49.

35. A. Flew: *New Essays in Philosophical Theology*, p. 147.

36. A. Farrer: *Love Almighty and Ills Unlimited*, Collins (Fontana), 1966, p. 88.

37. *ibid.*, p. 57.

38. *ibid.*, p. 99.

39. Cited in Vladimir Lossky: *In the Image and Likeness of God*, Mowbray (Oxford), 1975, p. 127.

40. For an excellent treatment cf. Edmund Hill, O.P.: *Being Human*, Chapman, London, 1984, p. 197 et seq.

41. Gen 9:6.

42. Michael Schmaus: *God and Creation*, Sheed and Ward, New York, 1969, p. 114.

43. Cited in Lossky, *In the Image the Image and Likeness of God*, p. 129.
44. *ibid.*, p. 139.

FIVE: ORIGINAL SIN

1. J.P. Mackey: *Life and Grace*, Gill and Son, Dublin and Sydney, 1968, second edition p. 152.

2. Karl Rahner, *Foundations of Christian Faith*, Seabury Press, New York, 1978, p. 112.

3. C. G. Jung, *The Undiscovered Self*, Mentor, Boston, 1957, p. 107.

4. K. Marx: 'Le Communisme de "l'Observatuer rhenan"' in *Gazette Allemande de Bruxelles*, n. 73, 12 September 1847, cited in J. L. Segundo: *Evolution and Guilt*, Gill and Macmillan, Dublin, 1980, p.63.

5. Segundo, *ibid.*, p. 61.

6. Edward Yarnold: *The Theology of Original Sin*, Mercier Press, Cork, 1971, p. 33.

7. John XXIII in his opening address to the Second Vatican Council, 11 October 1962.

8. Gabriel Daly, 'The Problem of Original Sin', *The Furrow*, (Maynooth), January, 1973, p. 14.

9. J. H. Newman: *Apologia Pro Vita Sua*. A. Koestler: in *The Observer*, 28 September 1969. Both citations are to be found in Yarnold: *The Theology of Original Sin*, p. 10.

10. Karl Rahner: *Foundations of Christian Faith*, pp. 109-110.

11. Louis Mondin: *Sin, Liberty and Law*, Sheed and Ward, New York, 1966, p. 72.

12. 2 Cor 5:19.

13. Yarnold: *The Theology of Original Sin*, p .50.

14. There is an immense literature on this point. Cf. especially S. Lyonnet: 'Le pêché originel et l'exegèse de Rom 5:12-14' in *Recherches de Science Religieuse*, (440) 1956, pp. 63-84; also by the same author: 'Le pêché' in *Dictionnaire de la Bible (Suppl)* 7 pp. 481-567).

15. M. Flick and Z. Alszeghy: *Il Peccato Originale*, Queriniana, Brescia, 1972, capitolo secondo, pp. 35-70.

16. D. Petavius: *Dogmata Theologica - De Incarnatione* 14: 2:1.

17. J. N. D. Kelly: *Early Christian Doctrines* third edition, A. and C. Black, London, 1965, p. 350.

18. *ibid.*, p. 349.

19. Basil: *Hom. in Ps. 94*:3 (P.G. 29.489). Cf. also Cyril of Jerusalem: *Catech.* 2: *De Poen.* 4 (P.G. 33.398); Gregory Nazianzen: *Orat.* 19:14 (P.G. 35.1060).

20. Athanasius: *De Incarn. et contra Arianos*, c.8 (P.G. 26. Col.996 C).

21. On this question cf. D. Grasso: *Bisogna ancora battezzare i bambini*, Assisi, 1973; W. Kasper: *Christsein ohne Entscheidung, oder, soll die Kirche Kinder Taufen*, Mainz, 1970; E. Schlink: *Die Lehre von der Taufe*, Kassel, 1969.

22. *Epist.* 64:2 (CSEL I:718).

23. Gregory of Nyssa in P.G. 46. 161-192.

24. Augustine: *De Diversis Quest. ad Simplicianum* (P.L. 40.106-107). *De Peccatorum Meritis et Remissione* (P.L. 44. 114-145). Cf. A. Sage: 'Pêché originel. Naissance d'une dogme' in *Revue des Études Augustiniennes* (13), 1967, pp. 211-248. J. De Blic: 'Le pêché originel sêlon S. Augustin' in *Recherches de science religieuse* (16), 1926, pp. 97-119 and (17), 1927, pp. 512-531. J. Pepin: 'L'orientation actuelle des recherches Augustiniennes' in *Recherches de philosophie* (2), 1956, pp. 345-351. H. Rondet: *Essais sur la théologie de la grace*, Paris, 1964.

25. *De Vita Christiana* 6 (P.L. 40. 1037).

26. A. Vanneste: 'Le decret du Concile de Trente sur le pêché originel' in *Nouvelle Revue Theologique* (88), 1966, pp. 598-600.

27. Alszeghy and Flick: *Il Peccato Originale,* esp. p. 110.

28. Cf. *Concilium Tridentinum. Diariorum, Actuum, Epistolarum, Tractatuum* nova collectio. S. Ehses. Freiburg, 1911, 5:162-256. Cf. also Hefele-Leclerc: *Histoire des Conciles* 9 (1-2), Paris, 1930-1. and again, the series of articles by A. Vanneste: *Nouvelle Revue Theologique (86), pp. 355-368; (87), pp. 688-726; and (88), pp. 581-602. Cf. also E. Gutwenger: 'Die Erbsunde und das Konzil von Trient' in Zeitschrift für Theologie und Kirche* (89), 1967, pp. 443-446.

29. Canon 1. If anyone does not confess that Adam, the first man, by his transgressions of God's commandments in paradise immediately lost the sanctity and justice in which he had been constituted, and by the offence of this sin drew upon himself the wrath and indignation of God and the death with which God had threatened him, and with death captivity in the power of him who had the empire of death, i.,e. the devil, and that the whole Adam by the offence of this sin was changed in body and soul for the worse, *anathema sit.*

Canon 2. If anyone assert that Adam's sin harmed only himself and not his posterity, and that the holiness and justice which he lost, was lost for himself alone, and not for us too; or that he passed on to all mankind death and bodily punishment but not sin as well, which is the death of the soul, *anathema sit.*

Canon 3. if anyone assert that this sin of Adam, which was one in origin and is passed on by propagation not by imitation, and is in each and proper to each, can be taken away by the powers of human nature or by any remedy other than by the merits of the one Mediator Our Lord Jesus Christ ... or deny that this merit of Christ Jesus is applied, to adults and children, in the sacrament of Baptism duly administered in the Church's form, *anathema sit.*

Canon 4. If anyone deny that children newly come from their mother's womb should be baptized even if they come from baptized parents; or says that they are baptized for the remission of sin but bear nothing of the original sin from Adam ... whence it follows that in their case the form of Baptism 'for the remission of sins' is not understood in the true sense but in a false sense, *anathema sit.*

Canon 5. If anyone deny that the guilt of original sin is remitted by the grace of our Lord Jesus Christ conferred in Baptism or assert that everything that has the true and proper nature of sin is not taken away but is erased or not reckoned, *anathema sit.*

30. *Opera Calvin1* (Braunschweig) 7:43-425.

31. Alszeghy and Flick: *Il Peccato Originale,* 156-7.

32. *Formulations of Christian Faith,* p. 111.

33. Rahner develops this point in 'Theological Reflections on Original Sin' in *Theological Investigations,* Vol. I, esp. pp. 240-247; cf. J. De Fraine: *The Bible and the Origin of Man,* Desclee, New York/Paris/Rome, 1962, p. 72.

34. *Aliter* de Nobili: in Ehses: *Concilium Tridentinum,* V. 198.

35. P. Smulders: 'Evolution and Original Sin' in *Theology Digest,* (Autumn) 1965, p. 175.

36. There is a vast literature. A small sample is offered here: U. Baumann: 'Erbsünde' Ihr traditionelle Verstandnis in der Krise heutiger Theologie, Freiburg, 1970. A. Hulsbosch: *God's Creation,* Sheed and Ward, London, New York and Melbourne, 1965. P. de Rosa: *Christ and Original Sin,* Chapman, London, Dublin and Melbourne, 1967. P. Schoonenberg: *Man and Sin,* Sheed and Ward, London, New York and Melbourne, 1965. K. H. Weger: *Theologie der Erbsunde,* Freiburg, 1970. Two excellent articles: Gabriel Daly: 'The Problem of Original Sin' in *The Furrow,* January 1973, pp. 13-26. M. Hurley: 'The Problem of Original Sin' in *The Clergy Review,* October 1967, pp. 770-776. Cf. also Gabriel Daly: 'Theological Models in the Doctrine of Original Sin' in *The Heythrop*

Journal, (XIII, 2) April 1974, pp. 121-142. Karl Rahner: 'Original Sin' in *Sacramentum Mundi* Vol 4.

37. Cf Alszeghy and Flick: *Il Peccato Originale*, p. 371; K. Rahner: *Theological Investigations*, Vol. I. pp. 246-247. Je. De Fraine: *op. cit.*, p. 74.

38. Teilhard's references to original sin are unsystematic and scattered in widespread fashion throughout his writings. For treatments of Teilhard's views on original sin cf. D. Clarke: 'Original Sin in the thought of Teilhard de Chardin' in *Laurentianum* (9), 1968, pp. 353-394; P. Smulders: *La Vision de Teilhard de Chardin*, Paris, 1965, pp. 174-210. Cf. K. Schmitz-Moormann: *Die Erbsünde. Uberholte Vorstellung bleibendes Glaube*. Olten, 1969.

39. P. Lengsfeld: *Adam and Christus*, Essen, 1963.

40. G. Daly: 'The Problem of Original Sin', *The Furrow*, January 1973, p.22.

41. J. P. Mackey: *Life and Grace*, p. 152.

42. Karl Rahner: *Foundations of Christian Faith*, p. 109.

43. Mackey: *op. cit.*, p. 191.

44. Henri Rondet: *Le Péché originel dans la tradition patristique et theologique*, Paris, 1967, esp. 307-329. *Idem.* with E. Boudes and G, Martelet: *Péché originel et péché d'Adam*, Paris, 1969.

SIX: EVOLUTION AND HOMINISATION

1. A. Hulsbosch: *God's Creation,* Sheed and Ward, London/Melbourne/New York, 1965, p. 105.

2. Cited in E. Rideau: *The Thought of Teilhard de Chardin*, Desclee, New York, 1967, p. 54.

3. C. Tresmontant: *Introduction a la théologie chrétienne*, Seuil, Paris, 1974, p. 69.

4. R. North: *Teilhard and the Creation of the Human Soul*, Bruce, Milwaukee, 1966, p.36, n.2.

5) Teilhard de Chardin: 'Man's Place in the Universe' in *The Vision of the Past*, New York, 1967, p.231.

6. E. Nemesszeghy and J. Russell: *Theology of Evolution*, Mercier, Cork, 1972, p.14.(7) ibid., p.21.

8. For a good treatment of the empirical and philosophical aspects of evolution cf. (i) Anthony Flew: *Darwinian Evolution*, Paladin, London, 1984; (ii) Bernard Ryan: *The Evolution of Man*, Paulist, New York, 1965; (iii) D. Forristal: *The Mystery of God*, Veritas, 1980, p. 49.

9. W. Harrington: *Genesis and Evolution*, p. 96.

10. Nemesszeghy and Russell, *op. cit.* p. 18.

11. Council of Cologne (Titulus IV, Cap. 14), *Collectio Lacensis*, V, 292.

12. Cited by J.D. Holmes: 'Newman and Mivart' in *The Clergy Review*, November, 1965, p.854, n. 1.

13. *eo. loco.*

14. G. Daly: 'The Problem of Original Sin' in *The Furrow*, January 1973, p. 19.

15. W. Heisenberg: 'Scientific Truth and Religious Truth' in *Cross Currents* Winter 1965, p.463.

16. J. H. Newman: *The Idea of a University*, Discourse III, Longmans Green & Co., London, 1902, p. 67.

17. *Constitutio Dogmatica De Fide Catholica*, cf. especially Denzinger 3017-19.

18. J. De Fraine, *The Bible and the Origin of Man*, p. 28.

19. J. F. O'Grady, *Christian Anthropology*, Paulist, New York/Toronto, 1976, p. 98.

20. Nemesszeghy and Russell: *op. cit.*, p. 34.

21. Denzinger, 3864.

22. *Dei Verbum,* par. 12.

23. Denzinger, 3898.

24. Michael Schmaus: *God and Creation,* Sheed and Ward, New York, 1969, p. 123.

25. ' ... the teaching of the Church leaves the doctrine of evolution an open question, as long as it confines its speculations to the development, from other living matter already in existence, of the human body. (That souls are immediately created by God is a view which the Catholic faith imposes on us). In the present state of scientific and theological opinion, this question may be legitimately canvassed by research, and by discussion between those who are expert on both sides ... ' *Humani Generis.* In Denzinger (33rd edition) no. 3896.

26. *Man's Place in Nature,* Collins, London, 1966, pp. 63-4.

27. Denzinger, 3896.

28. G. Ryle: *The Concept of Mind,* Hutchinson, London, 1949; cf. A. Koestler: *The Ghost in the Machine,* London, 1967.

29. *The Phenomenon of Man,* Collins, London and New York, 1959, p. 176.

30. *ibid.,* p. 186.

31. *ibid.,* p. 189.

32. *ibid.,* p. 175.

33. *ibid.,* p. 173.

34. *ibid.,* p. 176.

35. *ibid.,* p. 66.

36. *Man's Place in Nature,* p. 65.

37. *The Phenomenon of Man,* p. 206, n. 6; *Man's Place in Nature,* p. 65, n. 1.

38. *The Phenomenon of Man,* p. 183.

39. *eo. loco.*

40. *ibid.,* p. 187.

41. J. V. Kopp, *Teilhard de Chardin Explained,* Mercier, Cork, 1964, p. 43.

42. *The Future of Man,* Collins, London, 1964, p. 13.

43. *The Phenomenon of Man,* p. 188, n. 4.

44. *Acta Apostolicae Sedis* 31 (1939), 490.

45. K. Rahner and P. Overhage: *Hominisation,* Herder and Herder, 1965; P. Schoonenberg: *God's World in the Making,* Gill and Son, Dublin, 1965; R. North: *Teilhard and the Creation of the Human Soul.* (cf. footnote 4 *supra*).

46. Rahner: *Hominisation,* p. 53.

47. *ibid.,* p. 59.

48. *On The Theology of Death,* Seabury, New York, 1961.

49. K. Rahner: 'Hominisation' in *Sacramentum Mundi,* Vol. 2, p. 296.

50. P. Schoonenberg: *God's World in the Making,* pp. 62-3

SEVEN: HUMAN RIGHTS OBSERVED – A SERVICE OF THE CREATOR

1. Maurice Cardinal Roy: Foreword to *The Church and Human Rights,* Pontifical Commission for Justice and Peace, Vatican City, 1975, p. 1.

2. *Octogesima Adveniens,* Apostolic Letter of Paul VI, AAS 73 (1971), paragraph 23.

3. Dennis Lloyd: *The Idea of Law,* Pelican, Harmondsworth, 1964, p. 84. Cf. *ibid.,* p. 141.

4. J. M. Bonino: 'Religious Commitment and Human Rights' in *Understanding Human Rights* (ed. A. Falconer), Irish School of Ecumenics, Dublin, 1980, p. 24.

5. *ibid.,* p. 25.

6. Seán McBride: 'The U.N. Declaration – Thirty Years After' in *Understanding Human Rights,* p. 13.

7. *Universal Declaration of Human Rights,* art. 55. For a good treatment of the context of the Declaration cf. Sean McBride's article already cited. Cf. also Ian Brownlie: *Basic Documents on Human Rights,* O.U.P., London, 1971.

8. *ibid.,* article 1.

9. Ireland subscribed to the Covenants in October 1973, 'subject to ratification'.

10. McBride: *Understanding Human Rights,* p. 11.

11. Egon Schwelb: 'Human Rights and the International Community' in *The Roots and Growth of the Universal Declaration of Human Rights, 1948-63,* Quadrangle Books, Chicago, 1964, pp. 37 and 47, cited by David Hollenbach: *Claims in Conflict;* cf. footnote 16 *infra.*

12. For a lucid expose of these conditions cf. McBride: *Understanding Human Rights,* p. 15.

13. Report to the Council of Europe (Consultative Assembly), Document 3334, 13 Sept. 1973, Rapporteur, M. Peridier.

14. Maurice Cranston: *What Are Human Rights?* Taplinger Publishing Co., New York, 1973, p. 68.

15. Iredell Jenkins: 'From Natural Law to Legal to Human Rights' in E.H. Pollack ed. *Human Rights,* AMINTA PHIL. 1., Jay Stewart, New York, 1971, p. 213. (Cf. footnote 16).

16. David Hollenbach: *Claims in Conflict. Retrieving and Renewing the Catholic Human Rights Tradition,* Woodstock Theological Studies 4, Paulist, New York, 1979, p. 33. I wish to acknowledge my major indebtedness to this fine study at all points of this chapter.

17. *The Church and Human Rights,* p. 18, no. 18.

18. Tertullian: *Apologeticum* XXIV (ed. Tescari, Turin, 1951, p. 159).

19. *ibid.: Liber ad Scapulam,* 2. (P.L. 1, Col. 699).

20. Lactantius: *Divinarum Institutionum* V.21. (P.L. VI, Col. 619-20). *Epitome divinarum Institutionum* 54, (P.L. VI, Col. 1061).

21. Hippolytus: *Comment. in Danielem* III. Cf. citation in Gustavo Gutierrez: *Liberation and Change,* John Knox Press, Atlanta, 1977, p. 9.

22. Cf. Gutierrez's analysis in *Liberation and Change,* pp. 10 *et seq.*

23. *Epistola* 93, v. 16.

24. *Summa Theologiae* IIa IIae., q. 10, art. 8 ad 3.

25. *De Gubernatione Dei* in *Corpus Scriptorum Ecclesiasticorum Latinorum* VIII, 41, 20; 86, 25.

26. 'On the only way of bringing all people to the true religion'. Cf. the analysis, with copious citations, in G. Gutierrez: *Liberation and Change,* pp. 60-94. The 'encomienda' involved the expropriation and enslavement of Indians. it was given a religious justification by the pretext that the measure aimed at the evangelisation of the Indians.

27. Cf. encyclical *Inscrutabili:* (2 April 1878). Cf. also D. Dorr: *Option for the Poor,* Gill and Macmillan, Dublin, 1983, pp. 29-34.

28. Gabriel Daly: 'Church, State and the Ideal of Freedom' in *Understanding Human Rights,* p. 169.

29. *Pacem in Terris,* par. 158, C.T.S., London, 1963, p. 57.

30. E. McDonagh: paper read to the Fifth Triennial Assembly of Conference of European Justice and Peace Commissions, Chantilly, October, 1981. I am grateful to Dr McDonagh for permission to cite.

31. Cf. Reginaldo Pizzorni: 'Persona Umana e Diritti dell "Uomo" in *De Homine,* Officium Libri Catholici, Roma, 1972, pp. 245-249.

32. *Summa Theologiae* Ia, q. 29, art. 3. *Summa Theologiae* IIa IIae, q. 21, art. 4 ad 3.

33. For a useful treatment cf. E. McDonagh: 'The Worth of the Human Person'

in *Doing the Truth,* Gill and Macmillan, Dublin, 1979, pp. 112-118. A. Wilder: 'Community of Persons in the Thought of Karol Wojtyla' in *Studia in Honorem Caroli Wojtyla. Numero Speciale di Angelicum,* Pont. Universitas a S. Thoma in Urbe, Vol. 56, fascicula 2-3, 1979.

34. *The Church and Human Rights,* no. 14, p. 11.

35. Hollenbach: *Claims in Conflict, p. 14.*

36. Cf. Hollenbach's excellent presentation of the developing tradition in *Claims in Conflict,* pp. 41-100.

37. F. A. Olafson: 'Two Views of Pluralism: Liberal and Catholic' in *Yale Review* 51 (1962), p. 531: cited in Hollenbach, p. 112.

38. Maurice Cranston: 'Pope John XXIII on Peace and the Rights of Man' in *Political Quarterly* 34 (1963), p. 390.

39. Allen O. Miller ed.: *A Christian Declaration on Human Rights,* Grand Rapids, MI, 1977, p. 144.

40. *Gaudium et Spes* nos. 4-19. Cf. Paul VI's Message to Peoples of Africa in J. Gremillion ed.: *The Gospel of Peace and Justice Catholic Social Teaching since Pope John XXIII,* Orbis, New York, p. 422.

41. *Peace - The Desperate Imperative* alias *Baden Consultation on Human Rights,* 3-9/4/1970, Geneva, 1970, no. 83, p. 71.

42. *Baden Consultation,* no. 86, p. 72.

43. Hollenbach: *Claims in Conflict,* p. 91.

44. Cf. Hollenbach's expose of this development in chapters II and III of *Claims in Conflict.*

45. Again, Hollenbach is most helpful on this. Cf. his treatment of claims in conflict in *Claims in Conflict,* pp. 141-178. For a splendid analysis papal social teaching cf. Donal Dorr, *Option for the Poor,* Gill and Macmillan, Dublin, 1983.

46. *Pacem in Terris,* no. 13.

47. Seán McBride in *Understanding Human Rights,* p. 17.

48. D. M. Clarke, *Church and State, Essays in Political Philosophy,* Cork University Press, 1984, p. 155.

49. *ibid.,* p. 159.

50. *Mater et Magistra,* no. 75.

EIGHT: ECOLOGY AND CREATIVE STEWARDSHIP

1. 'Oecology' in Oxford English Dictionary.

2. E. McDonagh: 'Technology and Value Preferences' in *Doing The Truth,* Gill and Macmillan, Dublin, 1979, p. 119.

3. Cited by Hugh Montefiore: *The Question Mark: The End of Homo Sapiens,* Collins, London, 1969, p. 86.

4. *Octogesima Adveniens,* paragraph 21.

5. *Populorum Progressio,* paragraphs 22 and 25.

6. *Justice in the World,* in paragraph headed 'Justice and World Society'.

7. Cf. C. T. Kurien: 'A Third World Perspective' in *Faith and Science in an Unjust World,* editor Roger Shinn, Vol.1., W.C.C., Geneva, 1980, pp. 220-225. I should like to acknowledge my especial indebtedness to this splendid publication.

8. *North-South: A Programme for Survival,* Pan (World Affairs), London and Sydney, 1980. Alias *The Brandt Report. esp. chapter 6.*

9. *The Global 2000 Report to the President.* Being a report commissioned by President Carter of the U.S.A.

10. Cited by Seán McDonagh in 'The Good Earth', *The Furrow,* July 1984, p. 434.

11. John Carmody: *Ecology and Religion,* Paulist, New York, 1983, p. 27.

12. Barry Commoner: *The Closing Circle,* Bantam Books, New York, 1971.

13. Cited by Manuel Sadosky: 'Some Aspects of the Problem in Latin America' in *Faith and Science in an Unjust World*, p. 102.

14. Rubem Alves: 'On the Eating Habits of Science' in *Faith and Science in an Unjust World*, pp. 41-43.

15. C. S. Birch: 'Nature, Humanity and God in Ecological Perpectives' in *Faith and Science in an Unjust World*, p. 62.

16. J. R. Ravetz: 'The Scale and Complexity of the Problem' in *Faith and Science in an Unjust World*, p. 93.

17. *eo. loco.*

18. J. Moltmann: *'Creation as an Open System' in The Future of Man*, Fortress Press, Philadelphia, 1979, pp. 115-130.

19. J. R. Ravetz: 'The Scale and Complexity of the Problem' in *Faith and Science in an Unjust World*, p. 90.

20. *eo. loco.*

21. Charles Birch: 'Nature, Humanity and God in Ecological Perspective' in *Faith and Science in an Unjust World*, p. 70.

22. R. Reuther: *New Woman New Earth*, Seabury, New York, 1965. D. Dinnerstein: *The Mermaid and the Minotaur*, Harper and Row, New York, 1976.

23. R. Reuther: 'Crisis in Sex and Race' in *Mission Trends* (4), eds. G. H. Anderson and T. F. Stransky, Paulist and Erdmanns, New York and Grand Rapids, 1974, p. 187.

24. J. H. Newman: *An Essay in Aid of a Grammar of Assent*, Longmans Green and Company, London, 1898, p. 389.

25. C. Birch: 'Nature, Humanity and God in Ecological Perspective', in *Faith and Science in an Unjust World*, p. 70.

26. Seán McDonagh: 'The Good Earth', *The Furrow*, July 1984, p. 435.

27. Cf. Ursula King's fine analysis of this aspect of Teilhard's thought in her *Towards a New Mysticism: Teilhard de Chardin and Eastern Religions*, Collins, London, 1980.

28. Cited in Alan Watts: *Nature, Man and Woman*, Wildwood House, London, 1973, p. 38.

29. Bernard Häring: *Free and Faithful in Christ*, Vol. III, Crossroad, New York, 1981, pp. 15-16.

30. John A. Ryan: *Distributive Justice*, Macmillan, New York, 1927, p. 397.

31. *Trócaire*. Motif for Lenten Campaign 1983.

32. John Carmody: *Ecology and Religion*, p. 137.

33. Cf. Alan Watts: *Nature, Man and Woman*, Wildwood House, London, 1973. Patricia Snell: 'The Bible and Ecology' in *Bible Today*, 104. (November 1979), pp. 180-85. James Barr: 'Man and Nature: The Ecology Controversy and the Old Testament' in *Ecology and Religion in History*, eds. D. and E. Spring, Harper and Row, New York, 1974, pp. 74-105. Lynn White: 'The Religious Roots of Our Ecological Crisis' *Science* 155 (1967) pp. 1203-7.

34. Cf. T. S. Derr: *Ecology and Human Liberation*, W.C.C., Geneva, 1973. M.A. Neal: *A Socio-Theology of Letting Go*, Paulist, New York, 1977. P. Santmire: 'Ecology, Justice and Theology' in *The Christian Century*, 9217 (12-5-1976).

35. R. Reuther: *To Change the World*, S.C.M., London, 1981, p. 58.

NINE: JUSTICE AND THE GOODS OF THE EARTH

1. An immense literature exists on the concept of justice. This theoretical approach is not at the centre of concern in this chapter. A much noticed recent publication is John Rawls, *A Theory of Justice*, Harvard University Press, 1971. Cf. also John A. Ryan, *Distributive Justice*, Macmillan, New York, 1927.

2. Aristophanes: *Ecclesiazousae*, 590-594. Cited by Martin Hengel, *Property and Riches in the Early Church*, Fortress Press, Philadelphia, 1974, p. 4.

3. Peter McVerry, 'Wealth and the Christian' in *Doctrine and Life*, (April 1983), p. 211.

4. Hengel: *op.cit.*, p. 34.

5. E. Schillebeeckx: *Christ: The Christ Experience in the Modern World*, SCM Press, London, 1980, p. 559.

6. Cf. Schillebeeckx's excellent treatment of the New Testament experience of grace in relation to its attitude to social structures, in *Christ*, pp. 544-567.

7. W.J. Walsh and J.P. Langan: 'Patristic Social Consciousness – The Church and the Poor' in *The Faith That does Justice*, J.C. Haughey ed.: Woodstock Studies (2), Woodstock Theological Center, 1977, p. 113. Here I should like to acknowledge my indebtedness to this excellent article throughout the section on the Church Fathers' attitude to property and its responsibilities.

8. *The Lapsed*, 5-6.

9. Homily on Luke, 12-18.

10. *Fall of Eutropius*, 2-3.

11. *Paedagogus*, 2, 119-120.

12. *Duties of the Clergy*, 1, 132.

13. *Naboth* 55.

14. *On Lazarus*, Homily 2.

15. *On Matthew*, 50.4.

16. *Parables* 5, 3, 7-9.

17. *Commentary on Matthew* (Series 61) in R.S. Tollington: *Selections from the Commentaries and Homilies of Origen*, London, 1929.

18. A notable exception was the founder of the White Fathers, Cardinal Lavigerie.

19. *North-South: A Programme for Survival*, 1980, introduction.

20. *Octogesima Adveniens*, 46. Cf. Donal Dorr: *Option for the Poor*, Gill and Macmillan, Dublin, 1983, pp. 162-176 for an excellent analysis.

21. Final Document of Puebla Conference, 328. Cf. *Puebla and Beyond*, (eds. Eagleston and Scharper), Orbis, New York, 1979, p. 169.

22. D.A. Lane: *Foundations for a Social Theology*, Gill and Macmillan, Dublin, 1984, p. 111.

23. *The Work of Justice*, Veritas, Dublin, 1977, 116.

24. Synodal Document *Justice in the World*, Introduction.

25. Medellin, Final Document (n. 9) in *Between Honesty and Hope*, Orbis, Maryknoll, New York, 1970, p. 214.

26. AAS, 956, 6-9.

27. Cited by Dorr: *Option for the Poor*, p. 230.

28. Gustavo Gutierrez: *The Power of the Poor in History*, Orbis, New York, 1983, p. 76.

29. Cited by Pat O'Brien: *Hope Yes, But No Optimism*, Veritas, 1984.

30. J. B. Metz, 'The Church's Social Function in the Light of a "Political Theology" ' in *Concilium (36) – Faith in the World of Politics*, p. 16.

31. Pedro Arrupe, S.J., *Witnessing to Justice* (Pontifical Commission Justice and Peace), pp. 37-38. Cf. also Segunda Galilea: 'Liberation Theology and New Tasks Facing Christians' in *Frontiers of Theology in Latin America*, SCM, London, 1975, p. 168.

32. E. McDonagh: Book Review in *The Furrow*, November 1984, p. 739.

33. P. Arrupe: *Witnessing to Justice*, p. 51.

34. Una O'Neill, R.S.C., 'Educating for Justice' in *The Irish Catechist* (May 1982), p. 28.

35. P. Arrupe: *Witnessing to Justice*, p. 54.

36. Kathy Halvey, F.M.M., 'Participation in the Lives of the Poor', in *Ensign*, (Winter, 1984), p. 9.

37. I am unable to trace this reference: however, it stands in its own clarity and I should wish to acknowledge my debt to its author.

38. *The Universal Purpose of Created Things*, Pontifical Commission Justice and Peace, No. 2, Vatican City, 1977, p. 215.

39. David Hollenbach: 'Modern Catholic Teachings Concerning Justice' in *The Faith That Does Justice* (ed.: J.C. Haughey), p. 215.

40. Cf. the excellent chapter 12 of D. Dorr: *Option for the Poor*, pp. 252-275.

41. *Summa Theologiae*, IIa. IIae., q. 66, articles 1, 2 and 7.

42. *The Work of Justice*, 65.

43. Ml Cronin: in *St Thomas Aquinas*, ed. C. Lattey, S.J. Heffer and Sons, Cambridge, 1925, pp. 180-181.

44. *Summa Theologiae*, IIa, IIae, q. 66, article 2.

45. *ibid.*, art. 7.

46. *The Tablet*, 3 November 1984.

47. *eo. loco.*

48. Hollenbach: *The Faith That Does Justice*, p. 215.

49. *Laborem Exercens*, especially Chapter Three. Cf. Final Document of Puebla, nos. 975, 1224, 1281. For Pope John Paul's opening address at Puebla see *Puebla and Beyond*, pp. 57-71.

50. *The Work of Justice*, 65.

51. *ibid.*, 66.

52. Rawls: *A Theory of Justice*, p. 109.

Index

Index

ERRATUM

dex continues on following page.

n page 51 "The Heart of the Matter
rt of Matter".